From Eve to Esther

Gender and the
Biblical Tradition

Editorial Advisory Board
Ross S. Kraemer
Carol Meyers
Sharon II. Ringe

From Eve to Esther

Rabbinic Reconstructions of Biblical Women

Leila Leah Bronner

Westminster John Knox Press
Louisville, Kentucky

Grateful acknowledgment is made for permission to quote from the following sources:
Babylonian Talmud, ed. I. Epstein, Soncino Press, 1952.
Midrash Rabbah, trans H. Freedman and M. Simon, Soncino Press, 1983.
The Book of Jashar, ed. Mordecai M. Noah, © 1972 by Sepher-Hermon Press, Inc.
Mishnah, ed. H. Danby, © 1933, 1983 by Oxford University Press.
Pesikta Rabbati, trans. W. G. Braude, © 1968 by Yale University Press.
TANAKH: The New JPS Translation According to the Traditional Hebrew Text, © 1985 by The Jewish Publication Society, Philadelphia.

Chapter 1 is a revised version of a paper originally published as "The Changing Face of Woman from Bible to Talmud," in *Shofar*, © 1989 by Purdue Research Foundation, West Lafayette, IN 47907 and is used by permission.

Book design by Ken Taylor

Cover illustration by Pem Pfisterer Clark

First edition

Published by Westminster John Knox Press
Louisville, Kentucky

This book is printed on acid-free paper that meets the American National Standards Institute Z39.48 standard. ∞

PRINTED IN THE UNITED STATES OF AMERICA

94 95 96 97 99 00 01 02 03 04 — 10 9 8 7 6 5 4 3 2 1

Library of Congress Cataloging-in-Publication Data

Bronner, Leila Leah.
    From Eve to Esther : rabbinic reconstructions of biblical women / Leila Leah Bronner. — 1st ed.
        p.   cm.
    Includes bibliographical references and index.
    ISBN 0-664-25542-6
    1. Women in rabbinical literature.   2. Women in Judaism.   3. Women in the Bible.   4. Bible. O.T.—Criticism, interpretation, etc., Jewish. 5. Rabbinical literature—History and criticism.
    I. Title.
BM509.W7B76   1994
222'.1083053—dc20   93-48941

To my children
Themey, Moshe, Esther
and their families

Contents

Abbreviations

Orders and Tractates in Mishnaic and Talmudic Literature: To distiguish tractates of the same name in Mishna, Tosefta, Babylonian Talmud, and Jerusalem Talmud a lowercase letter is used before the title (e.g., *m. Ta'an. b. Sanh.*).

'Abod. Zar.	*'Aboda Zara*
Ber.	*Berakot*
B. Meṣ.	*Babba Meṣi'a*
B. Qam.	*Babba Qamma*
'Erub.	*'Erubin*
Giṭ.	*Giṭṭin*
Hag.	*Hagiga*
Ketub.	*Ketubot*
Meg.	*Megilla*
Ned.	*Nedarim*
Pesaḥ.	*Pesaḥim*
Qidd.	*Qidduŝin*
Roš. Haš.	*Roš Haššana*
Sabb.	*Sabbat*
Sanh.	*Sanhedrin*
Sebu.	*Sebu'ot*
Ta'an.	*Ta'anit*
Yebam.	*Yebamot*

Rabbinic, Targumic, and other Sources:

'Abot. R. Nat.	*'Abot de Rabbi Nathan*
Ant.	Josephus, *Antiquities of the Jews*
Midr. Prov.	*Midrash Proverbs*
Pirqe R. El.	*Pirqe de Rabbi Eliezer*
Rab.	Midrash Rabbah (preceeded by abbreviation for biblical book name, e.g., Gen.)
Tg. Job	*Targum Job*
Tg. Onq.	*Targum Onqelos*
Tg. Ps.-J.	*Targum Pseudo-Jonathan*

Journals

AJSR	*Association of Jewish Studies Review*
BAR	*Biblical Archaeological Reader*
HTR	*Harvard Theological Review*
JBL	*Journal of Biblical Literature*
JJS	*Journal of Jewish Studies*
JSJ	*Journal for the Study of Judaism in the Persian, Hellenistic and Roman Period*
JSOT	*Journal for the Study of the Old Testament*

Preface

      Though I began this project as a purely academic subject, I quickly realized how much more personal the undertaking was than I had imagined. It was a case, once again, of life approximating art. On the surface, this was to be an intellectual analysis of classical commentaries on a sacred text—in this case, Midrash, or rabbinic lore, on Hebrew Scriptures. Yet on a deeper level, one that I had not clearly articulated to myself at the outset, I discovered that I was investigating a subject that has deeply affected me all my life. The way biblical women were understood and appropriated in rabbinic Judaism had shaped my upbringing, self-perceptions, and, to some extent, choices of lifestyle.

      I come to this study from two worlds. My growing up in a rabbinic family and a traditional community meant that a great love of the Bible was imparted to me. Its female personalities held a deep fascination for me. Sacred scripture was an integral part of life, and its heroes were as immediate to us as if they were our contemporaries. But as is characteristic of the traditional community, the Bible was never taught by itself; its every word was mediated through rabbinic sources. Thus the models set before me were both biblical and midrashic.

      My father was a Hasidic rabbi. I remember his response to me when, as a child, I would chafe at my role in the family, especially in comparison with my brothers' roles. He would remind me of the story in which God advised Abraham to hearken to the advice of Sarah. The rabbinic comment on this text is that Sarah's prophetic powers were superior to those of Abraham. My father would console me with the thought that when I was married, I would have a greater role. In citing these texts, he tried to endear me to a biblical model. He also followed the traditional manner of teaching and of communicating values through the tradition, values that were at times an apologia for women. If in the mundane role women appear inferior to men, in the realm of the spirit they are on a level equal to, if not higher than, that of men.

This childhood experience was a process that was replicated throughout the course of my formal education. Yet, happily, study was not censored. Though I accepted much of this learning uncritically, I was mildly aware of the lesser role of women in midrashic interpretation, of the discrepancies and inequities that existed. Thus, even before my horizons were expanded as an adult in academia, I felt a measure of ambivalence and frustration: love for sources that were nevertheless pockets of doubt; and an intense connectedness coming up against the parameters of respectful inquiry. Critique was not considered religiously inappropriate, but it was acceptable only up to a point.

As an adult, professional woman, I began to study and teach these sacred sources using critical, contemporary scholarship. Critical scholarship presented certain challenges to my faith, but these could be met by a firm belief and a rootedness in the traditional way of life. Thus, rather than irreparably impairing my faith, the new scholarship expanded my curiosity. It broadened my understanding and enabled me to approach traditional exegesis with a critical eye.

Then along came feminism, which contributed a whole new value system that I could now bring to bear on my understanding of Torah and Midrash. The more radical claims of feminism were too hostile and dismissive of texts that I felt offered so much wisdom, and these claims I could not espouse. However, I found myself increasingly able to combine scriptural critique and feminist perspective when analyzing a midrashic text. Feminist methodology tries to show that although many texts are strongly patriarchal, others, through the hermeneutic process of feminist reinterpretation, breathe an air of both authenticity and fairness. More important, I found that reinterpretation recognizes the diversity of the text. Awareness of textual multivalence makes it possible to uncover deeper levels of the text never before noticed or interpreted. In this way, our understanding of the sources is enriched.

Thus it was that I decided to revisit the sources with a critical bent, knowing that there was more to be found there than meets the eye. In addition to evoking so many personal feelings in encountering the data, I found there to be many surprises in the material itself. Although I was aware of many of the midrashim, I had never focused systematically on the bipolarization and ambivalence of rabbinic attitudes: upholding modesty as a virtue, yet exhibiting a certain tenderness and sympathy toward bad women; constraining to keep women within home and hearth, yet displaying occasional pride in women as significant leaders of the community. Clearly, embedded in the sources was a message that had been missed, an underlying message about multiple roles for women that could serve contemporary women quite well. Women were intended to be leaders as well as mothers. Better yet, they could choose not either/or, but both!

It seemed to me important to put all of this together in an accessible form. Understanding rabbinic perspectives on biblical women provides a fresh supplement to the numerous studies that have been undertaken on biblical women. It serves two purposes. First, biblical female figures—interpreted, embellished, and stereotyped throughout the generations—have exerted enormous influence on Western culture and have greatly affected the way women have been viewed and treated. It is important to get as full as possible a picture of the why and the how of women's inherited roles and status in society. Second, inasmuch as the Bible and Midrash will continue to have great impact on the values of their readers into future generations, it seems important to catalog the material in a way that clearly imparts new messages as well as old.

The ideas presented in this volume first began to be formulated by me in papers I presented at several conferences of the American Academy of Religion/Society of Biblical Literature and at the World Congress of Jewish Studies in Jerusalem. Two chapters were first published as articles in the journals *Shofar* and *Judaism* and appear here in revised form. As the research progressed, my ideas evolved. Consequently, those chapters as they appear in this book have been thoroughly reworked from any earlier established format.

Unless otherwise cited, translations of Hebrew biblical texts have been taken from the New Jewish Publication Society version; Babylonian Talmud and *Midrash Rabbah* from the Soncino editions; and the Mishnah from the Danby edition. Transliteration of the names of talmudic tractates and most midrashim follow the listing provided in the *Journal of Biblical Literature* style sheet. Transliteration of all other Hebrew words follows the simplified style of the *Encyclopaedia Judaica*, with the following exceptions: (1) *qof* has usually been represented with a *q* instead of *EJ*'s suggested *k*; and (2) both *'alef* and *'ayin* have been represented with apostrophes; the specialist will know which of the two is intended. A few Hebrew words, such as *mitzvah* and *kaddish*, have become standardized in English, and these spellings have not been altered.

Among the many feminist scholars who have influenced me, I am especially pleased to acknowledge the impact that Phyllis Trible has had on my thought. Her judicious treatment of the sources rejuvenates tradition without eroding it.

A number of friends and colleagues have been most kind in their readiness to discuss aspects of the work with me. Among these are Athalya Brenner (Technion and Catholic University of Nijmegon), Avigdor Shinan (Hebrew University), Eliezer Slomovic (University of Judaism), Steven Fine (Hebrew University), Marcia Reines Josephy (Curator, Martyrs Museum—L.A.), Marilyn Lundburg (Claremont), and Peter Petit (Claremont). David Hirsch, Jewish Studies Bibliographer of the Research Library of UCLA, was especially kind in granting me the benefit of his considerable expertise. Special appreciation is due to Carol Selkin (Duke University) for her assistance in researching various materials and in typing the manuscript.

Finally, I want to thank my husband, Rabbi Joseph Bronner, for his support and encouragement in this project, as in so many other endeavors in my life.

Introduction: "She Shall Be Called 'Woman' "[1]

This study focuses on female characters of the Bible as perceived through the aggadic traditions of Talmud and Midrash. Although study of women in the Bible has burgeoned in the last two decades, as has study of the halakhic and legal status of Jewish women, little work has been devoted to the analysis of rabbinic lore on biblical women.[2]

I believe such a study is important because rabbinic lore—which is essentially an interpretation and explanation of the biblical text—has significantly shaped human perception of heroes of the Bible for countless generations. As women today attempt to reappropriate past historical models, they are well served by understanding the values and inner workings of that process of interpretation. The rabbis were an elite culture that stood somewhat above and apart from the average Jewish person of that time.[3] How much of their reading into the biblical text was based on the actual status of women of their own times? How much was an idealized attempt to communicate to women the values and models they thought appropriate? Recent scholarship has begun to differentiate between what the rabbis said about women and what women's reality may actually have been.[4] As Ross S. Kraemer explains:

> Strikingly different portraits both of Jewish women and women's Judaism emerge from ancient rabbinic sources on the one hand, and inscriptional, archaeological, and neglected Greek literary sources from the Greco-Roman period on the other. Rabbinic

writings have led many scholars to conclude that Jewish women led restricted, secluded lives and were excluded from much of the rich ritual life of Jewish men, especially from the study of Torah. Evidence from the Greco-Roman Diaspora suggests, however, that at least some Jewish women played active religious, social, economic, and even political roles in the public lives of Jewish communities.[5]

Whether or not rabbinic literature is an accurate mirror of most women's lives of that time, this literature came to constitute part of the canon of Judaism in subsequent times. Consequently, it has had an impact for many centuries on the lives of actual Jewish women until today. It is therefore extremely important to obtain an accurate, balanced picture of what exactly classical rabbinic literature has to say about women.

Contrary to widely held belief, we will find that the sages' attitude toward biblical women in the aggadic, legendary literature of the Midrash and Talmud was not fixed or monolithic.[6] Rather, it was flexible, changing in accordance with the exegetical problem under discussion. Indeed, views expressed by the sages in a given midrashic context usually appear to have arisen out of the needs of the specific biblical text that they were analyzing.

But there is more to it than that. What appears to be a bipolarization of rabbinic attitudes toward biblical women—sometimes praising, sometimes criticizing—is quite likely the result of a tension between the sages' own social preconceptions about women and the demands of the written tradition guiding them. Behind rabbinic analysis also stands a good deal of intellectual curiosity and imagination, and these factors, too, influenced their method of argumentation. Thus the interaction between rabbinic society, midrashic method, individual sensibilities, and the inherited honor and awe of biblical text served to recast biblical woman into new and various images. It also explains another phenomenon. Even though many women of the Bible were revered as heroines and even though the rabbis adopted a more lenient attitude toward them than toward women of their own times, nevertheless they were occasionally critical even of these exceptional biblical figures. The rabbis could not help but view the women of the Bible, just as they viewed the women of their own day, according to preconceived notions regarding the limitations of the female sex.

I will endeavor here to study how the sages interpreted biblical verses dealing with women. Because my concern is with the midrashic texts, let me begin by defining what I mean by Midrash. I will discuss Midrash as a genre of literature below. For the moment I am concerned with Midrash as a method of inquiry. The word *Midrash* means to interpret or, on deeper level, to research select verses of scripture.[7] The Bible is a laconic, elliptical, and at times ambiguous text; thus it is open to a variety of interpretations of any one verse.

Midrashic analysis typically focuses on difficult words, inner contradictions, and problematical passages in the text. Much can be read into a text (eisegesis) through this sort of interpretation.[8] The sages, by viewing the text against the grain of their own ideology, formulated hermeneutics congruent with the preoccupations of their times. We can better understand what is meant by the word *hermeneutics* if we realize that different groups of people bring with them different presuppositions that influence how they understand the text. Group ideological stances as well as individual natures have a great bearing on exegetical projects. In this study, for example, I will show how the rabbinic valorization of female modesty often colored rabbinic readings of biblical texts about women.

The classical texts of rabbinic literature—Mishnah, Tosefta, Talmud, and Midrash—will constitute our primary sources for this study. Where applicable, I will also examine for comparative purposes Jewish literature that predates the rabbis; namely, the writings of Josephus and Philo, and other works of Hellenistic literature whose authors are unknown, some of which is typically designated the Apocrypha and Pseudepigrapha. Occasionally there will be reference to Christian texts. Although many centuries lie between these texts of the Second Temple Period and post–Second Temple rabbinic literature, there are affinities between them, as well as with classical Greek literature. Therefore reference will be made to these sources for purposes of comparison or contrast. But the main focus will remain on the rabbinic sources, so it is worthwhile to describe these briefly.

The Mishnah is a book primarily comprised of legal rulings; it was edited approximately 200 c.e. The Tosefta augments the rulings of the Mishnah and traditionally is believed to include materials contemporary with those of the Mishnah. It was edited slightly later than the Mishnah, however. There are two parallel but different commentaries on the Mishnah; namely, the Palestinian Talmud (completed circa 400 c.e.) and the more voluminous and authoritative one, the Babylonian Talmud (redacted circa 600 c.e.). Finally, Midrash, as I indicated above, is an inclusive term for a genre of exegetical literature commenting on scripture.[9] Some of the earliest collections of Midrash, such as *Midrash Genesis Rabbah*, are believed to be contemporary with the Tosefta, whereas others, such as *Midrash Numbers Rabbah*, extend well into the medieval period. At times I will make reference to the *Zohar*, a medieval mystical work that is not classified as a work of classical rabbinic Judaism but as one that sometimes develops ideas present in earlier classical texts.

Often the midrashic collections and the Talmuds contain overlapping material, sometimes in slightly different versions. Some of these differences reflect the differing environments and time periods in which the rabbis lived and taught.[10] Unfortunately, much of rabbinic literature cannot be precisely placed with regard to provenience, and this limits our ability to view specific rabbinic comments in a precise historical or social context.

Rabbinic literature contains both *halakhah*, which is codified legal discussion, and *aggadah*, which is folkloristic, narrative, and legendary. Whereas the Talmud is more heavily halakhic, the Midrash is more heavily aggadic. Both bodies of literature, however, contain both types of material, and there is continuous flow on every page from one type to the other. In sum, *halakhah* and *aggadah* stand for the law and lore of the Talmud and Midrash. The contrast between the legal and narrative discourses is described graphically—albeit exaggeratedly—by the famous poet Hayim Nahman Bialik:

> *Halakhah* seems to wears a frown. *Aggadah* a smile. The one is pedantic, severe, unbending—all justice; the other is accommodating, lenient, pliable—all mercy. On the one side . . . reason is sovereign. On the other side . . . emotion is sovereign.[11]

The distinction made by Bialik applies especially to the situation of women in rabbinic literature. Women generally appear as individual persons in the midrashic sources, whereas in halakhic discussion they are treated as depersonalized prototypes for case study. The legal corpus of the Mishnah, which contains a great deal of material about women, cites only three women by name, whereas many named women feature in the Talmuds and midrashic collections. Individual biblical females figure far more prominently in aggadic material than in halakhic material.

In the first chapter, "Aggadic Attitudes toward Women," I will survey the historical, social, and political factors contributing to the rise of exceptional women in biblical times who attained fame by their own action or profession despite the disabilities inherent in their legal status. This public dimension is completely lacking from the lives of women described in talmudic literature. I will explain how the absence of female participation in public affairs was controlled by a premise held by the majority of rabbis that modesty should rule the lives of women. Modesty became an overriding obsession in the rabbinic portrayal of women. The androcentric valorization of modesty transformed women into private persons, their lives and activities ideally restricted to the domestic realm. I will try to evaluate whether rabbinic rules of modesty presented the state of affairs of the society as they actually were. Or did they instead represent matters as most rabbis wished they would be?

The second chapter, "Eve's Estate: Temptation, Modesty, and the Valorization of Matrimony," will deal with the Eve narrative. It has always intrigued me that Eve, described in the Bible as the mother of all life, became the mother of death in so many androcentric analyses.[12] Many ancient exegetes, the sages included, were led by their interpretation of the Genesis story to attribute sin and death to this primeval female character. As part of this transformation, Eve became the archetype whose behavior supplied the sages with the rationale to formulate rules that, in the name of modesty, removed women from public life and leadership and restricted them to the domain of the home. The sages projected their cultural presuppositions onto the Eve character, thereby adding to the already stereotypic ideas informing the biblical characterization of the first woman. As a result of Eve's action, all her daughters were subjected to the rabbinic regime of modesty and were profoundly restricted in their lives as a result.

I will discuss a totally different sort of woman in chapter 3, "Serah bat Asher: The Transformative Power of Aggadic Invention." She will present a marked contrast to the stark image projected by the rabbis onto Eve. Serah bat Asher strikes me as the most unique and fascinating character to emerge from midrashic exegesis on a female biblical figure. No more than a mere name on genealogical lists in scripture, Serah is transformed by the rabbis into a visionary, an adviser heeded by no less a leader than Moses himself. The sages accord crucial redemptive powers to this obscure biblical woman. She is credited with having made possible the departure of the Jews from Egypt. Moreover, they also ascribe analogous powers of redemption to other women who figure in the story of bondage and redemption, in particular, the midwives who acted to save the male children condemned by Pharaoh.

Another woman highly favored in rabbinic exegesis is Ruth, great-grandmother of King David, who is the subject of chapter 4, "The Regime of Modesty: Ruth and the Rabbinic Construction of the Feminine Ideal." Midrashic interpretation goes into great detail about her conversion, marriage, and role in redemption. The rabbis wanted to legitimize the ancestry of David and show that Ruth, a Moabite woman, was worthy of her place as a progenitor of the messianic line. Rabbinic exegesis highlights the extraordinary *ḥesed* (loving-kindness) displayed by Ruth in the biblical story and ascribes to her certain additional qualities, including beauty and modesty, that are nowhere mentioned in the biblical text. In the Bible, Ruth is an archetype of loving-kindness, but in rabbinic lore she instead becomes the very paragon of the cardinal female virtue—modesty.

Hannah also points up rabbinic contradictions. Discussed in chapter 5, " 'Remember Thy Handmaid': On Hannah and Prayer," her story brings to the fore the interesting problem of women's place in cultic practice in biblical times and in liturgical practice in rabbinic times. Hannah prays in the public, ritual space of the biblical tabernacle; but the rabbis see the sincere, spontaneous, heartfelt—that is, private—quality of her prayer as what makes it an outstanding model of how one— man or woman—should try to pray.

Women's prayer is characterized in rabbinic literature as a spiritual but private act. Even when a woman is physically present and praying in the synagogue, such praying is different in a fundamental way from the normative, public liturgical practices of men. We see interesting—and unresolved—contradictions in the rabbis' attitude toward such private, noncommunal prayer—at once approving, for its spontaneity and sincerity, and disapproving, for its departure from the privileged canons of public, communal, synagogue worship. Paradoxically, women are not models of prayer in the rabbinic community, yet Hannah becomes the prototype for excellence in prayer.

In chapter 6 we turn our attention to the member of the Hebrew family accorded the lowest status: " 'The King's Daughter Is All Glorious Within': The Estate of Daughterhood." Biblical law clearly places daughters on a lower rung than it does sons. Few daughters are mentioned by name in the Bible, and these are mentioned only when they play dramatic roles as calamity befalls the family. Beginning with Dinah and the rabbis' censure of her alleged immodesty, the uneven saga of daughters begins to unfold. The daughters of certain notable biblical figures—of Lot, Jacob, Zelophehad, and Jephthah—are discussed. Some of these girls and women are given names in the Bible; others remain forever anonymous. Rabbinic indulgence in behalf of these piteous figures demonstrates the merciful, smiling quality that Bialik describes as distinguishing the aggadic from the halakhic mode and shows how in the individual human case the rabbis could bend their categorical rules and see through the confines of their own gender preconceptions.

Chapter 7, "Hope for the Harlot: The Estate of the Marginalized Woman," deals with the question of prostitution in ancient Israel and the rabbinic interpretation of harlots and harlotry. The social practice of prostitution posed a challenge to the normative institutions of marriage and family, and its existence in ancient Israel was something the rabbis had somehow to encompass within their moral framework. The aggadic traditions surrounding the biblical figures of Rahab, the former harlot who, according to the rabbis, eventually marries the hero Joshua, and Tamar, who ingeniously solves the predicament of her childless widowhood by using a ruse of harlotry, shed light on this subject. I will also discuss some illuminating stories about rabbis and disciples encountering prostitutes in their own day. Surprisingly, the rabbis hold out hope for the reintegration of such women into the sphere of propriety. They achieve this through repentance, a concept heavily emphasized throughout rabbinic literature.

The female prophets are an exceptional category of women, and aggadic treatment of them demonstrates the variety and complexity of the rabbis' attitudes. Chapter 8, " 'Deborah, Say Your Song': Female Prophecy in Talmudic Tradition," deals with the question of female prophecy. Quite striking is the fact that the sages clearly seem to have found the most exceptional personages, such as Deborah and Huldah, intimidating, even threatening, whereas the less powerful female prophets earned their unqualified approbation.

Also of interest is that, in contrast to most biblical women, the prophetesses are by and large not measured according to the criterion of modesty. They are not usually praised for embodying it, nor are they censored for failing to do so. Their prowess in public endeavors seems to exempt them from these considerations. Or perhaps it is more accurate to say that their achievements in the public realm were made possible by their acting outside the rabbinic rules governing female behavior, and the rabbis in this instance generally tolerated it.

Women in the aggadic traditions of Midrash and Talmud have not received the attention they deserve. This study explores some of this rabbinic material to gain a better and more complete picture of women as they appear in this vast and complex literature. We will see that although these bodies of rabbinic exegesis are rife with stereotypes of feminine qualities, the sages were also ready to appreciate admirable and even heroic qualities in female characters, sometimes even when such characteristics are not plainly evident in the biblical account.

I will show a frequent pattern whereby the rabbis' interpretation of scriptural material first discerns in it stereotypes of female weakness and sexual allurement, and then formulates codes of behavior to enforce female confinement to domestic roles. These rules, which relegate women to the private sphere of home and family responsibility, remove her from learning and leadership, the keys to power and prominence in the community. But even here there are significant complications and contradictions evident in the attitudes of the rabbis and in the scriptural material they are interpreting.

Today, women continue both to benefit and to labor under the impact of rabbinic interpretation of scriptural models. The way culture and texts interacted in the past still speaks to our lives today. The challenge today is for creative men and women to continue in the rabbinic tradition, and to reclaim biblical models in new and different ways, appropriate to our times. To do so, we must adequately understand the processes and the values that informed our teachers, whose work we need not reject in order to build new myths for future generations. In the pages that follow, I will try to explore rabbinic perspectives on biblical women with the care they deserve.

Reconsideration and reinterpretation constitute an exciting project. I hope that this study might be taken as part of a larger trend toward looking at the women of the Bible and Talmud afresh, and that it encourages further studies in the emerging tradition of depatriarchalizing interpretation.[13] I have taken pains to recognize and present what the aggadic traditions of Talmud and Midrash actually say, rather than what in retrospect we might like them to have said, so that the process of reinterpretation and recuperation can proceed on an honest and authentic ground.

Notes

1. Genesis 2:23.
2. Ross S. Kraemer ("Women in the Religions of the Greco-Roman World," *Religious Studies Review* 9 [1983]:130) stated in 1983 that study of women in rabbinic literature has been minimal. She subsequently encouraged study of the topic herself by including some pertinent source material in her sourcebook, *Maenads, Martyrs, Matrons, Monastics* (Philadelphia: Fortress Press, 1988). Since then other works have appeared, including a relevant chapter in Kraemer's own *Her Share of the Blessings: Women's Religion among Pagans, Jews, and Christians in the Greco-Roman World* (Oxford: Oxford University Press, 1992); *"Women Like This": New Perspectives on Jewish Women in the Graeco-Roman World*, ed. Amy-Jill Levine (Atlanta: Scholars Press, 1991); Betsy Halpern Amaru, "Portraits of Biblical Women in Josephus' *Antiquities*," *JJS* 39 (1988), 143–70; and Dorothy Sly, *Philo's Perception of Women*, ed. J. Neusner et al., Brown Judaic Studies 209 (Atlanta: Scholars Press, 1990), 218. Judith Romney Wegner is notable for her work on the legal status of women in rabbinic Judaism, e.g., *Chattel or Person? The Status of Women in the Mishnah* (New York and Oxford: Oxford University Press, 1988), and "The Image and Status of Women in Classical Rabbinic Judaism," in *Jewish Women in Historical Perspective*, ed. J. R. Baskin (Detroit: Wayne State University Press, 1991). My study is focused more specifically on women in the aggadic lore, rather than the halakhic law, in Midrash and Talmud.
3. Shaye J. D. Cohen, *From the Maccabees to the Mishnah*, Library of Early Christianity (Philadelphia: Westminster Press, 1987), 221–24; and Lee I. Levine, "The Sages within Jewish Society," in *The Rabbinic Class of Roman Palestine in Late Antiquity* (Jerusalem: Yad Izhak Ben-Zevi; New York: Jewish Theological Seminary of America, 1985).

4. Bernadette J. Brooten, *Women Leaders in the Ancient Synagogue: Inscriptional Evidence and Background Issues*, Brown Judaic Studies 36 (Chico, Calif.: Scholars Press, 1982); Kraemer, *Her Share of the Blessings*, 3–21; and Daniel Boyarin, "Reading Androcentrism against the Grain: Women, Sex and Torah Study," *Poetics Today* 12 (1991): 29–52.

5. Kraemer, *Her Share of the Blessings*, 93.

6. Jewish feminist scholars have addressed the tendency of some feminists to make rabbinic literature appear wholly negative toward women through the selective use of texts. See Judith Plaskow, "Blaming the Jews for the Birth of Patriarchy," *Lilith* 7 (1980): 11–13; and Susannah Heschel, "Anti-Judaism in Christian Feminist Theology," *Tikkun* 5 (1990): 25–28, 95–97.

7. For further information on Midrash as a genre or method of inquiry, see James L. Kugel, "Two Introductions to Midrash," in *Midrash and Literature*, ed. G. H. Hartman and S. Budick (New Haven: Yale University Press, 1986), 91; Renee Bloch, "Midrash" and "Methodological Note for the Study of Rabbinic Literature," in *Approaches to Ancient Judaism: Theory and Practice*, ed. William Scott Green (Missoula, Mont.: Scholars Press, 1978); and Jacob Neusner, *Midrash in Context: Exegesis in Formative Judaism* (Philadelphia: Fortress Press, 1983).

8. Exegesis is reading "out of" a text.

9. Cf. Avigdor Shinan and Yair Zakovitch, "Midrash on Scripture and Midrash within Scripture," in *Scripta Hierosolymitana*, ed. Sara Japhet, Studies in Bible 31 (Jerusalem: Magnes Press, 1986), 258–59.

10. In-depth analysis is required to elucidate how and why these variations originated, but this is beyond the scope of our study.

11. Hayim Nahman Bialik, *Halachah and Aggadah*, trans. Leon Simon (London: pamphlet published by the Education Department of the Zionist Federation of Great Britain and Ireland, 1944).

12. Cf. Elaine Pagels, *Adam, Eve, and the Serpent* (New York: Random House, 1988), esp. p. 68.

13. Phyllis Trible, "Depatriarchalizing in Biblical Interpretation," in *The Jewish Woman*, ed. Elizabeth Koltun (New York: Schocken Books, 1976), 218, 234–35.

1

Aggadic Attitudes toward Women[1]

The expanding role of women in modern, Western society has stimulated new interest regarding the place of women in the past. Most women of the ancient world held a status secondary to men. Although their experiences differed from society to society, a basic pattern of gender discrimination prevailed across class, tribal, and national lines. Biblical society was no different. Glaring inequalities or double standards between men and women prevailed in the areas of adultery, marriage, divorce, inheritance, vows, worship, leadership, and covenantal status. The language of the Bible is strongly masculine. The Bible primarily depicts men and their activities. The Israelite community is addressed as men, and even God is described primarily by andromorphic terminology.[2]

Yet despite disabilities imposed by law and custom, despite the hierarchy that is revealed in language, a number of exceptional women rose to real prominence in biblical times. The Bible attests to these special women acting in public spheres generally reserved for men. Some came to this by way of their familial relatedness to male heroes. But others came to positions of prominence through their own strength of personality or character, which enabled them to rise to a situation calling for an unusual response. Some of these women played leading roles in the political life of the nation.[3]

Such was not the case for women described within the talmudic system, where public position and leadership were deemed inappropriate for women. Women in the social and religious framework of the Talmud functioned primarily as daughters, wives, mothers, or sisters.[4] Rarely, if ever, did they surface in the literature as exemplary persons in their own right. Throughout the talmudic era, women leaders in the rabbinic world were rare.[5] By and large, they conformed to the roles established for them by law and custom. They were enablers, family oriented, and away from the centers of power and communal leadership. This is in contrast to the Bible, where despite their being ineffective in the legal realm, some women display active leadership in the narrative sources. One wonders how even a handful of women in a patriarchal, patrilineal, patrilocal society could rise to leadership, particularly those who got there by dint of their own personalities, such as Deborah, the judge.

Several ideas come to mind:

> The period described in the Bible covers a much larger span of time—1400 years as compared with 700 in rabbinic literature, twice as many centuries for exceptional women to rise. Moreover, much of biblical history takes place in a national home, whereas rabbinic history involved coping with national, political loss and exile.
>
> It may be that stories of exceptional women in biblical times were recorded but those of rabbinic times were not. Changing attitudes may be reflected in the shifting choice to exclude stories about women. Exclusion of such stories may in part be an extension of rabbinic proscriptions about avoiding unnecessary contact with women, an attitude which in turn lessened the possibility of a woman becoming a leader.
>
> The law was expanded and detailed in post-biblical times, and the hierarchy became increasingly fixed as the law was layered through centuries of life. Strict gender criteria for leadership and for being active and visible in public are more prominent in the Talmud than in the Bible. Thus exceptional women of biblical times performed no antinomian acts. They simply rose to leadership as the situation demanded.[6]

Although the rabbis virtually denied roles like these to women of their own times, they could look upon such biblical women with relative generosity. Much of this grew out of their total reverence for biblical texts. But some measure of their equanimity resulted from the fact that biblical women were not viewed as lawbreakers, but nation-savers.

The categories by which the rabbis judged and embellished female heroes of the Bible were less legal than value-oriented. Of course, as we will see below, where there was a challenge to legal structures, such as in the case of Deborah as judge, they recast her work to suit the *halakhah* of their own times. They dealt similarly with the laws of the convert in the story of Ruth and the laws of women and public prayer in the story of Hannah. But primarily, they brought to bear on the lives of biblical heroines a scale of values that was uppermost in their minds. In doing so, they not only endeared the characters of the Bible to folk of their own times, but they also used these unusual personalities both to teach the law and to convey the values they wanted to spread throughout the community.

Values and Law

To understand the context out of which the aggadic treatment of biblical personalities was rooted, let us examine briefly some aspects of rabbinic values and the laws they engendered.

In talmudic life and literature, the proper role of women was restricted to that of wife and mother—enabling roles. Talmudic sources praise women for being supportive of their menfolk and for obeying their husbands and fathers. The Talmud advises men to honor the woman who fulfills her feminine role well.[7] Frequently quoted is the passage in tractate *Berakot:*

> Whereby do women earn merit? By making their children go to the synagogue to learn Scripture and their husbands to the Beth Hamidresh to learn Mishnah, and waiting for their husbands till they return from the Beth Hamidresh.[8]

Whether this adage represented a socioreligious reality or was an effort to impose this viewpoint upon the women of their age, it would have served to guide the behavior of women in one direction—nurturing and serving.

An anecdote about the daughter of the emperor[9] exemplifies ideological female servility. When the emperor taunts Rabban Gamaliel II, saying that God was a thief because God stole a rib from Adam to make Eve, the emperor's daughter answers that theft of this nature is not only commendable but profitable, for God took a rib from Adam and gave him a woman to serve him instead.[10] This account is representative of a genre of "serving women" stories in rabbinic literature, wherein even high-ranking women are depicted as having internalized the enabling and constricted role laid out for women.

In addition to her role as enabler—or perhaps because of it—a host of laws limiting the options available for women were promulgated. Many discussions in the Talmud begin with the phrase "women, slaves, and children." The basis for the association of the three classes in this common collocation is their restricted freedom of action and their lack of political, economic, or social independence.

Women are restricted in the acts they must, or must not, perform. Religious tradition lays down strictly and clearly which laws men and women are obligated to observe. All negative commandments are applicable to men and women, and both are liable to equal punishments for violating them. Women, however, are exempt and de facto excluded from participating in commandments contingent upon time, such as communal prayer. Women thus do not count for the communal *minyan*, and this further removes them from public contact or position. They are instead encouraged to pray privately.[11]

Women are likewise not to engage in study of Torah, though this is not an activity that is really contingent upon time. The reason given by later apologists for this exclusion—namely, that women are busy with domestic responsibilities—was in fact never explicitly given in the talmudic sources. In tractate *Soṭa,* which deals with the laws relating to married women accused of adultery, the sages discuss whether women should be permitted to study Torah. Ben Azzai says that a man *should* teach Torah to his daughters, so they will know how to defend themselves against their husbands in case they are ever accused of adultery. Rabbi Eliezer disagrees and retorts that to teach Torah to one's daughter would be a grossly unseemly act.

Rabbi Eliezer's opinions in this matter carried great weight throughout history, even until modern times. They had the effect of applying brakes to women's educational opportunities.[12] He was the most virulent opponent of woman's Torah study; he taught: "Let the books of Torah be burnt rather than be given to a woman."[13] A woman once dared to pose some questions about Torah to Rabbi Eliezer. He rudely brushed her aside, declaring that men study Torah, whereas "women's wisdom is to ply the spindle."[14]

Another example of restricted behavior for women can be found in this talmudic teaching: "All obligations of the son, which lie upon the father to do to his son, men are bound, but mothers are exempt. The father is bound to circumcise his son, redeem him, teach him Torah, take a wife for him, and teach him a craft."[15] Education of young males was thus transformed into a male prerogative. The Talmud further states: "Whoever is commanded to study is commanded to teach."[16] The mother, being exempt from the obligation to study, cannot teach. Once the woman became unlearned in Torah, she was limited in her ability to rise in community life.

Yet the biblical book of Proverbs had clearly stated: "My son, heed the discipline of your father, and do not forsake the instruction of your mother" (Prov. 1:8). Moreover, it was the advice of the mother of King Lemuel to her son that was preserved, not that of his father (Prov. 31:1). Nevertheless, the gender differentiation prescribed in the Talmud for the role of teaching children became in talmudic sources the pattern for social and religious life.

Another primary value was that of female modesty. The modesty code is known in current religious terminology as *zni'ut*. Although the nomenclature of *zni'ut* is not yet present in classical rabbinic literature, the structural framework of modesty laws did exist. In classical rabbinic Judaism, women were required to reduce their natural seductiveness. When in public, they had to cover themselves and their hair (considered a powerful *'ervah*, "sexual incitement").[17] They were also forbidden to sing in the presence of men outside their family.[18] Even a code of dress and manners for women was developed in talmudic and midrashic sources. Women were expected to observe this code of behavior, and men were expected to respect it. There are stories in the Talmud in which men removing the head covering of women in the street are fined for the violation.[19] The rabbis say that Kimhit, the mother of the High Priest Simeon b. Kimhit, deserved the blessing of having seven sons because of her meritorious practice of keeping her hair covered so continuously that "not even the beams of her house have seen the plaits of her hair."[20] So great was her merit that all seven sons became high priests. Biblical sources show concern for women's sexual allure. The rabbis heighten this anxiety in their exegesis. The consequence is the extreme emphasis on women's modesty as a form of social control in Jewish tradition. This trend also led to highly complicated attitudes toward beauty, as will be shown later.

The concept of modesty in rabbinic literature, which is often exemplified by the biblical passage "the king's daughter is all glorious within" (Ps. 45:13), became increasingly entrenched as a means of restricting women's behavior.[21] This verse from Psalms became the peg on which the rabbis hung their claim that a woman's glory is in the modest seclusion of her home. A major cluster of regulations emerged from the concept of *zni'ut* and developed around the issue of keeping men and women from mingling in situations that could lead to indecent behavior, or even the possibility of indecency. These laws were called *yihud.* Talmudic sources show that a man was normally to avoid speaking with women, especially in public, not even with his own wife—and certainly not with other women. One rabbi discouraged men from engaging in discussions with women on the grounds that such talk would expose them to temptation.[22] Samuel the Sage refused even to countenance the sending of regards to a woman.[23] Nevertheless, one sage is recorded as having sent his greetings to Yalta, the wife of Rabbi Nachman,[24] showing that dissenting voices always had their say in such matters.

Another counterexample is often cited. The Talmud records discussions between Rabbi Jose and a Roman *matrona*, an important woman of the ruling class. This does not, however, prove that the sages sanctioned conversation with women. The stories about Rabbi Jose and the *matrona* are a genre of literature and may very well have no historical basis. Such stories could be told because they would not imperil the rabbinic notion that men were not to speak with women, because the *matrona* was not an ordinary woman. Underlying the story is the suggestion that had an important woman of the ruling class wanted to engage a Jewish sage in conversation, political considerations might have impelled the sage to comply.[25]

Certain ritual practices centered around the important matter of "family purity"—the set of laws regarding menstrual cleanness that ordained specified periods of abstention from marital relations, based on the rules in Leviticus. These laws are grouped under the term *niddah*. The laws of *niddah* emphasize not only purity and rhythm to sexuality, but also modesty in sexual behavior.

The (Limited) Amelioration of Women's Status

Given the emphasis in rabbinic thought on women's domestic role, it should be mentioned that in areas such as marriage and divorce, women's legal status did improve somewhat over that of women in biblical times. Simeon ben Shetah, possibly under the influence of Queen Salome Alexandra, is credited with having introduced the *ketubah* (marriage contract), which made a husband's entire estate guarantor of his wife's *ketubah*. This represented a substantial improvement in social and economic status of woman. In theory, by requiring the husband to repay the *ketubah* upon divorce, the institution of the *ketubah* was intended to discourage divorce, which could be initiated solely by the husband.

In practice, however, divorce still remained easy for men to obtain. The discussions between the schools of Shammai and Hillel are most telling in this connection. The School of Shammai allowed divorce only on the grounds of adultery by the wife. The School of Hillel permitted a man to divorce his wife even if it were for no better reason than that she burned his food or, as Rabbi Akiva later ruled, even if he simply found a more beautiful woman.[26] The Shammaite ruling may have reflected the improved status of women in upper-class society, for their husbands could not divorce them as easily as could the husbands of women of the lower classes.[27] Another factor working in favor of talmudic women was the abolition by Rabbi Yohanan ben Zakkai of the rite of bitter waters, a trial by ordeal to determine if a woman had been guilty of adultery.[28] As a practical matter, the rite would have already ceased to exist once there no longer was a temple or a high priest to officiate at the ritual. Some sages said that the rite had in fact been abolished because adultery had increased and the ritual was no longer efficacious, [29] which might indicate that abolition of the rite occurred while the Temple yet stood.

A woman had to perform certain duties for her husband. The Mishnah enumerates in detail her obligations to her husband:

> These are works which the wife must perform for her husband: grinding flour and baking bread and washing clothes and cooking food and giving suck to her child and making ready his bed and working in wool. If she brought him in one bondwoman she need not grind or bake or wash; if two, she need not cook or give her child suck; if three, she need not make ready his bed or work in wool; if four, she may sit [all the day] in a chair. R. Eliezer says: Even if she brought him in a hundred bondwomen he should compel her to work in wool, for idleness leads to unchastity.[30]

Additionally, the wife's dress had to conform to certain modest standards, covering body and head. If she disobeyed, she could be divorced and even lose her *ketubah*, which was supposed to give her some economic security in case of divorce.

Individual Women
Cited in the Talmud

It is not surprising that there was great conformity on the part of women to the roles set out for them. Thus the Talmud yields only a very few individual characters with which to work.

On the other hand, the tradition includes a number of devoted women who, by giving themselves completely to ensuring the success of their husbands, exemplify the supportive "helpmeet" prototype. An outstanding instance of this type was Rachel, the self-sacrificing wife of R. Akiva, who readily abandoned the rich life of her father to promote the growth and development of the ignorant shepherd Akiva.

> R. Akiva was a shepherd of Ben Kalba Sabua. The latter's daughter, seeing how modest and noble [the shepherd] was, said to him, "Were I to be betrothed to you, would you go away to [study at] an academy?" "Yes," he replied. She was then secretly betrothed to him and sent him away. When her father heard [what she had done] he drove her from his house and forbade her by a vow to have any benefit from his estate. [R. Akiva] departed, and spent twelve years at the academy. When he returned home he brought with him twelve thousand disciples. [While in his home town] he heard an old man saying to her, "How long will you lead the life of a living widowhood?" "If he would listen to me," she replied, "he would spend [in study] another twelve years." Said [R. Akiva]: "It is then with her consent that I am acting," and he departed again and spent another twelve years at the academy.[31]

It is true that upon his return Akiva acknowledged that he owed his achievements to the assistance and many sacrifices of his wife, telling his disciples: "[My learning] and yours are hers."[32] In other words, R. Akiva admitted that it was thanks to her advice, encouragement, and especially her readiness to sacrifice that he went to study and achieved greatness. Yet, although he became the renowned scholar and leader of the nation, she spent the better part of her life in obscurity and loneliness.[33]

The maid of Rabbi Judah Ha-Nasi was a devoted servant to her master and displayed erudition on many occasions, assisting the students who came to learn with Rabbi Judah by hinting at translations of difficult terms. Even though the maid was obviously learned, we do not even know her name. As has been wryly observed, had this savant servant been male, he surely would have been pulled from servile status and brought into the ranks of rabbinic students. And it is likely that he would then not have remained nameless or the anonymous servant of an eminent man.[34] Even if this character is fictional, the account reflects the truth of woman's subordination and the failure to give status to her learning.[35]

Both Imma Shalom and Yalta, wives of well-known rabbis, are depicted as intelligent, lively women; but the Talmud does not say that they were learned in Torah. Nor did they play any role in public life. The anecdotes describing their activities generally refer to their roles in family life.[36]

The only woman in talmudic literature who *is* described as learned in Torah is Beruriah.[37] The stories about this most prominent female of the Talmud indicate that the rules forbidding conversation between women and men disturbed her. When Beruriah encountered Rabbi Jose the Galilean and he asked her for directions—"By what road do we go to Lydda?"—she answered him, "Galilean fool, did not the rabbis teach, 'Engage not overmuch in talk with women'? You should have asked, 'How to Lydda?' "[38] Her sharp, ironical response, I think, indicates her general resentment at women's status in a male-dominated world.

In talmudic anecdotes, Beruriah is always pitted against men and is shown engaging them in learned discussions and debates. The brilliance of her scholarship is demonstrated when Rabbi Simlai comes before Rabbi Johanan and asks to be taught the Book of Genealogies in three months. Rabbi Johanan responds by throwing a clod of earth at him, saying, "If Beruriah, wife of Rabbi Meir and daughter of Rabbi Teradyon, who studied three hundred laws from three hundred teachers in one day, could not do her duty in three years, how can you possibly do it in three months?"[39] This discussion accords Beruriah an important place in Torah learning, yet she is never given the title of Rabbi and thus never had the authority accorded other sages. Her sex must have debarred her from ordination, yet her opinions on halakhic matters are cited in the talmudic text and held in high regard.[40]

A story arose about Beruriah's demise that may have been an attempt by some rabbis in later history to annihilate the image. This story was related by Rashi, who lived a thousand years later, from an unknown source. It tells of a bitter quarrel between

Beruriah and her husband, Rabbi Meir.[41] Beruriah mocked the saying of the rabbis in *b. Qiddušin*, which states: "Women are temperamentally light-headed."[42] Rabbi Meir is said to have warned her that her impudence will bring her tragedy; and, according to this story, it did. Supposedly, R. Meir sent a student to seduce her and eventually she succumbed to his advances. When she realized what she had done she committed suicide. What can we conclude about such a story? Beruriah represented a learned, intelligent, and independent woman who dared question the stereotype. It seems implausible that Rabbi Meir would attempt to cause his wife to sin. Further, there is nothing in the intelligence and moral character of Beruriah to make this story acceptable. More likely, it was contrived by men of a later generation who grew uncomfortable with the legacy of such a woman. This story was the rabbinic way to warn women against following Beruriah and studying Torah. Later tradition preferred the image of the self-sacrificing and self-effacing Rachel above the assertive, intellectual Beruriah.

One of the two female leaders that the Talmud does refer to favorably is Queen Salome Alexandra, [43] who ascended the Hasmonean throne during the Second Jewish Commonwealth upon the death of her ruthless husband, Jannai. Though she ruled for only nine years, 76 to 67 B.C.E., her reign was characterized by peace and prosperity in Judea. Despite the general approbation of the rabbis for Salome Alexandra's successful rule, the Midrash remarks that you can appoint a king but not a queen.[44] Later halakhic rulings, following this lead, flatly barred women from leadership positions.

It is well to remember, though, that Salome was not appointed queen by the sages, but rather by her husband, a Sadducee strongly influenced by Hellenistic ways. Anthropologists have shown that elitist groups prefer to appoint a woman from their own class over a male from a lower class.[45] Jannai apparently did not trust in his two sons and, not wanting an outsider, appointed his wife.

The only other queen mentioned in the Talmud, Queen Helena of Adiabene (who ruled in the first century C.E.), was a convert to Judaism and won high praise from the rabbis for her meticulous observance of Jewish tradition.[46]

Though the list of women specifically mentioned in the Talmud is a short one, certain individual women of talmudic times—like certain biblical ones—managed to leave their mark in the male-dominated world of the sages.

Biblical Models and Values: The Wise Woman

Having established the character of women's roles as reflected in talmudic literature, let us now consider how the rabbis viewed those biblical women who challenged their conceptions about the restricted role of woman. As we will see throughout the course of this work, the biblical models were conceded considerably more latitude than the talmudic ones, particularly in the areas of intellect and leadership.

The book of Samuel introduces us to the activities of two women designated by the title "wise woman" (*'ishah ḥakhamah*) (2 Sam. 14:1–22; 20:17–22).[47] The two narratives—one concerning the wise woman of Tekoa; the other, the wise woman of Abel—describe the counsel rendered by these two women to David and show that there were women in biblical Israel who were active in public life, advising kings and leaders and not just people in their own family circle.

The first of these wise women appears in the story of Absalom, who murdered his half-brother Amnon for raping his sister Tamar. The murder causes Absalom to become alienated from his father, King David. Joab, commander-in-chief of David's army, senses that David longed to be reconciled with Absalom, so Joab contrives a plan involving the help of a wise woman from the city of Tekoa. Joab brings the woman to the king. The discussion between the two is somewhat complex, but the narrative makes it clear that she succeeds by the use of proverbial language in persuading the king to bring back his rebellious son (2 Samuel 14). Her handling of the matter is masterful, suggesting that she was experienced in managing such delicate situations with tact and diplomacy.

Another *'ishah ḥakhamah* of the Bible, the wise woman of

Abel, spoke up fearlessly in a dangerous situation, thereby saving her city from destruction by Joab and his army (2 Samuel 20). She leads the inhabitants of her city, men and women alike, to the wall to confront Joab, and through her skillful oratory persuades him to withdraw. Who was this wise woman who successfully directed her people at a time of national emergency? No information is offered in the Bible to explain how this woman acquired the education and skills needed to negotiate in difficult political situations. As in the case of the wise woman of Tekoa, we must assume that she had some training for the sensitive political task she is shown carrying out, which required great wisdom. There are three similar instances in the Bible in which leaders negotiate at the city wall, but this is the only episode showing a woman as leader.[48]

Another image of female leadership is found in Judges (9:53), in a story about the death at the hands of a woman of the ruthless Abimelech, who contrived to make himself king. When Abimelech approached the fortress of Thebez to burn it and the people within, an unnamed woman, presented simply as *'ishah 'aḥat* ("one woman"), had the courage and quick sense to cast a piece of millstone upon his head, breaking the miscreant's skull.[49]

Though the stories about these women are brief, they convey the important information that not all authority roles were defined as male. Whereas in talmudic times women were not seen in negotiator roles, nor as wise advisers to leadership, and certainly not in or near combat, in biblical times they apparently were not thus restricted and could therefore rise to leadership when extraordinary circumstances called for it.

In addition to the existence in biblical lore about "wise women," there is also the image presented in Proverbs of women in educational roles.[50] As we have seen, a most significant aspect of the educational teachings of Proverbs is that it depicts both fathers and mothers alike acting in the capacity of instructors of their children.[51] For example, King Lemuel is shown being taught ethical behavior by his mother.[52] The model woman described in the famous acrostic poem on the "woman of valor," though deprecated by some modern writers as a mere homemaker, deserves to be appreciated as offering the image of a woman playing an important role both inside and outside the home.[53]

Women as Leaders in the Bible: Deborah, Huldah, and Esther

A few outstanding women leaders of the Bible achieved a stature unparalleled by any woman of rabbinic literature. These figures will be amplified more fully in chapter 8. Perhaps none is more multifaceted than Deborah, who functioned as judge, political leader, and also religious teacher in her capacity to compose inspiring liturgical songs. Through wisdom, initiative, and forthright leadership, she saves the nation from conquest.

Esther too is renowned for having saved the people from extinction. She further served in another unusual capacity—as a female authenticator of written tradition. The book of Esther, which tells the story of her deliverance of the Jews from the Persians, reveals that three parties were involved in the establishment of Purim: Esther, Mordecai, and the Jews of Persia. The Jews undertook to observe the new festival, relying on what was written in the letter of Mordecai and on the command of Queen Esther.[54] When Esther joins Mordecai in writing a second letter and finally issues a command on her authority alone, the codification of the festival is complete.[55] The biblical scroll (*megillah*) about Purim is named for Esther. In this sense, Esther, like the other wise women, represents an oral tradition being written down.[56]

The prophetess Huldah was a Jerusalemite woman, the wife of Shallum, who was the keeper of the king's wardrobe during the reign of Josiah (639–609 B.C.E.). Huldah figures in the dramatic discovery of a scroll that greatly influenced Josiah's reign (2 Kings 22:14–20).

The country was in the midst of a religious reform when Hilkiah, the high priest, announced that he had discovered "a scroll of Moses" in the Temple storage. Most scholars maintain that he had discovered either the partial or complete book of Deuteronomy, which foretold imminent destruction of the land and people. King Josiah was greatly distressed by this find.

He tore his garments and sent his emissaries to consult the prophetess Huldah regarding the meaning of the scroll.

Huldah responded in prophetic fashion, "Thus said the Lord," issuing dire warnings of evil doings and foretelling the destruction of Jerusalem, adding that Josiah would not live to witness the great calamity.[57] Nothing is made of the fact that it was a *woman* who was consulted by the king concerning a religious-legal problem. No one suggests asking another opinion from another source. No one even brings up the idea of seeking out a male prophet.

The preceding examples suggest that biblical literature was not as inflexibly gender-conscious regarding leadership as was the Talmud. The female figures whose activities have thus far been described acted in an extraordinary capacity for women in the Bible. Nonetheless, act they did, and their stories were accepted into the tradition and recorded for posterity. Moreover, there is no mention in biblical sources of anyone in authority discussing the propriety of women acting in a leadership role, as the later talmudic sages would do centuries later when discussing Deborah, Huldah, and others.

In all of these instances, aggadic exegetes examined these biblical heroines under their own unique lenses. The rabbis had to find a way for biblical women to fulfill their leadership roles while obeying the strictures demanded of women in the name of modesty. As noted above, rabbinic literature is not characterized by a uniform, systematic philosophy. It reflects different and sometimes inconsistent points of view. This is not only to be expected of a literature that was composed over a vast period of time, but is indicative of the problematical nature of the rabbinic attitude toward women, an attitude riddled with inconsistencies and contradictions and one that reveals the tensions and fissures in their ideological project.

Conclusion

Many factors—social, political, economic, and religious— contributed to the changes in the role of women that occurred between biblical and talmudic times. Historians maintain that Jewish life altered dramatically with the destruction of the Temple and the loss of political power. The loss of the Temple along with the loss of sovereignty constituted a profound and far-reaching crisis in the structure of Jewish life. After the fall of Jerusalem, the Jewish community became more focused on the Book and, concomitantly, became more hierarchical from within, focusing its life on the functions of study and worship. An effort was made to preserve these activities as male prerogatives by imposing social controls upon women in the name of modesty.

The societal and religious structure placed women outside the corridors of influence and power and gave them only the limited instruction they would need to function as homemakers. No formal educational institutions or opportunities were open to them. As the Talmud harshly puts it: "Women lived a restricted life, wrapped up like a mourner, banished from the company of all men and confined within a prison."[58] A prostitute was a woman who went abroad,[59] whereas respectable women were expected to obey the laws of modesty, stay at home, and mind the affairs of the household.

Given this societal and halakhic context, it is remarkable that the aggadic treatment of biblical women who ventured beyond these circumscribed spheres was so forthcoming.

Notes

1. This chapter is a revised version of a paper originally published as "The Changing Face of Woman from Bible to Talmud," *Shofar* 7 (1989): 34–47.

2. However, it must be noted that a countertradition of female metaphors for the Deity exists; see Trible, "Depatriarchalizing in Biblical Tradition." As Trible states it, "The hermeneutical challenge is to translate biblical faith without sexism" (p. 218). See, too, Leila L. Bronner, "Gynomorphic Imagery in Exilic Isaiah," *Dor Le Dor* 12 (1983/84): 71–76.

3. Jo Ann Hackett, "Women's Studies and the Hebrew Bible," in *The Future of Biblical Studies: The Hebrew Scriptures*, ed. Richard Elliott Friedman and H. G. M. Williamson, SBL Semeia Studies (Atlanta: Scholars Press, 1987), 141; and Susan Niditch, "Portrayals of Women in the Hebrew Bible," in *Jewish Women in Historical Perspective*, ed. Judith R. Baskin (Detroit: Wayne State University Press, 1991), 25–42.

4. The Hellenic environment may well have exerted some negative influence on the status of women in Jewish society, and its influence may have seeped into talmudic law itself. The extent to which Hellenistic culture influenced the attitudes of the rabbis toward women has been a matter of lively disagreement among contemporary scholars. Whereas some scholars explain the changed role and lower status of talmudic women compared with biblical women as being the result of cultural influences emanating from Greece and Rome, Leonard Swidler (*Women in Judaism: The Status of Women in Formative Judaism* [Metuchen, N. J.: Scarecrow Press, 1976], 7–9, 22–24, 167–69) claims that the reverse is true—the Jews negatively influenced the Greeks on

this score. I do not think that the historical evidence we now possess enables us to decide this question.

5. Theodore Friedman, "The Shifting Role of Women, from Bible to Talmud," *Judaism* 36 (1987): 480–82; and Brooten, *Women Leaders in the Ancient Synagogue*. Although Friedman's observations accurately reflect the literary approach, Brooten's study offers suggestive evidence from epigraphic and archaeological sources indicating that women's disappearance in the nonrabbinic world may have been less than complete.

6. If classical rabbinic authority was as circumscribed as some current scholars believe (e.g., Cohen, *From the Maccabees to the Mishnah*, 221–24), one would have to draw a distinction between the desire of the rabbis to restrict female leadership and the social reality that the public may not have listened to them. We know that there were at least some women in public life, as, for example, Queen Salome Alexandra.

7. See Moshe D. Gross, *Ozar HaAgadah*, 1:1 n. 268 (Jerusalem: Mosad HaRav Kook, 1960), 266–68 [Hebrew]; C. G. Montefiore and H. Loewe, *A Rabbinic Anthology* (n.p.: Meridian Books, 1970), 507–9.

8. *b. Ber.* 17a.

9. The Aramaic text reads only "*his* daughter" and is vague about *whose* daughter, whether the emperor's or R. Gamaliel's. A case could be made in either direction, but it is less plausible that R. Gamaliel's daughter would have cause to be in the emperor's presence.

10. *b. Sanh.* 39a; *Gen. Rab.* 17:7.

11. More on women and prayer can be found in reference to Hannah in chapter 5.

12. *m. Soṭa* 3:4; *m. Ned.* 4:3; *b. Soṭa* 20a, 21a. Even now, in Orthodox circles, it is a daring matter to suggest teaching the oral law to women. Professor Yeshayahu Leibowitz, quoted in Rachel Biale, *Women and Jewish Law: An Exploration of Women's Issues in Halakhic Sources* (New York: Schocken Books, 1984), 38, is a forceful advocate of overturning these traditional proscriptions: "After repeated discussions of this question in the history of Halakhah it was determined that . . . women are exempt from [learning Torah]. And this is a grave error and a great misfortune in the history of Judaism. . . . Barring women from the study of Torah is not freeing them from an obligation (as is the case of some other *mitzvot*) but rather a denial of a basic Jewish right. Women's 'Jewishness' thus becomes inferior to that of men."

13. *y. Soṭa* 3:4, 19a.

14. *b. Yoma* 66b. This recalls Telemachus in the Greek Odyssey telling his mother that she must "go to [her] wiferies" because speech belongs to him alone, as man of the house. Although the Odyssey

reflects much more ancient times, the attitudes and pattern of female subordination it depicts persisted in Greek society; see Homer, *The Odyssey*, Book 21, Harvard Classics (1909), 304.

15. *b. Qidd.* 29a.

16. *b. Qidd.* 29b.

17. *b. Ketub.* 72a.

18. *b. Ber.* 24a.

19. *m. B. Qam.* 8:6.

20. *t. Yoma* 4:20; *y. Yoma* 1:1, 38d; *y. Meg.* 1:12, 72a; *b. Yoma* 47a; *Num. Rab.* end of chapter 2.

21. *b. Yebam.* 77b; *b. Git.* 12a; *b. Šebu.* 30b; *Lev. Rab.* 20:11; *y. Yoma* 1:1, 38d; *y. Meg.* 1:12, 72a; *Lev. Rab.* 2:11; *Tanhuma, WaYislaḥ* 36.

22. *m. 'Abot* 1:5; *b. Ned.* 20b.

23. *b. Qidd.* 70a.

24. *b. Ber.* 51a.

25. Eliezer Slomovic and Rosalie [Shoshana] Gershenszon, "A Second Century Jewish Gnostic Debate: Rabbi Josi Ben Halafta and the Matrona," *JSJ* 16 (1985): 1–41.

26. *m. Git.* 9:10.

27. On this theory, see Louis Finkelstein, *Halachah and Agadah* (New York: The Jewish Theological Seminary of America, 1960), 266 [Hebrew].

28. *m. Soṭa* 9:9; *t. Soṭa* 14:2 (Saul Lieberman, *Tosefta Ki-fshutah* [New York: The Jewish Theological Seminary of America, 1955–88], 235–36).

29. Ibid.

30. *m. Ketub.* 5:5; see also 5:7 for mutual sexual obligations.

31. *b. Ketub.* 62–63a.

32. *b. Ketub.* 63a.

33. Although Rachel is depicted in rabbinic literature as the epitome of the supportive wife, Shulamit Valler, in her recent book, discusses how a husband's Torah study, which led to prolonged absence from the home, affected his wife, and whether she had any right to prevent his departure; see her *Women and Womanhood in the Stories of the Babylonian Talmud* (Israel: Hakibbutz Hameuchad, 1993), 56–80 [Hebrew].

34. *b. Ketub.* 104a; Swidler, *Women in Judaism*, 110.

35. Cf. Rabban Gamaliel's female slave Tabitha, *y. Nid.* 2:1, 49d.

36. *b. Šabb.* 116a–b; *b. Ned.* 20b; *b. B. Meṣ.* 59b; *b. Qidd.* 70a–b; *b. Ber.* 51b; *b. Nid.* 20b; *b. Ḥul.* 109b; Raphael Loewe, *The Position of Women in Judaism* (London: SPCK, 1966), 30.

37. *b. Pesaḥ.* 62b; cf. *Midr. Prov.* 31:10, where Meir's wife is not given a name.

38. *b. 'Erub.* 53b.

39. *b. Pesaḥ.* 62b.

40. *t. Kelim B. Meṣ.* 1:6; Aharon Hyman, *Toldoth Tannaim Ve'Amoraim* (London: Express Press, 1910), 294 [Hebrew]. For further discussion on Beruriah, see David M. Goodblatt, "The Beruriah Traditions," in *Persons and Institutions in Early Rabbinic Judaism*, ed. William Scott Green, Brown Judaic Studies 3 (Missoula, Mont.: Scholars Press, 1977), 207–35; Rachel Adler, "The Virgin in the Brothel: The Legend of Beruriah," *Tikkun* 3 (1988): 28–31, 102–5; repr. *Vox Benedictina* 7 (1990): 7–29; and Daniel Boyarin, "Reading Androcentrism against the Grain," 40–48, and *Carnal Israel: Reading Sex in Talmudic Culture* (Berkeley: University of California Press, 1993), 181–96. Goodblatt argues that the traditions ascribing an advanced rabbinic education to Beruriah stem from later Sassanian Babylonia, where the notion of an exceptional, learned female was more acceptable than in Roman Palestine. Boyarin, on the other hand, believes that the tradition of Beruriah existed in both Palestinian and Babylonian contexts. In both settings, the idea of a learned woman was "atypical, but only in one [i.e., the Babylonian] does she become a scandal" (Boyarin, *Carnal Israel*, 189 and 183 n. 16).

41. Rashi on *b. 'Abod. Zar.* 18b; *b. Šabb.* 33b.

42. *b. Qidd.* 80b.

43. *Sipra, Beḥuqqotai* 1:1; *Sipre Deut.* 42; *b. Ber.* 48a.

44. *Sipre Deut.* 17:15; Maimonides, *Mishneh Torah, Sefer Shoftim, Hilkhot Melakhim* (New York: Shulsinger Bros., 1947), 1:5.

45. Hackett, "Women's Studies and the Hebrew Bible," 149.

46. *m. Yoma* 3:10; *m. Nazir* 3:6; *t. Sukk.* 1:1; *b. B. Bat.* 11a; *b. Yoma* 3:10; Josephus, *Ant.* 20.21–20.43 [17–96].

47. It should be noted that these women are respected for their counsel, whereas Eve is regarded as having given evil counsel. See chapter 2.

48. 2 Kings 18:18; 1 Sam. 36: see also 2 Sam. 11:18–28.

49. Judg. 9:53. See chapter 6.

50. The exalted role of wisdom personified as woman is discussed by Claudia V. Camp, *Wisdom and the Feminine in the Book of Proverbs*, Bible and Literature Series 11 (Decatur, Ga.: The Almond Press, 1985).

51. Prov. 1:8; 4:1–3; 6:20; 10:1; 15:20; 23:22–25.

52. Prov. 31:1ff.

53. See Swidler, *Women in Judaism,* 35, for a different point of view about the role of the woman of valor.

54. Esth. 9:29–31.

55. Esth. 9:32. See also various commentators on the book of Esther: *The Interpreter's Bible,* "Book of Esther," 1952; *Soncino Bible,* Book of Esther, 1946; etc.

56. Camp, *Wisdom and the Feminine,* 145–46.

57. 2 Kings 22:14–20.

58. *b. 'Erub.* 100b.

59. *m. Kelim* 28:9; see the Hebrew commentary of Chanoch Albeck, *Shishah Sidre Mishnah, Seder Toharot* (Tel Aviv: Mosad Bialik/Dvir, 1958), 116. This understanding is not expressed in the Danby translation.

2

Eve's Estate: Temptation, Modesty, and the Valorization of Matrimony

The story of Adam and Eve has long been the topic of intense discussion and interpretation in the religious traditions of the West. In all of them, Eve emerges as archetype or prototype of woman;[1] thus every religion takes her as the beginning of its discussion on womanhood. Values and attitudes toward the class of women are often derived from these early understandings of biblical Eve.

In Judaism, much of that discussion can be found within the pages of Talmud and Midrash, within the extracanonical texts such as the Apocrypha and Pseudepigrapha, and within other early sources such as Philo and Josephus. In Christianity, the early and formative understanding of Eve can be found in the New Testament and the patristic literature. But in contrast to all other literatures, where the Eve figure is a basis for theology, in Talmud and Midrash she serves primarily as a basis for *halakhah and for women's values*. Rabbinic exegesis of Eve became the rationale for rules and regulations guiding women's behavior, a Jewish catechism of do's and don'ts for females. And because Eve was regarded as a source of sin in Talmud and Midrash, there was a need to rein her in, to harness that dangerous energy, to create areas of female seclusion and subordination. Thus, the *halakhah* concerning woman that flows from interpreting Eve is at times limiting. It is obvious, then, that an analysis of the attitudes of the sages toward Eve is of great consequence to living Jewish women of every generation.

Below we will examine several examples of this unique rabbinic process, of interweaving law and lore, *halakhah* and *aggadah*. Rather than separate them, we will treat the sources as they exist—an admixture of theology and history, linguistics, construction of values, sociological observations, and law.

Eve and Evil

The rabbis were not alone responsible for making of Eve an archetype of sin. Long before their time, there existed in the literature of the Second Commonwealth a well-developed notion of Eve as a sinful influence.[2] Among these writers, for example, was Ben Sira, who apparently was the first to point to Eve (inferring women in general) as the author of death and sin.[3] Another prerabbinic Jewish source, the pseudepigraphic *Life of Adam and Eve* (first century c.e.), depicts Eve as remorsefully indicting herself for causing Adam to sin and thus bringing death into the world.[4] There is a countervailing force in the biblical text emphasizing Eve's significance as the source of all life (Gen. 3:20), but this was no match for the growing negative construction in prerabbinic times of protowoman as sinner. By now, the previous balance maintained in the Bible was tilted, and the story became increasingly a cultural justification for male dominance and female subservience, both in Judaism and Christianity. Thus, subsequent rabbinic literature and nascent Christianity emphasized not her significance as a source of life, but more as the source of evil and death.

The Story of Eve and Its Rabbinic Retelling

And God said, "Let us make man in our image, after our likeness. They shall rule . . . the whole earth, and all the creeping things that creep on earth." And God created man in His image, in the image of God He created him; male and female He created them. God blessed them and God said to them, "Be fertile and increase, fill the earth and master it" (Gen. 1:26–28).

The Lord God formed man from the dust of the earth. He blew into his nostrils the breath of life, and man became a living being. . . . The Lord God said, "It is not good for man to be alone; I will make a fitting helper for him." . . . So the Lord God cast a deep sleep upon the man; and, while he slept, He took one of his ribs and closed up the flesh at that spot. And the Lord God fashioned the rib that He had taken from the man into a woman; and He brought her to the man. Then the man said, "This one at last is bone of my bones and flesh of my flesh. This one shall be called Woman, for from man was she taken" (Gen. 2:7, 18, 21–23).

These two accounts in Genesis concerning the creation of man and woman differ greatly in language, style, and content.[5] In both, woman, like man, is the direct intentional creation of God. Only in the first version, however, is it stressed that both man and woman are created equal in the image of God and given the mandate by God to populate the earth and have dominion over it (Gen. 1:26–28). In the second version, Eve is created from Adam and both are placed in the Garden of Eden. Both Adam and Eve disobey the command of God, and both are punished. The second version can be read etiologically, as explaining the primary characteristics of the human-divine relationship among God, man, and woman. The enunciation of the punishments, including the words "he shall rule over you," can likewise be understood as a simple description of how things *would* be, rather than as a command saying that this is how things *must* be.

Most traditions down through the ages, including the mid-rashic tradition, evince a deep-seated conviction that Eve tempted Adam to commit sin. The exact nature of the sin is unclear in both the biblical text and rabbinic interpretation. Rather, it was simply a given upon which the rabbis proceeded to analyze the parts of the story. Their analysis, therefore, is not a sweeping theological statement or series of cosmic questions. Instead, they focus on issues such as her name, her creation and physiognomy, her individual actions, and her punishment. Out of this, or one might say, from inside out, they construct a midrashic and halakhic reality much larger than the sum of its parts.

Eve's Name

To the sages, names were regarded not only as labels but also as symbols—magical keys to the nature and essence of the person or object to which they referred. In this they took their cue from Hebrew Scriptures, including its problematic reference to Eve's name: "The man named his wife Eve, because she was the mother of all the living" (Gen. 3:20). In sound but not derivation, the name *Eve* in Hebrew resembles the Hebrew word for "life."[6] Thus, rabbinic etymologies for the name *havvah* (Eve) are popular rather than scientific. Instead of attempting to derive its linguistic root, they create puns around it, relying on its sound to invent its sense.

One midrash connects the root *havvah* ("to declare"), to make Eve an "adviser" to Adam. Eve is thus placed in a very negative light, because she, like the serpent, was a presenter of bad advice and evil counsel.[7] This midrash also plays on a connection to the Aramaic word *hivya*, meaning "serpent," for Eve was the "tempter" of Adam.[8] Not so subtly, this midrash recasts the narrative material of Eve's having been seduced by the serpent and presents her as the serpentlike tempter of Adam.[9]

This serpent/seduction theme comes up many times in rabbinic discussion about Eve, often connecting it with her name or her manner of coming into being. For example, one midrash states that the letter *samekh* appears for the first time in Genesis 2:21, in the word *sagar* ("to close"), which is used in connection with the closing of Adam's flesh after Eve's creation. The word *sagar* is taken to be suggestive of the word *Satan*. Note here the wide latitude taken by the rabbis as they relied on sound and pun in their exegesis: the word *Satan* and the root *sagar* are only connected by sound, the first being written with the Hebrew letter *sin* and the other with a *samekh*.[10] By using a wordplay to suggest that Eve and sin (Satan) entered the world together, Eve is made responsible for the introduction of lust into creation.[11]

Such linguistic connections gave rise to numerous rabbinic remarks positing that Satan harbored sexual desire for Eve.

> We thus find it with the primeval serpent [in the Garden of Eden] which set its eyes on that which was not proper for it; what it sought was not granted to it and what it possessed was taken from it. . . . It said, "I will kill Adam and marry Eve"; but now, "*I will put enmity between thee and the woman, and between thy seed and her seed*" (Gen. 3:15).[12]

Some sages actually claimed that Satan "injected his lust into her," a somewhat obscure phrase that may mean that he had sexual intercourse with her, or perhaps more abstractly that he infused her with sexual urges.[13] Some sages related that Satan was jealous of Adam (presumably for possessing Eve) and that Satan's jealousy brought death into the world.[14] Because the serpent's jealousy was seen to have started the whole process, it would appear that he was viewed as responsible for bringing death into Eden. Nevertheless, it was because of Eve's presence that the serpent became jealous, and this has been used to justify placing the responsibility (blame) with her.

Overall, then, rabbinic exegesis of Eve's name reinforces the theme not of connecting the first woman with life, but rather with forbidden knowledge, lust, temptation, sin, and death.

One thing the rabbis never do, but that Christian traditions of roughly the same period imply, is to say that because Adam named Eve, he therefore ruled over her (and by implication, *ought* to have done so).[15] This conclusion comes out of the ancient notion holding that to name someone or something is to have power over that person or thing. The rabbis offer other justifications for Eve's subordination, but reject this particular one.[16]

"Male and Female Created He Them"

In discussing the story of the creation of the first humans, the rabbis expend considerable energy on the question of androgyny. It was not only the first version that bothered them—that is, the creation of two sexes from one being. It was also the discrepant accounts that begged the question.

In attempting to make sense of the first version of the creation of the first man and woman, the rabbis made use of the concept of androgyny, which in rabbinics ordinarily means to possess complete sets of both male and female genitalia. The rabbis speak of two bodies, male and female, joined together:

> When the Holy One, blessed be He, created Adam, He created him an hermaphrodite [bi-sexual], for it is said, *Male and female created He them and called their name Adam* (Gen. 5:2). R. Samuel b. Nachman said: When the Lord created Adam He created him double-faced, then He split him and made him of two backs, one back on this side and one back on the other side.[17]

> When the Holy One, blessed be He, created the first man, he created him an hermaphrodite. R. Levi said: When man was created, he was created with two body-fronts, and He sawed him in two, so that two backs resulted, one back for the male and another back for the female.[18]

We see that Adam and Eve are described as having been created at the same time, possessing a shared body with a male face and body front on one side, and a female face and body front on the reverse side. The Adam side was the "front," and the Eve side was the "back." The hermaphrodite was sawed in half, leaving two separate bodies, one male and one female. The sages contemplated just how this androgyne was configured, and they discussed which part of the original androgynous being became Eve when separated. Such explanations of an original hermaphrodite accommodate the more egalitarian thrust of the first creation story (Gen. 1:27–28).

The second creation story (Gen. 2:7, 21–22)—the "rib" story— gave rise to even greater midrashic speculation, first as an attempt to reconcile this account with an androgynous being,[19] and then as an understanding of the relationship between male and female.

The word *zela*, ordinarily translated as "rib," becomes a key word in the sages' inquiry. They strenuously interpret this word, generating abstruse discussions in which different verses from scripture are cited to determine whether the word means a "face," "side," or "tail." For example, they observe that the word *zela* is used to describe the Tabernacle and that there it must mean the "side" of the Tabernacle (Ex. 26:20) and certainly not "the rib."[20] Although the use of Adam's "side" for Eve's creation lends itself to a more egalitarian understanding, use of the "tail" is demeaning. As the reader will observe, such interpretive maneuvers construe the creation of Eve as having been formed from a mere part of Adam—not even half, just a small part, whether that be his tail, a rib, his face, or whatever.[21]

Their interpretive manipulations had two results: first, they helped to reconcile the dissonance between the two stories; second, they pushed the interpretation of the Genesis story in a direction that jibes with a view of Eve as subordinate to Adam, and consequently woman as subordinate to man. In addition, though the specific meaning of the term *zela* is never resolved, the speculations it gave rise to become a point of departure for favorable remarks regarding Eve's physical qualities, a matter discussed in greater detail below.

Constructing Eve and Constructing Woman

A phrase appears in the second creation story that captivated the attention of the sages. The passage in question appears in Genesis 2:22 in which it is said that God "built [Eve] from the rib." *Wayyiven*, the verb used, is accurately translated as "and he built."[22]

The sages play on the word *build* to explain Eve's purpose as childbearer, and their tone in doing so is one of praise. They elaborate the metaphor of Eve as a built object to note that a woman's body is structured like a *binyan* ("storehouse") for a purpose:

> It teaches that [God] built Eve after the fashion of a storehouse. Just as a storehouse is narrow at the top and broad at the bottom so as to hold the produce [safely], so a woman is narrower above and broader below so as to hold the embryo.[23]

To the sages' way of thinking, this comparison of a woman's body to a storehouse—from the same root as the Hebrew for "to build"—was a great compliment, for motherhood was considered to be the highest purpose of a woman's life.

The sages also connect *wayyiven* with *binah* ("understanding"): " '*And the Lord God built (wayyiven) the rib.*' . . . She was endowed with more understanding (*binah*) than a man."[24] The force of the compliment here is somewhat undercut by their characterization of the nature of feminine intelligence as a matter of mastery of domestic practicalities, in contrast to the intellectual demands faced by men venturing out into the world and learning understanding from people. Unfair circular reasoning may be detected here. The sages promulgate regulations that restrict women to the home—using the generally negative qualities they have ascribed to women to justify this—while giving away in passages like these their recognition that such restrictions on women's lives lead to their intellectual and social inferiority.

Two additional midrashim based on the rib story inform the nature of interpersonal relationships: "One should love one's wife as oneself and honor her more than oneself"[25] and, "His wife is like himself."[26] Though these ethical constructs are founded on Eve's having been taken from Adam's body and are on the surface entirely positive, a second look raises other questions. Are they telling the reader that the wife is to be loved not for her own qualities, but rather because she is part of her husband? Was there a message here that diminished women's persona?[27] On the other hand, "Honor her more than himself" is unequivocal; I believe the first passage can be taken romantically and complimentarily.

Another midrash, with its lovely image of God plaiting Eve's hair, emphasizes the importance of a woman's role in marriage. Commenting again on *wayyiven*, "and the Lord God built the rib that He took from man into a woman and he brought her unto the man," the rabbis say: "[This verse] teaches that the Holy One, blessed be He, plaited Eve's hair and then brought her to Adam, for in the seatowns they describe net-work as *binyata.*"[28] Thus, the making of nets is likened to braiding hair by virtue of employing the word *binyata*. So highly esteemed by the sages was the state of matrimony, that their midrashim depict God preparing Eve for marriage to Adam. In this rabbinic story, God performs the familiar functions carried out in later Jewish tradition by the important men and women in the bride's life. Not only does God give away the bride in the manner of a father; God also beautifies Eve. Moreover, just as the woman is herself a storehouse, built for childbearing, so she will, in marriage, build the home (rabbis called their wives, their "houses").[29]

Rules, Regulations, and the Meaning of Eve

The midrashic tradition does not so much concern itself with abstract theological matters as with clarifying guidelines for daily life. Here we see the interweaving of *halakhah* and *aggadah.* The rules of conduct are dealt with in narrative midrashic texts, in rabbinic legends that also serve to explain the necessity of observing such rules. Stories and commentaries that interpret biblical verses also levy and justify ritual obligations. It is, as the last midrash might suggest, a plaiting of its own kind.

As exalted as the state of marriage and motherhood is made out to be by the rabbis, matrimony for Eve (and hence all women) entailed specific rituals and obligations laid out by the rabbis to atone for Eve's sin. For example:

> "And why was the precept of menstruation given to her?" "Because she shed the blood of Adam [by causing death]." . . . "And why was the precept of 'dough' [*hallah;* Num. 15:19ff.] given to her?" "Because she corrupted Adam, who was the dough (*hallah*) of the world." . . . "And why was the precept of the Sabbath lights given to her?" "Because she extinguished the soul of Adam."[30]

This *aggadah* introduces three of the primary *mitzvot* associated with women: family purity, separating the dough for consecration, and lighting the candles for Sabbath and holidays. It is difficult to comprehend why these precepts find such negative explanations in this *aggadah*. Ross Kraemer suggests that the passage may have been polemical, representing a minority backlash against the increasing prominence of women in religious life.[31] Happily, history has seen more positive contexts for these women's rituals. Use of narrative makes the legal material more accessible and pedagogically forceful. One cannot say that it was done this way only to convince women; this was the pattern for laws that concerned men as well.

Eve and Modesty

As will become increasingly apparent throughout this work, the rabbis sought to project the value of modesty at every opportunity. They found such an opportunity in the story of Eve's creation. The Midrash again takes as its point of departure the expression *wayyiven*, once again connecting it to *binah*, meaning "understanding or intelligent consideration of a matter." "*Wayyiven* is written, signifying that He considered well from what part to create her."[32] God, this midrash tells us, considered various parts of the body and rejected them because they would result in undesirable traits:

> [God said], "I will not create her from [Adam's] head, lest she be swell-headed; nor from the eye, lest she be a coquette; nor from the ear, lest she be an eavesdropper; nor from the mouth, lest she be a gossip; nor from the heart, lest she be prone to jealousy; nor from the hand, lest she be light-fingered; nor from the foot, lest she be a gadabout; but from the modest part of man, for even when he stands naked, that part is covered." And as He created each limb He ordered her, "Be a modest woman." Yet in spite of all this, *But ye have set at nought all My counsel, and would none of My reproof* (Prov. 1:25).[33]

Yet despite the care taken by the Creator to create woman free of the possible faults anticipated, and despite the command to "be a modest woman,"[34] Eve and, by extension, all women are guilty of these failings and remain in need of rules and regulations to ensure their modest demeanor and conduct. The masculine discourse simultaneously creates an ideal of female virtue and a stereotype of feminine shortcomings and culpability, thus explaining the necessity of the prescribed corrective—rules and regulations to govern women's lives. One of these rules was the covering of one's hair.

There are many talmudic passages dealing with hair covering, some of which are connected to Eve. The commonly held notion was that women's hair is an irresistible sexual lure. For example, one passage speaks of woman's hair as being sexually provocative and says that this is why one must not recite the *shema* prayer in front of a woman with uncovered hair.[35] Women, then, must cover their heads so as to not distract men from their prayers.

Another section of the Talmud states that it is deemed a transgression if a married Jewish woman goes outside with her head uncovered.[36] The covering of the hair, one of the most obvious of the rules comprising *zni'ut*, implies the married woman's submission to the authority and control of her husband. This was most explicitly spelled out in the New Testament, which indicates that hair covering was to show that a woman "was made out of man" and not vice versa, and that therefore it is woman's duty to have a "symbol of authority on her head" (1 Cor. 11:2–15). Hair covering was probably also a token of her unavailability to other men. Hair covering and related customs, such as veiling, were widespread throughout the ancient world, as was women's submission to the control and authority of their fathers and subsequently their husbands. The Midrash stipulates that women should keep their hair covered because of Eve's sin:

> Why does woman cover her head and man not cover his head? A parable. To what may this be compared? To a woman who disgraced herself and because she disgraced herself, she is ashamed in the presence of people. In the same way Eve disgraced herself and caused her daughters to cover their heads.[37]

The Midrash continues in this vein, explaining that women walk before the bier at funeral processions, presumably with heads covered, to atone for Eve's having brought death into the world.[38] The connection is not obvious but rather implicit: Eve's attractiveness, having contributed to her temptation and seduction of the man, made it her responsibility to modestly cover her hair.

The custom of hair covering underwent further development and became deeply entwined in the rules and customs known as *zni'ut*—the laws of modesty. The explanations in Talmud and Midrash as to why women are obliged to cover their hair, although differing somewhat on the surface, all reference a basic, consistent discourse that assumes that women are responsible for their sexual allure (which men cannot be expected to resist) and must therefore lead a confined, private life, obeying restrictive laws of dress, demeanor, and behavior. Whether or not these texts refer to the Eve story explicitly, they draw on the same set of assumptions about female seductiveness and the need to control it by requiring modesty on the part of women.

It should be kept in mind that in the aggadic traditions of Midrash and Talmud, the focus was kept on very pragmatic considerations to guide daily conduct through rules and rituals, rather than on abstract theological questions. Thus there is great convergence of purpose in all of these midrashim around the archetypal figure of Eve: a woman's primary (if not entire) significance lies in her role as wife, mother, and homemaker. Although the sources do indict women for their seductiveness, the emphasis is on valorizing marriage and motherhood, and the rules are designed to enforce the modesty that will support these exalted functions. Eve's potential sexual threat is moved into safe marital guidelines.

Lilith: A Rebellious Eve

No discussion of the aggadic interpretation of the Eve story would be complete without some mention of the fascinating and controversial character Lilith. This figure is vaguely mentioned in early midrashic literature, but her image is not fully developed until medieval and kabbalistic sources.[39] These traditions describe Lilith as the first wife of Adam, like him made from the dust of the earth. Unlike her canonical successor, she refused to be obedient to Adam and insisted on being his equal. A medieval source has her arguing with Adam over who should take the superior position during sexual relations. Refusing to accept the female inferior role, Lilith flew away and refused to return to Adam. God tried to persuade her to return, but she would not relent. Consequently, God made another wife for Adam when Lilith ran off, and she was called Eve.

The medieval sources transform Lilith into a demon who harasses men and children at night. She is said to tempt men sexually, to be promiscuous, to give birth to legions of demon babies, and to bring death to human babies; in short, she is the antithesis of female virtue.

The Lilith figure is interesting insofar as she is a type contrary to the prescribed female role; she rebels against the submissive behavior expected of women and enforced by the rules and regulations applicable to them. The fact that medieval sages can imagine her rebellion, even though they do not countenance it, at least shows that they were aware of the constrictions and limitations women suffered under rabbinic rule. They even display some contradictory attitudes toward the ideal standard of femininity they construct, with tensions and ambiguities in several directions. The Eve figure, although blamed for bringing evil, also introduced the exalted role of subservient matrimony and motherhood—the "mother of all life" theme. Lilith is a female character who was imagined as even more sexually dangerous and untrammeled than Eve, and who is so compelling that her image lingers and haunts the tales of generations of commentators. The power of this antiheroine is a measure of the unease engendered by the strictness of the female role deemed proper by the rabbinic authorities themselves, a tradition to which Lilith serves as a potent countercurrent. Lilith is the paradigm for the rebellious woman.

Eve and Christianity

In comparison with the Eve described in rabbinic literature, the New Testament and later patristic literature may take an even harsher attitude toward sin, sexuality, suffering, and death. The connections among these subjects are made closer; and the interest in drawing theological implications is stronger, while Eve is drawn more emphatically as a seducer to evil (2 Cor. 11:3; 1 Tim. 2:13). One should not draw too emphatic a dichotomy between Jewish and Christian attitudes toward female sexuality. Just as the rabbis channel Eve's potential sexual threat into safe marital guidelines, 1 Timothy 2:15 states that a woman is saved through motherhood. Yet, although marriage and procreation are positive, divine commandments in Jewish tradition, the Christian view sees them as concessions rather than compulsory; and, for some, the demands of the kingdom might involve a celibate life. Paul, who according to Acts 22:3 was a disciple of Rabban Gamaliel (though many modern New Testament scholars dispute this), advocated celibacy. He believed that family responsibilities interfered with a person's ability to serve the kingdom. His advice was: "It is better to marry than to be aflame with passion" (1 Cor. 7:9). The Jewish Eve led to the exultation of matrimony, whereas the Christian Eve led to a darker view of sexuality and procreation even within marriage and to a pronounced strain of asceticism, a trend that never took strong hold in Judaism apart from small sects like the Essenes and Therapeutae. In the Jewish and Christian traditions alike, however, the category of woman is constructed in a male discourse.

Conclusion

From the figure of Eve and the creation story there emerged in the aggadic traditions of Talmud and Midrash a particular construction of the category of woman that represents the mainstream view in rabbinic Judaism. In the literature of the early second century (in the writings of the Apocrypha and Pseudepigrapha) and also in some of the medieval Jewish texts, there are elements in the interpretation of Eve that depart from the rabbinic perspective in ways that demonstrate tensions and contradictions both within and without the tradition, and sometimes suggest the possible influence of Hellenistic and Christian sources. The talmudic and midrashic traditions are male discourses that depict Eve as the tempter of Adam. Unlike the Hellenistic and, even more, the Christian traditions, the emphasis is not on formulating a theology of seduction, sin, temptation, and death. Rather, the aggadic sources concentrate on formulating guides to daily observance and conduct for women to follow in order to atone for Eve's sin and to achieve the modesty required for the fulfillment of their roles in marriage and matrimony.

A detailed set of practices is constructed embracing virtually the whole of women's lives. The ultimate goal, which was practical rather than philosophical, was the achievement of holiness and awareness of God's presence throughout daily existence— the essence of Jewish practice in general. The rabbis' rules regulating the daily life and rituals of women, which were justified as being necessary because of Eve's sin and the seductive dangers of all women, enabled them to restrict women's activities according to their social, cultural, and religious preconceptions. These restrictions to home and hearth, promulgated under the regime of modesty, cut women off from public leadership, learning, and communal prayer, resulting in their isolation and subordination.

In the search for a reconstructed but still authentically Jewish view of Eve and her daughters, some women have taken a new look at the Genesis verses. They have discerned in the opening lines of the first creation story the possibility of imagining an androgynous moment of existence and a more egalitarian view of men and women.[40] Although some may find the androcentrism of the Bible and rabbinic tradition too pervasive and the role granted to women too thoroughly limiting, others find that the tradition holds enough room for a reconstructed view that recuperates the tradition's overall power and beauty.

Notes

1. Beverly Moon, "Archetypes," in *The Encyclopedia of Religion,* vol. 1 (New York: Macmillan Publishing Co., 1987), 387ff.

2. Bernard P. Prusak, "Women: Seductive Siren and Source of Sin?" in *Religion and Sexism: Images of Woman in the Jewish and Christian Traditions,* ed. Rosemary R. Ruether (New York: Simon & Schuster, 1974), 97; and Léonie J. Archer, "The 'Evil Woman' in Apocryphal and Pseudepigraphical Writings," in *Proceedings of the Ninth World Congress of Jewish Studies,* Division A: *The Period of the Bible* (Jerusalem: WUJS, 1986), 239–46.

3. Ben Sira 25:24; cf. Jack Levison, "Is Eve to Blame? A Contextual Analysis of Sirach 25:24," *Catholic Biblical Quarterly* 47 (1985): 617–23; and John R. Levison, "The Exoneration of Eve in the Apocalypse of Moses 15–20," *JSJ* 20 (1989): 135–50.

4. The Book of Jubilees also deals with Adam and Eve; but it merely repeats the Genesis story, with little elaboration apart from the mention of a few purity regulations from Leviticus.

5. In contemporary scholarship, the first story is identified as belonging to the P source and the second, to the J source. The rabbis, of course, see them both as of one source, the word of God, with the second story merely a detailed elaboration of the earlier, more abstract, one; see, for example, Nehama Leibowitz, *Studies in the Book of Genesis,* trans. Aryeh Newman (Jerusalem: World Zionist Organization, 1972), 1; and Joseph B. Soloveitchik, "The Lonely Man of Faith," *Tradition* 7 (1965): 5–56.

6. The meaning of the name Eve is, according to linguistic scholars, uncertain and very controversial. Nine different possible etymologies are offered by L. Koehler and W. Baumgartner, *Lexicon in Veteris*

Testamenti Libros (Leiden, Neth.: E. J. Brill, 1958), 280. See also Phyllis Trible, "Eve," in *Harper's Bible Dictionary* (San Francisco: Harper & Row, 1985), 286.

7. *Gen. Rab.* 20:11; John A. Phillips, *Eve: The History of an Idea* (San Francisco: Harper & Row, 1984), 166–67.

8. *Gen. Rab.* 20:11; see *Midrash Rabbah: Genesis*, trans. H. Freedman (London and New York: Soncino Press, 1983), 70 n. 1.

9. This brings to mind the two comments about Eve in the New Testament (2 Cor. 11:3; 1 Tim. 2:13), especially the passage in 2 Corinthians that speaks of the seduction of Eve by the serpent, in which the emphasis on Eve herself as serpentlike seducer is even more marked.

10. *Gen. Rab.* 17:6.

11. Similar indictments of women as seductive sirens are made in many literatures of the Semitic, Greek, Roman, and Christian worlds. Hesiod, in *Works and Days* 81, describes Pandora as possessing the finest gifts, but also as having been made by Zeus deceitful and mischievous to punish men; see Linda S. Sussman, "Workers and Drones: Labor, Idleness and Gender Definition in Hesiod's Beehive," in *Women in the Ancient World: The Arethusa Papers*, ed. John Peradotto and J. P. Sullivan (Albany: SUNY Press, 1984), 79–93; Samuel Tobias Lachs, "The Pandora-Eve Motif in Rabbinic Literature," *Harvard Theological Review* 67 (1974): 341–45.

12. *b. Soṭa* 9a.

13. *b. Šabb.* 146a; *Gen. Rab.* 18:6; *b. Soṭa* 9b; *b. Yebam.* 103b; *b. 'Abod. Zar.* 22b. Cf. 4 Macc. 18:7, 8, which implies that the serpent sexually seduced Eve.

14. *b. Sanh.* 59b; Ephraim E. Urbach, *The Sages: Their Concepts and Beliefs* (Jerusalem: Magnes Press, 1975), 147.

15. Gen. 2:19–23; cf. 1 Tim. 2:13. Some modern scholars have suggested that by naming the animals the man exerts his mastery over them, so by naming woman he extends his rule over her; see Gerhard von Rad, *Genesis, A Commentary*, rev. ed., The Old Testament Library (Philadelphia: Westminster Press, 1973), 83; cf. Phyllis Trible, *God and the Rhetoric of Sexuality* (Philadelphia: Fortress Press, 1978), who is among those arguing against this premise.

16. The Greek story of Pandora resonates with themes similar to those being discussed, yet the overall import of the Eve and Pandora narratives is different. Briefly put, the Pandora story entails a capricious god who punishes man for disobediently stealing something forbidden by creating woman, who brings with her all evil and death into the world. The parallels are clear, but the theological frameworks are

utterly different. The biblical story entails a monotheistic worldview in which human beings exercise free will, whereas the Greek story represents a polytheistic perspective in which fate and determinism are the decisive forces. See further Lachs, "The Pandora-Eve Motif in Rabbinic Literature," 341–45.

17. *Gen. Rab.* 8:1.

18. *Lev. Rab.* 14:1; *b. ʾErub.* 18a; *b. Ber.* 61a; *Gen. Rab.* 8:1. Plato has a similar concept of creation in the *Symposium* (189d–190b), where he speaks of three generations: the masculine, the feminine, and the androgynous.

19. In contrast to the rabbis, Philo solves this exegetical problem by employing his philosophic-allegorical method. He explains that the first version is the idea of man, which is incorporeal, hence neither male nor female; whereas the second account treats the material creation of the human, which has definite form, either man or woman.

20. *Gen. Rab.* 14:1.

21. Esp. *Gen. Rab.* 8:1; *b. ʾErub.* 18b; *b. Ber.* 61a.

22. This usage has considerable resonance for modern scholars in the humanities who speak of the socially constructed nature of various categories by which to understand, organize, and interpret the world. Feminists in particular have been concerned with the socially constructed quality of the category of woman; the Genesis text and its rabbinic interpretation provide a rich source of material for observing not only the construction of this category but also the concomitant controls and restrictions of the female role that emerge therefrom. In this context, it is noteworthy that the verse states "*He* built," indicating that it is the masculine subject who constructs Eve, the first and prototypical woman. The masculine subject is, of course, the Hebrew God, but the surrounding interpretive discourse of the rabbis is also wholly a discourse of men.

23. *b. Ber.* 61a.

24. *Gen. Rab.* 18:1; *b. Nid.* 45b.

25. *b. Yebam.* 62b.

26. *b. Ber.* 24a; *b. Sanh.* 38b.

27. Among the Christian writers, a similar double meaning can be discerned in material, such as Paul's injunction in which he exhorts men to "love each one his wife as his very self" (Eph. 5:33). Yes, this exalts women, but really only insofar as she belongs to, is part of, her husband.

28. *b. Nid.* 45b.

29. *b. Šabb.* 118b.

30. *Gen. Rab.* 17:8. The meaning of the metaphor of Adam as dough is rather obscure, and an examination of the aggadic sources does not clarify the matter.

31. Kraemer, *Her Share of the Blessings,* 99–100.

32. *Gen. Rab.* 18:2; cf. for a variation of the same theme also *Gen. Rab.* 45:5; *Gen. Rab.* 80:5.

33. *Gen. Rab.* 18:2.

34. Ibid.

35. *b. Ber.* 24a; Louis M. Epstein, *Sex Laws and Customs in Judaism,* rev. ed. (Hoboken, N.J.: Ktav, 1987), 46–48.

36. *b. Ketub.* 72a. The Mishnah describes the duty to cover hair as a "Jewish practice," but the Gemara says it is a "Pentateuchal prohibition": "And he shall uncover the woman's head" (Num. 5:18). For a discussion of technical differences between the two levels of observance and a complete study of women's hair covering in Judaism, see my article "From Veil to Wig: Jewish Women's Hair Covering," *Judaism* 42 (Fall 1993), 465–77.

37. *'Abot R. Nat. b.* 9:25, cited from Anthony J. Saldarini, *The Fathers according to Rabbi Nathan,* Studies in Judaism in Late Antiquity 11 (Leiden, Neth.: E. J. Brill, 1975), 83; *Gen. Rab.* 17:8. *'Abot R. Nat. b.* 42:117 goes on to discuss the ten curses pronounced on Eve according to its exegesis. Among these curses is the following: "When she goes out to the marketplace her head has to be covered like a mourner." There must have been an association between Eve and all women underlying this restriction. See also *b. 'Erub.* 100b.

38. This custom is no longer followed in the Jewish community. Moreover, in ultraorthodox Hasidic circles, women are discouraged altogether from attending funerals because, it is said, the Angel of Death dances before her (*b. Ber.* 51a). Women are expected to prepare food and bring it to comfort the bereaved.

39. Isaiah 34:14 contains the only reference to the word *Lilith* in scripture, and this reference has nothing to do with the female Lilith figure of later literature. Although there are midrashic sources from the first millennium c.e. that mention "the first Eve" and that may be referring to Lilith (or a Lilith-type figure), these references are obscure. See, e.g., *Gen. Rab.* 22:7; *b. Pesah.* 88a; and Louis Ginzberg, *The Legends of the Jews* (Philadelphia: The Jewish Publication Society of America, 1947), vol. 1, p. 65, and vol. 5 n. 40, which provide further instances. In medieval midrashic sources, however, Lilith is spoken of explicitly. For further details, see Barbara Black Koltuv, *The Book of Lilith* (York Beach, Me.: Nicolas-Hays, 1987), 61–72, 78–85.

40. R. David Freedman has published a paper that recuperates the *second* set of creation verses as capable of supporting an egalitarian reading; see his "Woman: A Power Equal to Man." *BAR* 9 (1983): 56–58. See also Berel D. Lerner, "And He Shall Rule over Thee," *Judaism* 37 (1988): 446–49.

3

Serah bat Asher:
The Transformative Power
of Aggadic Invention

Serah bat Asher is an exceptional figure in aggadic tradition because she represents a nearly unique instance in which this male-oriented literature fashioned a woman in the role of leader. I say "fashioned" because Serah is transformed through aggadic exegesis from a mere name in the Bible to a measure of prominence in rabbinic sources. She is one of the few female characters in the Talmud and Midrash who ventured beyond the limited spheres to which women were relegated in order to participate in activities ordinarily restricted to men, such as learning and political leadership.[1] Moreover, and perhaps equally unusual, she achieved this through her own merit, not as the wife or mother of a great man.

Still, Serah bat Asher remains little known. Ask anyone reasonably well educated in Jewish texts and the name Serah bat Asher will draw a blank, whereas the very same person will probably know several stories about another remarkable woman in talmudic literature, Beruriah.[2] Indeed, very few studies have been done on this intriguing figure in the Talmud.

From a Name to a Heroine

Who was this woman? She appears three times in scripture— each time as a name on a genealogical list:

42

1. "Asher's sons: Imnah, Ishvah, Ishvi, and Beriah, and their sister *Serah*" (Gen. 46:17).
2. "The name of Asher's daughter was *Serah.*—These are the clans of Asher's descendants" (Num. 26:46).
3. "These are the sons of Asher, Imnah, Ishvah, Ishvi, and Beriah, and their sister *Serah*" (1 Chron. 7:30).

Genealogical lists bear great significance in scripture. They are understood as a means of showing that the history of Israel was no human accident but was, from the beginning, shaped by the sure and sovereign will of God. That is why the genealogies are set forth in such meticulous detail. To the modern reader, these long lists of names may seem tedious; but to the sages, they were both symbol and guarantee of Israel's divine purpose in history, an unbroken link with the remote past, and hence also a firm basis from which to build the future.

Biblical lineage is usually traced through the male; females are mentioned only in rare instances. The fact that she is mentioned no less than three times by name in genealogical lists is remarkable in itself; and this may be what made her seem extraordinary in the eyes of the sages, enough to embroider marvelous, even mythic stories about her. Another factor in explaining why they ascribed such significant activities to her may be the period in which she lived. She was a woman of the Exodus—a period of great crisis in Israelite history, a period that produced an impressive number of prominent women. The sages in tractate *Soṭa* comment on this phenomenon stating:

> [A]s the reward for the righteous women who lived in that generation [Exodus] were the Israelites delivered from Egypt.[3]

Despite that, the rabbis, who are given to speculating on the meaning of biblical names and often build their exegesis from etymological conjecture, never discuss the meaning of the name Serah.[4] Their failure to do so is even more remarkable when one considers that this name appears nowhere else in the Bible and that its occurrence on these lists constitutes the only information scripture gives us about her. Surely that should have provided a midrashic opportunity. To bridge this gap, I will offer a modern midrash in keeping with the figure that emerges from the sage's narrative embellishment.

Semitic scholars interpret the root of her name, *srḥ*, as meaning "to overhang," by analogy "abundant" (like the overflowing curtains of the Tabernacle).[5] Others look to Arabic to translate the word as meaning "one who explains, opens, or extends."[6] Although the sages never glossed her name, their narrative embellishments transformed Serah into a woman who enjoyed abundance in every sphere: age, activity, and importance. One midrashic source gives her name as Segulah[7] rather than Serah. Although this may represent a corruption in the text, its meaning—the "treasured," "chosen," or "redeemed" one—is favorable and also compatible with the image fashioned in rabbinic exegesis, that of a redemptive, quasi-immortal figure given a key role in the deliverance from Egypt.

"Serah, Daughter of"

Further striking about the aggadic evolution of the Serah tradition is that the sages make no attempt to ascribe to her a husband or children. It is true that in two of the three genealogical references to Serah in the Bible, she is described by the word "sister," while the third reference speaks of her as "daughter" (Num. 26:46); but in rabbinic literature she is always referred to as Serah, daughter of Asher.

In both scriptural and rabbinic literature, the marital status of women is usually given. In addition, aggadic sources have a propensity to invent, through narrative expansion, marriages for those not described in scripture as married. The most prominent female leaders in the Bible, such as Deborah and Huldah, are identified in scripture as being married; even the names of their husbands are given. A good example of a woman whose personal status in the Bible is single but who is given a husband in the Talmud is Miriam.[8] Yet, strangely enough, the question of Serah's marital status is not even discussed by the rabbis. It may be that in the evolution of the Serah tradition the sages accepted the extraordinary figure they had fashioned by her own merit, the wisdom they had ascribed to her elevating her to a status even greater than their own. And they were so awed of their own creation that they did not feel the need to marry her off.

The Evolution of the Serah Tradition

According to aggadic sources, Serah was raised in the house of her grandfather Jacob. God gave her beauty and sagacity, and she walked in the ways of the pious. In the Aramaic translation of the Pentateuch known as *Targum Pseudo-Jonathan,* one reads:

> And Serah their sister, who spoke and was therefore worthy of entering Gan Eden [Paradise], because she brought good tidings to Jacob, saying: "Joseph lives."[9]

Late tradition further elaborates her story. The midrashic *Book of Jashar* (thirteenth-century Italy?) speaks of Serah in great detail.

> And . . . [the sons of Jacob] went along until they came nigh unto their houses, and they found Serah, the daughter of Asher, going forth to meet them, and the damsel was very good and subtle, and knew how to play upon the harp. . . . And they took her and gave unto her a harp, saying, go now before our father [meaning Jacob], and sit before him, and strike upon the harp, and speak these words. . . . She took the harp, and . . . she came and sat near Jacob. And she played well and sang, and uttered in the sweetness of her words, "Joseph my uncle is living, and he ruleth throughout the land of Egypt, and is not dead." And she continued to repeat and utter these words, and Jacob heard her words and they were agreeable to him.[10]

The *Book of Jashar* thus described Serah as being blessed with spiritual and prophetic qualities, and able to inform her grandfather Jacob that her uncle Joseph was alive. Accordingly, Jacob blessed her:

> And Jacob blessed Serah when she spoke these words before him, and he said unto her, "My daughter, may death never pre-

vail over thee, for thou hast revived my spirit; only speak yet
before me as thou hast spoken, for thou hast gladdened me with
all thy words."[11]

Serah thereafter acquired the powers of blessing and saving
people in distress. She also received the secret knowledge of
how to identify the Redeemer. She was the only woman to receive this secret password, otherwise transmitted through the
males of the family.

> The sign of [God's] visitation which He communicated to them,
> for they had this as a tradition from Jacob, Jacob having handed
> down the secret to Joseph, and Joseph to his brothers, while
> Asher, the son of Jacob, had handed down the secret to his
> daughter Serah, who was still alive. This is what he told her:
> "Any redeemer that will come and say to my children: 'I will
> surely visit you' shall be regarded as a true deliverer."[12]

Midrash Exodus Rabbah, another late source (tenth century),
clearly states that the secret of how to recognize the Redeemer
was passed down by her father Asher to Serah. The Midrash
narrates that the people were reluctant to accept Moses as their
redeemer until Serah gave them the proper password.[13] In addition, she helps Moses locate the bones of Joseph, so that they
can return them to their homeland. These two acts of assistance to Moses on the part of Serah made possible the Exodus.

Seventy Souls

The Bible tells us that the total number of Jacob's family
who went down into Egypt was seventy (Gen. 47:27). The first
biblical mention of Serah is in this genealogical list of the Israelites going into the land of Egypt (Gen. 46:17). Because the
female family members are not generally named, as is Serah,
the rabbis argue whether she merited mention because she was
the one who brought to seventy the number of Israelites who
entered Egypt.

The rabbis construe the number seventy as portentous because of the great importance attached to the events that unfolded from the going into Egypt. To be designated as the one who brings the group to that total implies great significance and honor. The problem is discussed at length, but no consensus is reached. Some traditions accorded this honor to Serah:

> Some say that Serah the daughter of Asher made up the number [of seventy]. Thus it is written, *Then cried a wise woman out of the city: Hear, hear; say, I pray you, unto Joab: Come near hither, that I may speak with thee.* . . . (2 Sam. 20:16ff.).[14] Thy name is Joab, she said to him, meaning that thou art a father (*ab*) to Israel, whereas in fact thou art but a destroyer, and dost not fit thy name. . . . [Joab says to her,] "Who art thou then?" . . . [She replies,] "It is I who made up (*hoshlamti*) the numbers (*minyan*) of Israel in Egypt; it is I who delivered (*hoshlamti*) the faithful (*ne'eman*) to the faithful, Joseph to Moses."[15]

But other commentators disagree, claiming that Jacob or Jochebed or even God accounted for the seventieth.[16] Some commentators have even claimed that Serah, because of her longevity, counted for two people on the list.[17] The rabbis base their assertion of Serah's longevity on the fact that she is the only person listed not only among those entering Egypt, but also among those leaving it (Num. 26:46). Rabbinic focus on Serah was spurred by the textual problem of why she was mentioned in the genealogical lists, a prominence accorded very few biblical females. The midrashic basis of their inquiry is typical of one means by which rabbinic thought developed.

Serah and the Bones of Joseph[18]

Serah's most important activities in Egypt are invented by the sages to credit her with a role in facilitating the Exodus. The Bible records that Joseph asked his brothers to promise him that on departing from Egypt, they would take his bones back to the land of Canaan.

At length, Joseph said to his brothers, "I am about to die. God will surely take notice of you and bring you up from this land to the land that He promised on oath to Abraham, to Isaac, and to Jacob." So Joseph made the sons of Israel swear, saying, "When God has taken notice of you, you shall carry up my bones from here." Joseph died at the age of one hundred and ten years; and he was embalmed and placed in a coffin in Egypt (Gen. 50:24–26).

In the book of Exodus it is further written: "And Moses took with him the bones of Joseph, who had exacted an oath from the children of Israel, saying, 'God will be sure to take notice of you; then you shall carry up my bones from here with you' " (Ex. 13:19).

What was the problem for the rabbis, and why did they feel the need to enlarge upon the story of the elusive bones? It grows out of the Jewish concern for burial of the dead. Genesis mentions only the embalming of Joseph and the placement of his body in a casket, but not the location of burial. This left a gap that rabbinic midrash moved in to fill.[19]

Three versions tell the tale of Moses' recovery of Joseph's bones. They are found in the Mekilta, the Tosefta, and the Talmud. That of Mekilta may be the most elaborate. The Mekilta, describing the Israelites' preparations to leave Egypt, depicts them taking booty from the Egyptians, while Moses was occupied with finding the bones of Joseph. Various rabbinic sources inform us that Moses could not redeem the people and leave Egypt, because he could not find the place of Joseph's grave. How did Moses eventually discover where Joseph was buried? In all three sources the sages tell us that Serah, daughter of Asher, survived from the time when Joseph died and was buried, and that she showed Moses where Joseph's casket was to be found. She told him that the Egyptians had fashioned a metal casket and dropped it into the middle of the Nile. The Mekilta reads:

> *And Moses Took the Bones of Joseph with Him.* This proclaims the wisdom and the piety of Moses. For all Israel were busy with the booty while Moses busied himself with the duty of looking after the bones of Joseph. Of him Scripture says: "The wise in heart takes on duties" (Prov. 10:8). But how did Moses know where

Joseph was buried? It is told that Serah, the daughter of Asher, survived from that generation and she showed Moses the grave of Joseph. She said to him: The Egyptians put him into a metal coffin which they sunk in the Nile. So Moses went and stood by the Nile. He took a table[t] of gold[20] on which he engraved the Tetragrammaton, and throwing it into the Nile, he cried out and said: "Joseph son of Jacob! The oath to redeem his children, which God swore to our father Abraham, has reached its fulfillment. If you come up, well and good. But if not, we shall be guiltless of your oath." Immediately Joseph's coffin came to the surface.[21]

The Tosefta is also earlier than the Talmud. Its version reads:

How did Moses know where Joseph had been buried? They tell: Serah daughter of Asher was [a survivor] of the generation [of Joseph], and she went and said to Moses, "In the River Nile Joseph is buried. And the Egyptians made for him metal spits and affixed them with pitch (to keep him down)." Moses went and stood at the Nile River and said, "Joseph, the time has come for the Holy One, blessed be He, to redeem Israel. Lo, the Presence is held up for you, and the Israelites are held up for you, and the clouds of glory are held up for you. If you show yourself, well and good, and if not, we are free of the oath which you have imposed upon our father." Then the coffin of Joseph floated to the surface and Moses took it and went his way.[22]

The talmudic version reads:

It is related that Serah, daughter of Asher, was a survivor of that generation. Moses went to her and asked, "Dost thou know where Joseph was buried?" She answered him, "The Egyptians made a metal coffin for him which they fixed in the river Nile so that its waters should be blessed." Moses went and stood on the bank of the Nile and exclaimed, "Joseph, Joseph! the time has arrived which the Holy One, blessed be He, swore, 'I will deliver you,' and the oath which thou didst impose upon the Israelites has reached [the time of fulfilment]." . . . Immediately Joseph's coffin floated [on the surface of the water].[23]

In neither of the earlier sources, the Mekilta and the Tosefta, is Moses described as going to the Tribe of Asher looking for Serah. Rather, in both sources she is mentioned without any introduction at all. She simply appears suddenly and immedi-

ately acts in an advisory capacity, instructing the great leader
Moses where to direct his footsteps. Only in the talmudic version does it state that Moses went to her. In all versions, he
follows her direction with no hesitation and locates Joseph's
river-bottom tomb.

Moses still faced the problem of how to raise the coffin from
the bed of the Nile. Serah plays no role here. The text of the
Mekilta describes Moses standing over the Nile and throwing a
tablet into the water. He does not pray but rather calls on Joseph to reveal himself. To paraphrase the Mekilta, Moses says to
Joseph that the time of redemption has come.[24] He goes on to
ask Joseph not to hold up the redemption, or the people of
Israel will be forced to leave without him. Thereupon Joseph's
coffin floated to the surface and Moses took it.

In the Tosefta and in the Talmud, as in the Mekilta, the
coffin floats to the surface; but in these two other sources there
is no mention of a tablet being tossed into the Nile. The account in the Mekilta has a magical quality because of the added
detail of a golden tablet inscribed with God's name. Both the
Mekilta and the Tosefta go on to quote a similar miraculous
story from the book of Kings that describes the prophet Elisha
assisting one of his disciples in a miracle that causes an iron ax
head to float up on the water.

> So they went to the Jordan and cut timber. As one of them was
> felling a trunk, the iron ax head fell into the water. And he cried
> aloud, "Alas, master, it was a borrowed one!" "Where did it
> fall?" asked the man of God. He showed him the spot; and he
> cut off a stick and threw it in, and he made the ax head float.
> "Pick it up," he said; so he reached out and took it (2 Kings
> 5:4–7).[25]

Perhaps the rabbis bring up the story of Elisha to reinforce
the idea that miracles of this magnitude were not exaggerated
and had occurred before. If the midrashic story of how Moses
raised the casket seems incredible, the rabbis are saying, just
look at the biblical account of Elisha, who was merely Elijah's
student, yet had performed a similar miracle. How much more
plausible, then, that Moses, teacher of Elijah and Elisha, could
accomplish such a miraculous deed.

Another narrative account of Serah's involvement in the Joseph incident is external to rabbinic sources, appearing in the *Tebat Marqa*, a collection of Samaritan writings dating from the fourth century C.E. This account describes the Israelites sacrificing at Raamses and moving on to Sukkot. When they wanted to leave Sukkot, a pillar of fire stopped in front of them, blocking their way. Moses and the elders were frightened, wondering what wrong they might have done. The elders went to speak to all the tribes and ascertained that no sin had been committed. When they came to the tribe of Asher, Asher's daughter Serah went to meet them. Gifted with special insight, she was able to inform them that no evil had been committed; the problem was simply that Joseph's bones had been forgotten.

> Serah the daughter of Asher went hurrying out to them. "There is nothing evil in your midst. Behold, I will reveal to you what this secret is." At once they surrounded her and brought her to the great prophet Moses and she stood before him . . . [saying,] "Hear from me this thing that you seek: Praise to those who remembered my beloved [Joseph], though you have forgotten him. For had not the pillar of cloud and pillar of fire stood still, you would have departed and he would have been left in Egypt. I remember the day that he died and he caused the whole people to swear that they would bring his bones up from here with them." The great prophet Moses said to her, "Worthy are you Serah, wisest of women. From this day on will your greatness be told." . . . Serah went with all the tribe of Ephraim around her, and Moses and Aaron went after them, until she came to the place where he was hidden.[26]

"Wisdom Is Better"

The texts we have discussed are highly unusual in that they introduce us to Serah while she is performing a most extraordinary function for a woman: she is advising a man—and no ordinary man, but Moses the great teacher, leader, and prophet. No other woman in rabbinic literature is cast in an analogous role.

An important later rabbinic source, the *Pesiqta de Rav Kahana*, describes Serah looking down from heaven and listening to the discussions of the rabbis in the house of study, while important religious matters were being discussed. Rabbi Johanan was explaining the problem of how the waters formed a wall for the Israelites when they went out of Egypt.

> From the teacher's seat R. Johanan sought to explain just how the waters of the Red Sea became a wall for Israel. Even as R. Johanan was explaining that the wall of the water looked like a lattice, Serah, daughter of Asher, looked down and said: I was there. The waters rising up like a wall for Israel were shining because the radiance [of such personages as Moses and Aaron, who had drunk deep of Torah's waters,] made the waters shine.[27]

During the scholarly discussions that ensued, Serah bat Asher boldly interrupted, contradicting R. Johanan. In all of rabbinic literature there is no other instance of a woman entering a house of study and correcting a sage.[28] Beruriah, the female scholar of the Talmud par excellence, is often depicted as discussing and differing on legal matters with male scholars, but she appears always to be outside the house of study.

A midrashic gloss on the verse "Wisdom is better" (Eccl. 9:18) says that this refers to the wisdom of Serah the daughter of Asher.[29] This midrash identifies Serah with a wise woman from the Bible who lived hundreds of years later, namely, the wise woman of Abel, who saved that city from slaughter at the hand of Joab, King David's commander-in-chief (2 Sam. 20).

From where do they get this association with a biblical figure from much later times? It stems from the aggadic interpretation of the genealogical information about Serah given in scripture. The fact that she entered Egypt and was still alive during the census taken prior to the Israelites' entry into the land of Canaan (Num. 24:46) led the rabbis to declare that she lived for hundreds of years. Aggadic sources in the Midrash and Talmud discuss seven biblical figures whose successive lifetimes span the whole history of humankind. Serah appears on the list in one of these sources, together with the prophet Ahijah the Shilonite (1 Kings 11:29; 14:1–18; and 2 Chron. 9:29).[30] In some ways, Serah and Ahijah the Shilonite are alike in that both enjoy longevity and a greatly expanded role in rabbinic history, tradition, and folklore.

The extraordinary longevity of Serah implied in scripture was eventually glossed by the rabbis into the statement that Serah "did not taste death" and was "one who entered paradise." We recall that *Targum Pseudo-Jonathan* describes her as "one who entered paradise,"[31] and the *Book of Jashar* elaborates how Serah came to merit entry into Paradise. She is movingly described as singing good tidings to Jacob about the fate of his son Joseph. Jacob is so comforted that he blesses her, saying, "My daughter, may death never prevail over thee, for thou hast revived my spirit."[32] By suggesting that she never tasted death and that she entered Gan Eden (the Garden of Eden, a term often equated with Paradise), giving her quasi-immortal status, the rabbis place her in an exalted category nearly on a par with Elijah, the eternal prophet.[33]

Another Feat of Aggadic Conjuring

Another female figure from the Bible and Midrash, Naamah, sheds some interesting light on Serah, for she too is a character scarcely mentioned in the Bible, yet is greatly embellished by the Midrash. Naamah (Gen. 4:22), the sister of Tubal-Cain, undergoes an aggadic embellishment in which the rabbis use methods similar to those they employ in the midrashim on Serah. Naamah's image in rabbinic stories, however, is a negative one.

The Bible records two women bearing the name Naamah. The one in Genesis is the one who concerns us. Her name is said in the Midrash to mean "pleasantness."[34] The rabbis denigrate the image of this Naamah. The sages explain that although the name Naamah means "pleasantness," Naamah's charms were improperly used to serve idolatrous ends. Naamah is described by the rabbis as the mistress of dirges and songs, playing to the idols in the temple that were made by her brother. Later rabbinic literature further develops the negative image of Naamah, claiming that she led the angels astray with her beauty and that from her union with Shamdon sprang the devil Asmodeus. She is even transformed into a Lilith figure, slaying little children and appearing to men at night to frighten and fool them.

The great differences between the midrashic Serah and the midrashic Naamah may be explained by their ancestries in the biblical text. In the ancient world, family bloodlines and traditions were believed to determine to a great extent a person's character. For women, subject as they were to male authority, this was even more true. The wickedness of Naamah's brother and father, implied in scripture, caused the sages to shape Naamah along the same wicked lines. The scriptural information that Serah's closest male relations were among the giants of Israelite history—Jacob (her grandfather), Joseph (her uncle), and Asher (her father)—gave her from the outset an important status. Thus the midrashic images of Serah, the saint, and Naamah, the sinner, reflect those of their male relations. Consciously or not, the sages may have created a binary opposition between Serah and Naamah. Because they had fashioned an exceptional woman from the merest mention of a name in scripture, perhaps they felt compelled to create, from similarly scant materials, an odious one.[35]

Ardent Wives and Defiant Midwives: The Brave Generation of the Exodus

As with all biblical heroes, one must understand Serah in the context of her times. She belongs to the women of the generation of the Exodus. Scripture portrays many women of that era playing crucial roles in saving their people from extinction under the cruel edicts of Pharaoh. The rabbinic retelling of the Exodus embellishes the deeds ascribed to the women of the time of the bondage in Egypt and the Departure. The Talmud tells us that it was through the merit of the righteous women that Israel came to be redeemed from Egypt.[36] The sages offer various examples and elaborations of the bravery and redemptive actions credited to the women of the days of the Exodus. This Amoraic source located the women's merit in their fulfilling their function as women—feeding and nurturing—to ensure the continuity of life. A more dramatic gloss claims that the women went into the fields to have sexual relations with their husbands despite the great danger this entailed, thus assuring the continuity of the nation. In their actions, the women displayed not only conventional female fortitude but also unprecedented courage on a par with that shown by men.

The midwives are also given credit in the Bible for securing the continuity of the Israelites by refusing to obey Pharaoh's command to put to death the male children of the Hebrews. In the Bible it is not clear whether Shiphrah and Puah (Ex. 1:15), the midwives, were Hebrew or Egyptian. The midrashic sources identify them as Hebrews (according to which Shiphrah was Jochebed; Puah, Miriam) and try to discover the meaning of their names, relating these meanings to their behavior in caring for the children.[37] Whatever their national identity, they defied the Pharaoh's command to kill every male child. Not only that, they went further and supplied the babes with water and food.

This behavior on the part of the midwives shows great courage. When Pharaoh demanded to know how they had dared to ignore his edict, the midwives asserted that the Hebrew women had no need for their services—that Hebrew women were vigorous and sturdy, unlike pampered Egyptian women, and they would give birth before the midwives arrived (Ex. 1:19).[38] The bravery of the women of that age was also credited to Egyptian women, acting in female solidarity to save the endangered children. Thus the daughter of Pharaoh is included in this tradition of female courage and defiance. Midrash, in explicating scripture (Ex. 2:5), records that in rescuing Moses from the bulrushes she dared to challenge her father, the king and ruler, who had absolute power over her, in order to save a male Hebrew child. Pharaoh's daughter is traditionally identified with the Bithiah mentioned in 1 Chronicles 4:18. The Midrash comments that her name indicates that she was a daughter of God (*bat-Yah*): "The Holy One, blessed be He, said to Bithiah the daughter of Pharaoh: 'Moses was not your son, yet you called him your son; you, too, though you are not My daughter, yet I will call My daughter.' "[39]

Other instances of women of the Exodus period playing redemptive roles include Jochebed, the mother of Moses, who hid the newborn child from the Pharaoh (Ex. 2:3), and Miriam, who watched from afar and waited until the daughter of Pharaoh rescued him from the river (Ex. 2:4). Zipporah, the wife of Moses, also performs a redemptive act by circumcising their child and thereby preventing her husband's death (Ex. 4:24–27). Eileen Schuller, in a recent paper on the women of the Exodus, sums it up well when she says that "Moses is surrounded by six women and, in fact, owes his very life to them."[40] No other biblical age records the names and deeds of so many masterful women, all of whom provided potential scope for rabbinic discourse. It is definitely a generation to which Serah belongs!

Conclusion

Something about Serah sparked the interest of the sages. Why, they wondered, did she warrant her place in scripture? Why does her name, above all other women, appear on three genealogical lists? Whatever the divine reason, it brings out in them the propensity for hyperbole and exaggeration. She enters Egypt and lives long enough to advise Moses and play a key role in enabling the redemption to proceed. She is a prototype of the biblical wise woman at Abel who saved the city from slaughter. Serah is unique in other ways; she is a woman who is said to have entered the sanctum sanctorum of rabbinic Judaism, the house of study. And all of this she achieves on her own merit, not through someone else, not behind the sages. The rabbis created an exemplary woman. For women of our times, she is a gift to reclaim.

Notes

1. Bronner, "The Changing Face of Woman from Bible to Talmud."

2. This probably can be explained by the fact that a student of Talmud and Midrash, though enjoined to do otherwise regarding rabbinic statements, made relative judgments about fact and myth. That is, the reader understands that with a literal reading Serah played a far more significant role in the history of the Jewish people than did Beruriah; but the latter's deeds held historical veracity, whereas Serah's powers and deeds were a figment of the rabbinic imagination, not a live tradition from her generation to theirs. For more on Beruriah, see chapter 1.

3. *b. Soṭa* 11b. See discussion below.

4. Of interest to Hebrew scholars, the name Serah is spelled differently in the Bible and the Talmud. It is written with a *sin* in the Bible but a *samekh* in the Talmud.

5. F. Brown, S. R. Driver, and C. A. Briggs translate "the excess which remains over" as "to go free, be unrestrained, overrun, exceed," in *A Hebrew and English Lexicon of the Old Testament*, repr. (Oxford: Clarendon Press, 1951), 710. Koehler and Baumgartner translate it as "to overhang," "set free," "grow luxuriantly," or "abundance," in *Lexicon in Veteris Testamenti Libros*, 667. See also M. Jastrow, *A Dictionary of the Targumim, the Talmud Babli and Yerushalmi, and the Midrashic Literature* (New York: Pardes Publishing House, 1950), 1024–25.

6. *The Interpreter's Dictionary of the Bible*, vol. 4 (Nashville: Abingdon Press, 1962), 278.

7. *Deut. Rab.* 11:7.

8. *b. Soṭa* 12a; *Ex. Rab.* 1:17. Josephus and the Talmud operated

out of the same tradition. He too ascribes a husband to Miriam; see Josephus, *Ant.* 3.2.4 [54]. See also chapter 8.

9. *Tg. Ps.-J.* on Gen. 46:17.

10. Quoted from Mordecai M. Noah, ed., *The Book of Jashar,* repr.(New York: Sepher-Hermon Press, 1972), 176–77; the Hebrew may be found in *Sefer Ha-Yashar* (Livorno: n.p., n.d.); see also *Tg. Ps.-J.* on Gen. 46:17; *Sefer Hadar Zekainim* (B'nai Brak: Institute for Dissemination of the Commentaries of the Ba'alei Tosafot, n.d.), 116; M. Z. Chefetz, ed., *Midrash 'Abot* (Minsk: n.p., 1896), 45, sec. 41.1.

11. Noah, ed., *The Book of Jashar,* 177.

12. *Ex. Rab.* 5:13–14.

13. Ibid.

14. Serah is thus identified with the wise woman of Abel, a fact we will return to shortly.

15. *Gen. Rab.* 94:9; *Eccl. Rab.* 9:18(1–2).

16. *Pirqe R. El.* 39; *Tg. Ps.-J.* on Gen. 46:27; Rashi on Gen. 46:26.

17. *b. Soṭa* 13a; for further information of the problem of the seventy souls, see *b. B. Bat.* 123a; *Jubilees* 44:11–34; Josephus, *Ant.* 2.7.4 [176–83, esp. 183]; Ginzberg, *Legends of the Jews,* vol. 5, p. 359 n. 321.

18. For more on the subject, see James L. Kugel, *In Potiphar's House* (San Francisco: HarperCollins, 1990), chap. 5. Kugel is primarily concerned with studying the image of Joseph in ancient aggadic sources and devotes some attention to Serah's part, insofar as it clarifies the Joseph problem. See also Joseph Heinemann, *'Aggadot v'Toldoteihen* (Jerusalem: Keter Publishing House, 1974), 49–63, who describes Serah as playing an important role in the midrashic episodes about Joseph's bones.

19. The Testament of Simeon, a pseudepigraphic source, handles the theme of Joseph's casket differently, asserting that it was hidden by the Egyptians, who had been told that should Joseph's body leave Egypt, they would be visited by darkness and plague. Howard Clark Kee, "The Testaments of the Twelve Patriarchs," in *The Old Testament Pseudepigrapha,* vol. 1, ed. James H. Charlesworth (Garden City, N.Y.: Doubleday & Co., 1983), 787–88.

20. A variant reading says "bundle" rather than tablet.

21. Quoted from J. Z. Lauterbach, *Mekilta de-Rabbi Ishmael,* vol. 1, Schiff Library of Jewish Classics (Philadelphia: The Jewish Publication Society of America, 1949), 176–77; the Hebrew text may be found in the editions of either M. Friedmann (Ish-Shalom) or Horovitz and Rabin, *Beshalaḥ* 1.

22. *t. Soṭa* 4:7; cited from *The Tosefta: Translated from the Hebrew, Order Nashim,* trans. Jacob Neusner (New York: Ktav, 1979), 162–63; the

Hebrew version may be found in Lieberman, *Tosefta Ki-fshutah,* 170, col. b; or M. S. Zuckermandel, ed., *The Tosefta* (Jerusalem: Wahrmann Books, 1962–63), 299–300.

23. *b. Soṭa* 13a.

24. Ibid.

25. Kugel, *In Potiphar's House,* 134–35, suggests that the association with the Elisha account is secondary.

26. Z. Ben-Hayyim, ed., *Tebat Marqua: A Collection of Samaritan Midrashim* (Jerusalem: Academy of Sciences, 1988), 98.

27. Quoted from *Pesikta de-Rab Kahana,* trans. W. G. Braude and I. J. Kapstein (Philadelphia: The Jewish Publication Society of America, 1975), 212; the Hebrew may be found in Solomon Buber, ed., *Pesiqta de Rav Kahana, Beshalaḥ* (Lwow: n.p., 1868; repr. 1963), 86 par. 117; and in Bernard Mandelbaum, ed., *Pesiqta de Rav Kahana,* vol. 1 (New York: The Jewish Theological Seminary of America, 1962), 188 par. 13.

28. The institutional context in which this incident occurred, whether synagogue, *beth hamidrash,* or somewhere less formal, is not specified in the account; but because the usual setting for rabbinic teaching was the house of study, *beth hamidrash,* it is justifiable to assume that this was the intended setting of the event.

29. *Gen. Rab.* 94:9; *Eccl. Rab.* 9:18 (2).

30. *'Abot R. Nat. b.* 38:103. In other sources, such as *b. B. Bat.* 121b, which also speaks of seven saints, Serah is replaced by the name of Amram, the father of Moses. The other saints enumerated in these sources with Serah (Amram) are Adam, Methuselah, Shem, Jacob, Ahijah, and Elijah; Ginzberg, *Legends of the Jews,* vol. 2, p. 116; vol. 5, p. 356 n. 294; p. 359 n. 321.

31. *Tg. Ps.-J.* Gen. 46:17.

32. Ibid. See also Noah, ed., *The Book of Jashar,* 54, 92–99; cf. Chefetz, ed., *Midrash 'Abot,* cited in note 10 above. For further information on those who entered Paradise, see Ginzberg, *Legends of the Jews,* vol. 5, p. 356 nn. 294–95.

33. Aggadic sources in the Talmud and Midrash enumerate a large number of men and women who were worthy of entering Paradise, but it is not always stated that they did not taste death, as is said of Serah. The following are mentioned in various sources: Abraham's servant Eliezer, Serah, Pharaoh's daughter Bithiah (1 Chron. 4:188), Othniel, Abigail and the matriarchs, Hiram, Elijah, Jonah, Baruch, Ezra (only in the Pseudepigrapha), Enoch, Jabez, Ebedmelech the Ethiopian, Jonadab ben Rechab.

34. *Gen. Rab.* 23:3, where Naamah is also identified with Noah's wife.

35. Although there are very few examples of women fashioned by rabbinic exegesis—almost out of whole cloth into figures of significance, good or bad—there are numerous instances of midrashic creativity regarding obscure biblical men. One interesting example is Hur (Ex. 17:10–12; 24:14), who took part alongside Aaron in certain key actions in the Exodus story. Hur appears and disappears from the biblical scene; but like Serah, he becomes a very important figure in the aggadic traditions of Midrash and Talmud. Together with the priest Aaron, he held up the arms of Moses at Rephidim in the battle against Amalek (Ex. 17:10–12). He also helped Aaron judge the people when Moses went up to Mount Sinai (Ex. 24:14). After these deeds he mysteriously disappears from the biblical record, although he was ostensibly groomed to be Moses' successor. His sudden disappearance was explained by claiming that he was murdered by the people because he courageously opposed the Israelites by refusing to join them in making the Golden Calf (*Ex. Rab.* 48:3; *b. Sanh.* 7a). As a reward for his fortitude and devotion, he became the ancestor of both Bezalel, the architect of the sanctuary (Ex. 31:2), and Solomon, builder of the Temple (1 Kings 6:1ff.; *Tanhuma Buber* Ex. 12:1; *b. Sota* 11b).

36. *b. Sota* 11b; see also *Num. Rab.* 9:13; Ginzberg, *Legends of the Jews,* vol. 3, pp. 174ff.

37. See *b. Sota* 12b; *Ex. Rab.* 1:13ff.; *Midrash Mishle,* ed. S. Buber (Vilna: n.p., 1893; repr. Israel: n.p., 1973), 14:74–75. This midrashic tradition says that Shiphrah is Jochebed, and she was called thus because she straightened the limbs of the babe. Another explanation for Shiphrah is that the Israelites were fruitful and multiplied in her days. The other midwife, Puah, is Miriam, who is called thus because she cried out to the child and brought it forth. Another explanation for Puah is more spiritual, claiming that she cried out through the Holy Spirit, saying, "My mother will bear a son, who will be the savior of Israel."

38. See Rashi on Ex. 1:19; also Benjamin Mazar, ed., *Views of the Biblical World,* vol. 1 (Chicago: Jordan Publications, 1959), 130.

39. *Lev. Rab.* 1:3 (fifth century).

40. Eileen Schuller, "Women of the Exodus in Biblical Retellings of the Second Temple," in *Gender and Difference in Ancient Israel,* ed. Peggy L. Day (Minneapolis: Fortress Press, 1989), 178.

4

The Regime of Modesty:
Ruth and the Rabbinic
Construction of
the Feminine Ideal

The book of Ruth presented the sages of the Midrash and Talmud with a unique social and religious problem. In the figure of Ruth, they were faced with a Moabite woman, a descendant of a people that the Pentateuch emphatically proscribes from entering the congregation of the Lord (Deut. 23:4–5). Yet in the biblical verses she is depicted from the start as an exemplary woman—a heroine by the merit of her own actions—even before she entered the Israelite fold. Faced with the cognitively dissonant exemplary character of this foreign woman, who would become the ancestress of the Davidic line, the rabbis of the Talmud felt that they had to halakhically legitimize Ruth's conversion. Then, having accomplished her acceptance into the fold, they wanted to underscore her merit and extraordinary kindness and valor, making her a suitable figure to stand at the beginning of the Davidic, which is to say messianic, line.

The biblical book of Ruth is a short story that opens with an Israelite family leaving their birthplace in Bethlehem because of a drought. The man Elimelech, his wife Naomi, and their two sons go to settle in the neighboring land of Moab, across the Jordan. The sons eventually marry Moabite women named Orpah and Ruth. Elimelech dies, and not long thereafter the sons too die, leaving their wives childless. Naomi, hearing that the famine is over, informs her daughters-in-law of her intent to return to her homeland. They beg to accompany her, but she encourages them to return to their families, for she has little to offer them. Orpah accedes to Naomi's request, but Ruth insists upon accompanying her mother-in-law to a foreign land. Upon arrival in Bethlehem, they seek out the field of Elimelech's relative Boaz, for Israelite law permits the impoverished to glean leftovers from the fields. Naomi contrives a plan to arrange a marriage for Ruth with Boaz, which succeeds. From this union results the genealogical line of King David.

A very special woman, a paragon of piety and virtue, Ruth is the only convert to have a biblical book named after her—a profound and unparalleled honor. Moreover, she was, with Esther, one of only two women to have this distinction. Several themes in Midrash related to her life and character reveal a Ruth possessing the feminine virtues the rabbis want to hold up for emulation.

The Theme of *Ḥesed*

In the original biblical narrative and in the midrashic retellings, Ruth is seen to act out of love for Naomi, as well as a more general love and generosity, embodying the quality known in Hebrew as *ḥesed*, a term generally rendered in English as "loving-kindness."

This theme of kindness is central to the book of Ruth. Rabbi Zeira stressed this characteristic of the narrative:

> This scroll [of Ruth] tells nothing either of cleanliness or of uncleanliness, neither of prohibition or permission. For what purpose then was it written: To teach how great is the reward of those who do deeds of kindness.[1]

Ḥesed is indeed one of the key words controlling the Ruth text. The word occurs three times. At the beginning, Ruth does *ḥesed* for Naomi—from gleaning in the fields to bringing food—and further performs *ḥesed* in honoring the memory of the dead in Naomi's family (which became, by marriage, her own) (Ruth 1:8). In the middle we find: "And Naomi said to her daughter-in-law: 'blessed be he by the Lord, whose kindness (*ḥesed*) has not forsaken the living or the dead' " (Ruth 2:20). And at the end of the story, Boaz says to Ruth: "You have made this last kindness (*ḥesed*) greater than the first, in that you have not gone after young men, whether poor or rich" (Ruth 3:10). He promises to look after her needs.[2]

Almost every character in this brief story—from Naomi to Ruth to Boaz to some minor characters—behaves in a manner that demonstrates this heroic concept of some form of *ḥesed*. Some perform ordinary *ḥesed*, and some—especially Ruth—extraordinary *ḥesed*. The rabbinic sources emphasize the super-abundance of *ḥesed*, its more-than-enoughness—as described by Maimonides. Such *ḥesed* "includes two notions, one of them consisting in the exercise of beneficence toward one who deserves it, but in a greater measure than he deserves it. In most cases the prophetic books use the word *ḥesed* in the sense of practicing beneficence toward one who has no right at all to claim this from you."[3] Regarding Ruth, the latter meaning is used—to practice benevolence toward people who have no claim on her for it. Her exemplary behavior is somewhat reminiscent of the patriarchs and matriarchs. In some places, the Ruth narrative actually resembles the older narratives in language, content, and style (Gen. 24:12–14; Ruth 3:3–9). Ruth, like Abraham—the founder of the nation, the first of the proselytes—left the house of her father and mother and went to join a people who, as far as she knew, would not accept her because of her foreign origins.[4] Yet she would not be dissuaded and joined the Israelite nation, with no thought of reward for this act of affiliation, and in this lies her great *ḥesed*.

The Righteous Proselyte

Both the Midrash and the Talmud place great importance on the story of Ruth's conversion. Having recognized Ruth as a *zadeket* ("righteous person"),[5] the sages found themselves needing to "justify" her affiliation with the Jewish people;

hence they sought to make her conversion "kosher" by ratio-
nalizing it halakhically. The initial problem was Ruth's origins:
the Pentateuch forbade Moabites from entering the congregation of the Lord:

> No Ammonite or Moabite shall be admitted into the congrega-
> tion of the Lord; none of their descendants, even in the tenth
> generation, shall ever be admitted into the congregation of the
> Lord, because they did not meet you with food and water on
> your journey after you left Egypt, and because they hired [the
> renowned prophet] Balaam son of Beor . . . to curse you. . . .
> You shall never concern yourself with their welfare or benefit as
> long as you live (Deut. 23:4–7).[6]

The rabbis interpret this pentateuchal prohibition to mean
that *male* Moabites were forbidden to come into the congregation of the Lord, thereby basing this interpretation on the use
of the male singular form in the biblical text: "A 'Moabite,' but
not a Moabitess [is excluded]." Because it was the Moabite
male, not the Moabite female, who violated the laws of hospitality by denying assistance to the Israelites, women are permitted
in marriage, the rabbis explain. This enabled them to sanction
Ruth's marriage and conversion.[7]

The Talmud and the Midrash describe in detail Ruth's conversion, which is placed within the framework of the famous
scene in which Naomi begs her two daughters-in-law to return
to their own parents and people. Naomi tries to reason with
them and dissuade them from remaining with her—a course
that holds out no hope and no future for them. Orpah heeds
her advice and goes home to Moab. Ruth, by contrast, utters
the famous speech:

> "Entreat me not to leave thee, and to return from following
> after thee; for whither thou goest, I will go; and where thou
> lodgest, I will lodge; thy people shall be my people, and thy God
> my God; where thou diest, will I die, and there will I be buried"
> (Ruth 1:16–17).[8]

Commenting on this verse, the Midrash begins with Ruth telling Naomi that she has fully resolved to become converted to
Naomi's God under any circumstances, and it is better that her
conversion should be at Naomi's hands than at those of an-

other. Naomi responds by relating the laws of conversion, because she realizes how sincere Ruth is in her resolve.[9]

According to the Midrash *Ruth Rabbah*, Naomi began her response to Ruth with the following warnings: "My daughter, it is not the custom of daughters of Israel to frequent Gentile theaters and circuses, to which she replied, 'Where you go I will go.' "[10] The daughters of Israel, Naomi continues, dwell in homes that have a *mezuzah*, a scroll bearing certain biblical verses that is attached to the doorpost in obedience to Deuteronomic law (Deut. 6:9). Ruth indicates her acceptance of this precept by declaring that she will lodge only where Naomi will lodge, that is, in houses with *mezuzot*. The biblical phrase "your people shall be my people" is taken in the Midrash to indicate her acceptance of all the penalties and admonitions of the Torah. Her acceptance of all the remaining commandments, according to the rabbis' interpretation, is expressed by the rest of the sentence: "Your God [shall be] my God."

In the talmudic version of the story, Naomi begins the conversion ritual by teaching the importance of Sabbath observance.[11] She tells Ruth that Jews are prohibited from traveling beyond the set Sabbath boundaries (*teḥum shabbat*) on the day of rest. Ruth replies, "Where you go I will go." Naomi then turns to sexual matters between men and women. Private meetings (*yiḥud*) between men and women (besides husband, wife, and family members) are forbidden. Ruth replies, "Where you lodge, I will lodge." Naomi tells her that the Jews have been commanded to observe 613 (606 + 7) commandments. Ruth replies, "Your people shall be my people" (Ruth 1:16). Six hundred six commandments are incumbent only upon Jews. An additional seven, called by the sages the "Noahide Laws," are incumbent upon all the descendants of Noah, that is—all humanity.[12] According to the *gematria* (the talmudic tradition of numerology, in which each letter is given a numerical value), the name Ruth adds up to 606. Thus the sages claim that even Ruth's name indicates her acceptance of all the 613 commandments of the Torah.[13]

The talmudic passage in *Yebamot* continues to interpolate discussions about Jewish laws of conversion within the dialogue of Naomi and Ruth. The Talmud takes Naomi's behavior to-

ward Ruth as the paradigm to teach that one must not exces-
sively push away a proselyte. The talmudic sages cite the verse
"And when she [Naomi] saw that she [Ruth] was steadfastly
minded to go with her, she left off speaking unto her" (Ruth
1:18). This verse becomes scriptural justification for the principle that one should not overly dissuade a would-be convert.[14]
The selections from rabbinic sources describing Ruth's conversion present an image of a steadfast and determined person,
firm in her decision to join the Israelites. The image is in keeping with all the other depictions of her in the biblical sources
and in the rabbinic retellings. Once she has decided to cast her
lot with her mother-in-law's people, she displays no questioning
or doubts. She accepts all the duties and requirements with no
complaint and expresses her willingness to comply fully.

The process of Ruth's conversion, as described in the biblical verses, significantly differs from the conversion process
developed in later Jewish practice. The rabbis, in their interpretation of her story, tried to interpolate features of the "official"
process into their retelling of her story. One midrash actually
has Ruth immersing herself; this is based on the verse in which
Naomi says to her "go wash" (Ruth 3:3).[15] All this interpretive
labor had several motives: first, to show what constitutes a
proper conversion in the Jewish tradition (the convert had to
be sincere and determined, and willing to accept the intense
duties and obligations of Jewish law); second, to show a paragon of docile, loyal, compliant female behavior; and third, to
legitimize Ruth's conversion in order to bolster the legitimacy
of the Davidic line.

Although the rabbinic sources on Ruth emphasize the need
for a convert to assent to the host of ritual requirements of
Jewish law, they do not expend much attention on the relative
desirability of conversion itself.[16] This focus, on making certain
that a conversion is sincere and valid, calls to mind the sharply
contrasting attitude toward conversion in the books of Ezra and
Nehemiah. Both Ezra and Nehemiah call for the foreign wives
of the returning Israelite exiles to be sent back to their own
people.

Why do Ezra and Nehemiah insist on this? No adequate answer has been given, though several explanations have been

advanced. It is possible that the concept of conversion had not been formulated at the time of Ezra and Nehemiah.[17] Moreover, during their historical period, it may have seemed to Ezra and Nehemiah, as others have suggested, that it might be risky for a small, newly established, unstable province like Judah under the Persians to allow its members to intermarry with their neighbors. This could erode the identity of the people and undermine the relative independence and autonomy of the province. Because the Judeans had already been divided between those who had remained in the land and those who returned from Babylonian exile, to allow too many foreign women to marry into the nation, some feared, would further threaten the unity of the nation. Yet, another explanation that has recently been proposed suggests that the reason behind the expulsion of the foreign wives was economic. The laws of inheritance extant among the foreign peoples who had married Judeans gave women some rights to inherit land, which, if followed, might cause lands belonging originally to Judean men to fall into the hands of foreigners in the event of the husband's death.[18]

With this in mind, many scholars have seen the book of Ruth as having been written as a polemic against Ezra and Nehemiah—for the purpose of permitting foreigners into the congregation of the Lord. The book of Ruth was regarded as representing a universalistic trend among the Jews, in a similar vein to the exilic prophecy of Deutero-Isaiah. According to this view, "Ruth was a protest paper by the universalists against the stringency of Ezra-Nehemiah nationalism, based on a subtle reminder that David's grandmother was a Moabitess."[19] Recently, however, many scholars have rejected this view, adducing that the book's mild tone belies a harsh polemical intent.[20]

The Resonance of Names

The ancient peoples of the Near Eastern and Mediterranean world believed in the potency of names and their meaningful reflection on the person. "All study of names in the Old Testament, of the symbolism associated with them and the literary effects which they exercise, begins with the recognition of one central fact, namely, that a large proportion of Hebrew personal names are intelligible sentences or phrases."[21] This point is effectively illustrated by the book of Ruth. The sages comment that the names of the characters bear out some of the main themes in the book.

The name Naomi means "sweetness, pleasantness"; it personifies everything pleasant: "for her actions were pleasant and sweet."[22] She followed her husband, Elimelech, into a foreign land, where a multitude of calamities befall her, including widowhood and bereavement of her sons. Yet she does not become resentful or bitter, but on the contrary remains as her name implies—pleasant. She continues to demonstrate *ḥesed* in her behavior and, after some trying, bitter experiences, eventually enjoys an agreeable and sweet life. Their gloss of the word Naomi comes easy to the sages, for Naomi does it for them. In the biblical narrative she notes that during the sad and difficult part of her life her name seemed inapposite: "Do not call me Naomi, call me Marah [that is, "bitter"]; for the Almighty has dealt very bitterly with me. I went away full, and the Lord has brought me back empty. Why call me Naomi, when the Lord has afflicted me and the Almighty has brought calamity upon me?" (Ruth 1:20–21).

Boaz, too, has a name that is easily glossed: *bo'az* means "in him is strength."[23] And, indeed, Boaz is a man of substance and strength. Gallant in his actions, he sets *ḥesed* and justice on its correct course by redeeming his kinsman's inheritance, and goes beyond duty by marrying a widow—an outsider, a woman alone. In the first sentence in which he is introduced in the biblical narrative, Boaz is called a *gibbor ḥayil* ("a mighty man of valor"), the masculine equivalent of *'eshet ḥayil* ("woman of valor"),[24] a term of praise applied to Ruth, both in the scroll and by the rabbis.

The rabbis found the figure of Orpah difficult to characterize and explain, and this led them to treat her in ways that reveal much about the midrashic process in general. Orpah's name, according to Midrash, comes from *'oref*, which is the Hebrew for the nape of the neck; her name is said by the sages to refer to her turning her nape to Naomi when she agreed to Naomi's suggestion to return to Moab. That the sages point to this moment in her life as the one signified by her name indicates that they considered this the most important part of her story.

Orpah is loyal to Naomi; and, when faced with conflicting loyalties, she behaves well by submitting to Naomi's counsel *and* returning to her original family. But in the rabbis' eyes, the extraordinary ḥesed that Ruth demonstrates in actually rejecting Naomi's advice and electing to stay with her husband's people, whom she had adopted as her own, ranks far higher than Orpah's docile obedience to her mother-in-law and consequent return to her people.

The difficulty Orpah poses for the sages is answered by the energetic midrashic invention of embroidering the biblical account. Those rabbis who want to emphasize Orpah's goodness proffer stories that support such a view;[25] those who see her as more bad than good offer stories that show her in a negative light. For example, one midrashic tradition holds that Orpah is the mother of Goliath, an enemy of Israel and the main adversary of Ruth's descendant, David. They give such an evil son to a woman who seemed to have done nothing wrong in this story. Orpah is not only not-entirely-good; for some midrashic commentators, she is downright infamous. According to some midrashim, her son Goliath was derided as "the son of a hundred fathers," which implies a serious slur on his mother's character.[26] Some of this exaggeration of Orpah's failings may be the result of a process by which Ruth's goodness is constructed and presented in both scripture and Midrash—the establishment of binary oppositions being a widespread strategy in narrative construction.[27]

The character Elimelech bears a name that means "my God is king," but which also evokes the sentiment "to me belongs royalty." Elimelech is eager for the status of royalty; he seeks position and honor for himself but does not seem particularly eager to give of himself in behalf of the people.

> He [Elimelech] was one of the notables of his place and one of the leaders of his generation. But when the famine came he

said, "Now all Israel will come knocking at my door (for help,) each one with his basket." He therefore arose and fled from them. This is the meaning of the verse: "And a certain man of Beth-lehem in Judah went."[28]

He never demonstrates courage or *ḥesed*, and is denigrated by the sages for leaving Judah and evading his responsibilities as a leader in time of crisis. His behavior fails to live up to what his name would require of him; he claims the right of royalty but not its obligations. He serves in the narrative as the antithesis of the quality embodied in its heroines and heroes—that of *ḥesed*, both ordinary and extraordinary.[29] Elimelech had two sons—Mahlon (meaning "the sickly") and Chilion ("the one who came to an early end"); both died young, fulfilling the meaning of their names.

Glossing Ruth's name is more complex, for its root is ambiguous. There are a variety of interpretations given in Midrash for this name. Rabbi Johanan derived the word from *ravah* ("to saturate"): "Because she was privileged to be the ancestress of David, who saturated the Holy One, blessed be He, with songs and hymns."[30] The name Ruth can also be derived from the root *ra'ah* ("to see"), for Ruth "saw," or considered her mother-in-law's words.[31] Later sources, such as the *Syriac Targum*, as well as modern scholars working from etymological evidence, derive it from the root for *re'ut*: "friendship" or "female companion."[32] Unlike the midrashic explanations, which advance other agendas, including bolstering the legitimacy of the Davidic line, this latter derivation is in keeping with the biblical character of Ruth.

The sages describe Ruth's departure from the land of Moab into the land of Israel in language virtually identical to that used in describing the departure of the patriarch Jacob from the land of Canaan. By drawing a parallel with Jacob, they emphasize Ruth's specialness and her fitness to stand as foremother of David. The sages say that a righteous person's departure from a place leaves a void, because the saintly person is the "shining light," "brilliance," "distinction," and "glory" of a place.[33]

"And she went forth out of the place where she was" (Ruth 1:7). . . . Was she then the only one that went forth from the place?

Did not many camel-drivers and how many ass-drivers also go forth? And yet it says only "and she went forth"? R. Azariah . . . explained: The great [person] of a city is its shining light, its distinction, its glory, and its praise. When he departs, its brilliance, its distinction, its glory, and its praise depart with him. And so you will find with our father Jacob when he departed from Beer-sheba. . . . [This explanation is] justified in the former case since there was no other righteous person but her [i.e., Ruth].[34]

Ruth's departure is said by the rabbis to have depleted Moab of a great and saintly person; this high praise is said of no other woman in midrashic literature.

Ruth is shown throughout the biblical narrative as being consistently kind and giving, and that theme is maintained throughout the *aggadah*. Although some stress that Naomi also exudes the quality of *hesed*, as does Boaz, what is remarkable in the narrative and the commentary is that a foreigner/convert female is allowed to take the lead as the epitome of *hesed*. Indeed, her case is unique in all of scripture.

Modesty—The Mark of Feminine Virtue

Although the characteristic of *hesed* leaps off the page at every turn, the theme of modesty does not. Nevertheless, Ruth's modesty is given great emphasis by the sages, for this is a quality they consider very important, especially in a woman. The prophet Micah (6:8) said: "Walk humbly [modestly] with God." Modesty in midrashic thought is likewise a highly prized, beautiful quality that should be cultivated by both men and women. Yet women are commanded to develop this quality to a higher degree of perfection than is expected of men. "The king's daughter is all glorious within," from Psalm 45:13, is often quoted when proper female behavior is being prescribed.[35] The rabbinic notion of a woman's innate modesty, which supported the expectations of women in that society, evolved in connection with the laws of *zni'ut*, which literally means "being hidden." The rabbis attempted to enforce a social system in which woman's life would be highly private. It was felt that the laws of *zni'ut* should govern male-female relations to protect this natural, womanly phenomenon of privacy. Men and women were not to mingle except in very circumscribed situations, as we saw in the law of *yihud* (one of the laws of *zni'ut*). In fact, women must not be alone with any man but her husband or immediate family members.

It is interesting to note that, although the laws are designed ostensibly to protect a woman's modesty, they coexist with the contradictory rabbinical view that a woman is seductive. The duty then falls upon the woman to check her behavior and demeanor so as to preclude all situations in which a man will be tempted by her charms.

According to the rabbinic sources, Ruth was truly modest. In fact, the sages say that what attracted Boaz to Ruth was her modest walk and behavior:

> [Boaz asked,] "Whose damsel is this?" Did he then not recognize her? The meaning is that when he saw how attractive she was, and how modest her attitude, he began to inquire concerning her. All the other women bend down to gather the ears of corn, but she sits and gathers; all the other women hitch up their skirts, and she keeps hers down; all the other women jest with the reapers, while she is reserved; all the other women gather from between the sheaves, while she gathers from that which is already abandoned.[36]

In the rabbinic version of her story, Ruth displays several exemplary qualities while reaping in Boaz's field: not only was her modesty in evidence but her lack of greed, for she takes care not to take more than she was permitted according to the law of gleaning. Furthermore, she had knowledge of these laws and observed them.[37]

From their initial meeting in the field, both Ruth and Boaz demonstrated modest behavior and, moreover, mutually recognized one another's goodness. Boaz is magnanimous toward the strange woman gleaning in his field, and Ruth is careful not to exploit his kindness and his hospitality. Boaz was so impressed by the Moabite maiden that he encouraged her to stay and glean in his field,[38] and he admonished his workers not to touch or reprimand her in any way.

Ruth's modesty remains intact when, at Naomi's instruction, she goes to Boaz at night at the threshing floor. Modern readers are likely to see this scene as fraught with eroticism. Ruth's bold action might easily have been misconstrued by Boaz and by anyone who might have observed her. Yet Naomi dared to send her; and the sages, knowing the dangers of such a potentially brazen act, turn the scene into a heroic moment in which Ruth's modesty is proved once again, as is Boaz's continence and virtue.[39]

Naomi sends Ruth to the threshing floor to lie at Boaz's feet and attract his attention. She instructs Ruth thus: "Wash therefore and anoint yourself, and put on your best clothes, and go down to the threshing floor" (Ruth 3:3). The rabbis pick up the fact that when Ruth carries out Naomi's instructions, she reverses their order, " 'and she went down to the threshing floor,' and [only] subsequently, 'and did according to all that her mother-in-law bade her.' "[40] They explain that Ruth did not make herself attractive until after she went to the threshing floor because she feared that she might meet a man on the way and her beauty would excite him, or he might take her for a harlot. Ruth's modesty is thus preserved throughout.

Yet even in this paragon of female virtue, the sages find and note a flaw: Ruth reports that Boaz had told her to "stay with the young men" (Ruth 2:21), whereas he had actually said:

"Listen to me, daughter. Don't go to glean in another field. Don't go elsewhere, but stay here close to my girls" (Ruth 2:8).

What might have been passed over as no more than a slip of the tongue was taken by the sages as an indication of impure thoughts on Ruth's part, a lapse they attributed to her heathen or Moabite background, from which, they say, she had not entirely freed herself: "In truth she was a Moabitess, for Boaz said to her, 'Abide here fast by my *maidens*,' while she said, 'by my young *men*.' "[41] This criticism was, however, slight, and the rabbis continued to acclaim Ruth's virtue and modesty thereafter.

Boaz's initial appreciation for Ruth's fine qualities deepened into commitment as a result of their subsequent encounter in the threshing floor. Their meeting and marriage has such an air of aptness—despite all the elements of chance that entered into their meeting—that the sages see the gracious hand of providence guiding them toward one another.[42]

Was Ruth Beautiful?

Nowhere in the biblical text is Ruth said to be beautiful. Yet, as in other commentaries on exemplary female biblical figures, the sages ascribe to Ruth physical beauty. Why do they add beauty to her already long list of well-established admirable qualities? To answer this question, we must first consider the concept of beauty as it appears in rabbinic sources. Although neither the attractiveness of Adam nor that of Eve is spoken of in scripture, the sages claim not only that Adam was beautiful, but that he was even more beautiful than Eve.[43] Sarah too was bestowed with the gift of beauty. In Sarah's speech, "After I have grown old, shall I be young again" (Gen. 18:12),[44] Rav Hisda believes it was meant that "after the flesh was worn and the wrinkles multiplied, Sarah was rejuvenated and returned to her original beauty."[45] Not only biblical figures but also rabbis—for example, Rabbi Johanan[46] and many others[47]—are said in talmudic writings to be beautiful. Although there are some dissenting views and counterattitudes evident in Midrash, some holding that beauty is or can be vain and deceptive, as in Mishnah *Ta'anit*,[48] the rabbis generally consider physical beauty as a good thing. In fact, they created a blessing to recite upon seeing a beautiful woman, something to be appreciated, celebrated, and enjoyed—a gift from God.[49]

In general, the rabbis have a marked propensity to bestow beauty on the important female characters in scripture—underscoring the comeliness of characters said to be beautiful in the biblical text, and, as with Ruth, endowing with beauty characters the Bible had neglected to favor in this manner.[50]

There are patterned ways whereby the rabbis discover the

beauty of biblical women in the scriptural materials relating to them. One midrashic trope, as we have seen with Sarah, is to say that a woman looks far younger than her years. This convention is applied in closely parallel midrashic traditions concerning Ruth. For example, it is said that Sarah was as beautiful when she died at the age, given in the Bible, of one hundred and twenty-seven (Gen. 23:1) as she had been as a girl of twenty.[51] Similarly, the rabbis say that Boaz took notice of Ruth because, at forty, she looked like a girl of fourteen:

> "[Naomi] said unto her, 'Go my daughter.'" R. Jannai said: "She was forty years of age and yet you call her daughter? The answer is that she looked like a girl of fourteen."[52]

Although Ruth's age is not specified in the biblical text, as one who has been widowed after ten years of marriage, she is certainly a mature woman when she meets and marries Boaz. The rabbis give her age as forty, although the biblical narrative would be at least as plausible if she were a good ten years younger. This not only makes the youthfulness of her appearance more striking; it also makes her bearing a child somewhat remarkable, in a way that is reminiscent of Sarah's prodigiously late maternity at the age of ninety. Thus the Midrash also claims that Ruth was lacking the main portion of the womb, but the Holy One shaped a womb for her "and gave her pregnancy."[53] This is to suggest the miraculous nature of her maternity, just as was Sarah's.

There is also a curious midrash on Boaz: Boaz, who was eighty when he married Ruth, died on the wedding night, after his son was conceived.[54] These midrashic nuances suggest that the marriage between Boaz and Ruth was hampered by many obstacles that had to be overcome to engender the birth of an important figure. Hence, female beauty, rejuvenation, and somewhat miraculous maternity following protracted barrenness are all thematically connected in the Midrash.

How the rabbis go about scripturally substantiating Ruth's beauty is worth some attention. In the portion of the narrative where Naomi sends Ruth to glean in the field, there is a verse that runs "and her *miqreh* was to light on that portion of the field" (Ruth 2:4). Normally, the Hebrew word *miqreh* could be

translated as "hap" ("happening") or "chance," or "occurrence," meaning that she chanced upon that particular field of
Boaz. The rabbis, however, resort to a fairly strenuous bit of
textual interpretation, connecting the word *miqreh* with *qeri,* a
word from the same root, used in rabbinic literature to refer to
a nocturnal emission. Although in the context of the narrative
this latter meaning would seem to modern readers rather remote, one midrashic reading seizes on the word *miqreh* here
and takes the passage to indicate that Ruth was so beautiful that
any man who glimpsed her would have a sexual reaction (a
"pollution," as the rabbis would phrase it).[55] By this midrashic
process, beauty is bestowed upon Ruth, thereby idealizing her
persona, making her even more dear and pleasing in the mind
of the people and more worthy of engendering the Davidic
dynasty.

Royal Origins

Midrashic lore gives Ruth royal origins,[56] as they do to
other foreign women mentioned in the Bible. The story of
Timna, who appears in Genesis 36:12 as the concubine of
Eliphaz (one of the sons of Esau) and the mother of the
horrible Amalek, echoes that of Ruth, Orpah, and Hagar.
Midrashic lore holds that Timna "asked to be received into
the faith of Abraham, but they all, Abraham, Isaac, and Jacob,
had rejected her," whereupon she declares: " 'Rather will I
be a maidservant unto the dregs of this nation, than mistress
of another nation.' "[57]

Another midrash identifies Hagar as the daughter of Pharaoh:[58] Pharaoh, having been smitten by the beautiful Sarah
but then immediately falling ill and being forced to let her go,
was impressed by the God of Israel for saving her in this way; he
was also impressed by the character of both Sarah and her
husband. He later decided to give his daughter Hagar to Sarah
because he felt it better for her to be a maid in the house of
Abraham than a princess in his own land.[59]

According to the rabbis, Ruth and Orpah's father was Eglon, king of Moab. They portray Eglon as a person of high ethical standards and, though a heathen, a righteous man.[60] The judge Ehud went to Eglon in a ruse to kill him, saying, "I have a message for you from the Lord, the God of Israel." When Eglon rose to honor God's name, Ehud killed him (Judg. 3:20–21). The rabbis claim that the reward for his piety was to have sired Ruth from whom the messianic line would descend. Thus the line of David is royal on both sides, father and mother.[61] Orpah, as the supposed forebear of Goliath, does not fare as well.

The Laws of Levirate and Land Redemption

The entire Ruth narrative, though only four chapters long, moves consistently toward a climactic ending that results in the marriage of Ruth and Boaz followed by the birth of Ruth's child, from whom David—and the redemption of the Israelites —eventually will spring. The story describes Ruth taking courage and, at Naomi's bidding, going to the threshing floor, where she said to Boaz: "Spread your skirt over your maidservant, as you are next of kin" (Ruth 3:9). In other words, she is telling Boaz that, because he is the near kinsman of her husband's family, it is his duty to assist her and her mother-in-law in their plight by redeeming her deceased husband's land and marrying her. The question that follows is whether the book of Ruth is in fact a source for the halakhic laws on levirate marriage pertaining to the status of a wife whose husband dies without an heir (Deut. 25:5) or the possibly allied question regarding redemption of the land (Lev. 25:25).[62]

The answer to the *yibbum* question is no! In Deuteronomy, the rite of *yibbum* is described as obligatory: The woman *must* marry the levir, and only he can release her from the legal requirement by either marrying her (*yibbum*) or granting release (*ḥalizah*). The Talmud and Midrash never treat Ruth as a woman who needs to get *yibbum* (the fulfillment of the levir's duties toward her).[63] Naomi clearly tells her daughters-in-law to return to their parents' home, for she has no more sons to give them (Ruth 1:11ff.); that is, there were no surviving brothers to fulfill the levirate laws. The widows were free to act as they wished. Whereas Deuteronomy specifies that it was the brother who was to fulfill the levirate requirement, Boaz is only a distant relation. Moreover, there is a ritual known as *ḥaliẓah* that must be performed when a levir refuses to marry his sister-in-law. In this ritual the man takes off his sandal and must hand it to the woman whom he is to release. In the Ruth narrative, Ruth is not present during the episode in which the shoe is exchanged. This bolsters the (rabbinic) thesis that the shoe-removal ceremony described in Ruth is not a levirate rite, but is rather a legal procedure to redeem the land and transfer ownership from kinsman to redeemer.[64]

Furthermore, Ruth is not obligated to marry Boaz but does, though he is old. He notes the *ḥesed* this entailed, saying: "You have made this last kindness greater than the first, in that you have not gone after young men, whether poor or rich" (Ruth 3:10). Had she been a *yevamah* (one obliged to submit to levirate law), she would have been obliged to act in accordance with the requirements satisfied with *yibbum*, and there would be no *ḥesed* in fulfilling the legal requirements. Likewise, Boaz is not one who simply fulfilled the legal requirements of levirate marriage; he too has acted out of kindness beyond duty. As we saw, Boaz is not a true levir.[65] He is not in fact the brother of the deceased husband and has no legal obligation to marry Ruth under the levirate rule. In a legal category, he can be considered nothing but a distant kinsman willing to redeem the land when a nearer kinsman refuses. In marrying Ruth he also "raises up a name to the dead." Although exemplary, the willingness of both members of this couple to accept obligations not incumbent upon them by law or custom makes them paragons of righteousness, living embodiments of *ḥesed*, but according to this view, not actors according to the rabbinic view in the legal ceremony of *yibbum*.

Instead, the rabbis focus on the issue of redemption of land. Under the laws of *ge'ulah* (the laws of redemption of property codified in Leviticus), the kinsman must redeem Naomi's land. This matter of property—redemption, particularly the laws and customs governing inheritance rights where women were involved—is very complicated, but for our purposes it is sufficient to note that talmudic and midrashic discussions of these matters in the book of Ruth tend to focus on the redemption ceremony. The sages' comments stem from these verses of Ruth: "Now this was the custom in former times in Israel concerning redeeming and exchanging: to confirm a transaction, the one drew off his sandal and gave it to the other" (Ruth 4:7).[66]

The Talmud notes that it is not clear in the biblical text whether Boaz gave the shoe to the kinsman or the kinsman to Boaz, and they do not settle the question.

> This is disputed by Tannaim: *Now this was the manner in former times in Israel concerning redeeming and concerning changing, for to confirm all things; a man drew off his shoe, and gave it to his neighbor. . . . Who gave whom?* Boaz gave to the kinsman. R. Judah said: The kinsman gave to Boaz.[67]

What matters here is that the transference of the shoe in Ruth 4:7 appears related to the law of the *go'el*,[68] as described in Leviticus 25:25, in which a kinsman redeems a poor relative's land. In the Ruth story, a relative who is called the *go'el* in fact relinquishes the property to Boaz, who is not called a *go'el.* The shoe transfer formalized the property exchange—the only other kind of transaction besides the *yibbum* in which the shoe ritual was practiced. Both types of ceremony, in a sense, were a kind of divorce in which one party relinquished all rights of claim.

The theme of the redemption of the land is given in elaborate detail in the biblical narrative and has also evoked lengthy and complicated midrashic exegesis. I would venture to say that because the midrashic project regarding Ruth appears to be interested in legitimizing her as the ancestress of David, the line from which will spring the redeemer of Israel, the theme of the redemption of the land is perhaps best understood within this tradition as a foreshadowing of the theme of the messianic redemption of Israel.

Conclusion

The qualities Ruth displays in the biblical narrative itself, and even more, her qualities as developed in rabbinic interpretation—modesty, obedience, devotion to wifely and maternal duties—are not the qualities sought by feminists. Ruth is not independent, autonomous, and free of male control; she is docile and submissive, and this is why the sages laud and honor her.

The sages emphasize those qualities that will bolster Ruth's fitness as an ancestress of David and also as an ideal of feminine behavior. Thus, in addition to the loyalty, steadfastness, *ḥesed* and obedience that she displays in the biblical text, they add beauty, royal lineage, and a highly exaggerated modesty. Ruth is the paragon of all those virtues the sages believed a woman ought to embody. Ruth's role is to be a faithful, modest daughter-in-law and, by remarrying and bearing a male child, to continue the male line of her deceased husband.

It is in marriage and motherhood that Ruth fulfills her role; and by her dedication to these, the feminine functions and values respected and venerated by the sages, she wins their approval and esteem. They compare her to the matriarchs who built the house of Israel, whose merit also derives almost entirely from their fulfillment of the maternal role. The sages accord great respect to the exemplary women of the Bible, more than they ever show toward any actual women of their own day. Ruth is afforded especially high honor. She is, however, praised to a great extent for qualities the sages themselves ascribed to her —in particular, for sexual modesty and for committing herself to the wifely and maternal rule. An embodiment of *ḥesed*, a loyal and obedient wife, a righteous proselyte— she is fitting ancestress of the line of David.

The rabbis focused on values appropriate to their times. But in our day, one can look at Ruth as an independent-minded young woman, not fearful to leave the comfort and security of her home and people, for she felt a higher calling. One can see through the rabbinic reading of Ruth how important it is for each generation to reinterpret scriptural texts in light of its own values. Ruth's model can be reappropriated in keeping with modern reality. The biblical and rabbinic value of *ḥesed* need not be connected to a secondary status of women. Ruth's kindness, her steadfast friendship, loyalty, and yes, even a measure of her modesty, are traits that can be held up as exemplary for both sexes to follow.

Notes

1. *Ruth Rab.* 2:13.

2. Yair Zakovitch, "Ruth: Introduction and Commentary," in *Mikra LeYisra'el: A Bible Commentary for Israel,* ed. M. Greenberg and S. Ahituv (Tel Aviv and Jerusalem: Am Oved Publishers/Magnes Press, 1990), 10ff.

3. M. Maimonides, *The Guide to the Perplexed,* trans. Shlomo Pines (Chicago: University of Chicago Press, 1963), 631.

4. *Gen. Rab.* 59:9: *b. Sukk.* 49b.

5. *Ruth Rab.* 2:12.

6. The Ammonites are also included in the Deuteronomic prohibition, which was to apply for ten generations. The seven nations that occupied Canaan prior to Israelite entrance into the land can never intermarry and must be destroyed.

7. *b. Yebam.* 76b–77a.

8. We follow here the beautiful, poetic translation of the original Jewish Publication Society version, reprinted in the Soncino edition of Ruth (London: Soncino Press, 1946).

9. Ancient Judaism held differing attitudes toward conversion, but eventually active proselytizing was abandoned until relatively recently. When prospective converts present themselves, they are typically discouraged at first and must prove their sincerity and conviction. Nevertheless, it is prohibited to dissuade a proselyte *too much*; and here, because Naomi is now convinced of Ruth's determination, Naomi sets out the rules. This is a talmudic law that the sages derived from the Ruth and Naomi episode; it is discussed later in this chapter. See further *b. Yebam.* 47a.

10. *Ruth Rab.* 2:22; cf. 2:12. The mention of theaters and circuses

betrays the times when the Midrash was composed, and is anachronistic in the context of when the story of Ruth is set. "Gentile" is the translator's choice; the Hebrew *'avodat kohavim*, literally, "worshipers of the stars and constellations" would be better rendered as "pagans" or "idolaters."

11. *b. Yebam.* 47b.

12. The seven Noahide laws are considered in rabbinic tradition as the minimal moral duties enjoined by the Bible on all people; *b. Sanh.* 56a and following; Maimonides, *Mishneh Torah, Sefer Shoftim, Hilkhot Melakhim* 8:10; 10:12. Jews are obligated to observe the whole Torah, whereas every non-Jew is a son of the covenant of Noah (Genesis 9).

13. Feivel Melzer, "Ruth," in *The Five Scrolls*, ed. A. Mirsky et al. (Jerusalem: Mosad Harav Kook, 1973), 21.

14. *b. Yebam.* 47a–b; *Ruth Zuta* 49, v. 44, pp. 85 and 108; D. Hartmann, *Das Buch Ruth in der Midrasch-Litteratur* (Leipzig: n.p., 1901), 98.

15. *Ruth Rab.* 5:12. The Midrash explains as follows: "Wash yourself, clean yourself from your idolatry by ritual immersion." See also *The Book of Ruth*, ed. Meir Zlotowitz and Nosson Scherman, Art Scroll Tanach Series (New York: Mesorah Publications, 1976), 109.

16. The view toward converts is not always positive. One adage states that converts are as hard to endure as a sore; *b. Yebam.* 47b.

17. Shmuel Safrai, *The Jewish People in the Days of the Second Temple* (Tel Aviv: Am Oved, 1970), 32.

18. Tamara C. Eskenazi, "Out from the Shadows: Biblical Woman in the Post-Exilic Era," *JSOT* 54 (1992): 25–43.

19. Edward F. Campbell, Jr., *Ruth*, The Anchor Bible, vol. 7 (Garden City, N.Y.: Doubleday & Co., 1975), 26–27.

20. The very basic task of dating the book of Ruth confounds assessment of the book's purpose and motive. A wide range of dates, from preexilic times to a late postexilic date, are offered. And although the Talmudic sages (*b. B. Bat.* 14a) generally accept that the book of Ruth was written by Samuel, the book of Ruth is found not after Judges in the Hebrew biblical canon, but among the writings, indicating uncertainty as to its period.

21. James Barr, "The Symbolism of Names in the Old Testament," *The Bulletin of the John Rylands Library* 62 (1969): 1–29.

22. *Ruth Rab.* 2:5.

23. A. J. Rosenberg, "Ruth," in *Five Megillot*, rev. ed. (London: Soncino Press, 1984), 121.

24. Ginzberg, *Legends of the Jews*, vol. 5, p. 258 n. 271.

25. *Ruth Rab.* 2:20. Orpah's forty paces walking with Naomi caused

retribution to be suspended for forty days from her descendant Goliath.

26. *Ruth Rab.* 2:20; *b. Soṭa* 42b.

27. See chapter 3 on Serah bat Asher.

28. *Ruth Rab.* 1:4 toward the end.

29. *b. B. Bat.* 9a; *Ruth Rab.* 1:4.

30. *b. Ber.* 7b.

31. *Ruth Rab.* 2:9.

32. Brown, Driver, and Briggs, *A Hebrew and English Lexicon of the Old Testament,* 946.

33. *Ruth Rab.* 2:12.

34. Ibid.

35. *Lev. Rab.* 21:11; *Num. Rab.* 1:3; *b. Yebam.* 77a; *b. Giṭ.* 12a. The subject of modesty is also discussed in chapter 1.

36. *Ruth Rab.* 4:6; *b. Šabb.* 113b.

37. *m. Pe'a* 6:5. According to the book of Ruth, in ancient Israel the laws of alms for the poor (Lev. 19:9–10, 23–24), especially for strangers, orphans, and widows (Deut. 24:19–21) as outlined in the Pentateuch, were observed; and the sages suggest that when Ruth had chosen to stay with Naomi and to adopt the Israelite laws, she learned these laws and obeyed them.

38. The biblical scene in which Ruth meets her future husband for the first time in the field is rich with symbolism. A contemporary scholar, Robert Alter (*The Art of the Biblical Narrative* [New York: Basic Books, 1981], 58), sees the book of Ruth as a "betrothal narrative," full of symbols of fallowness and fertility. Ruth is fallow, barren, but like the food and water offered by Boaz that physically sustains her, when he becomes her husband he will make her fruitful—and thereby both will become progenitors of the Davidic dynasty.

39. According to the Midrash, Boaz is one of the three most chaste men in the Bible, the others being Joseph and Palti. *Lev. Rab.* 23:11; *Gen. Rab.* 15:16; *Ruth Rab.* 3:13.

40. Ruth 3:6, as explained by *b. Šabb.* 113b.

41. *Ruth Rab.* 5:11.

42. Rosenberg, "Ruth," in *Five Megillot,* 123.

43. *b. B. Bat.* 58a.

44. This is my own free translation to bring out the midrashic meaning.

45. *b. B. Meṣ.* 87a.

46. *b. Ber.* 20a.

47. *b. B. Bat.* 58a.

48. *m. Ta'an.* 4:8.

49. *y. Ber.* 9:2, 13b.

50. It is interesting to note here that the rabbis generally treat beauty as a desirable and admirable quality when discussing the exemplary women of the Bible, rather than when they discuss the women of their own day. For the rabbis, the beauty of the biblical characters is taken as something that shows them to be perfect creations of a perfect creator. When it comes to women of their own day, the picture becomes more complicated. The rabbis rarely mention individual women in the Talmud, and the physical appearance of the few that they do name is not discussed. This seems to reflect the rabbis' concern for sexual propriety: the beauty of the actual women around them is a dangerous matter, for it is fraught with the possibility of exciting uncontrollable and impure passions. The female characters of the Bible are evidently remote enough that this is not a problem where they are concerned.

51. *Ruth Rab.* 4:4.

52. Ibid.

53. *Ruth Rab.* 7:14.

54. *Ruth Zuta* 55; *Leqah Tov* on Ruth 4:17. This rabbinic story conjures up the image of Abraham, who begot his first child, Ishmael, when he was eighty-six years and was one hundred when he begot Isaac (Gen. 16:16; 21:5).

55. *Ruth Rab.* 4:6; cf. *b. Meg.* 15a, where the sages discuss beautiful biblical women and suggest that Rahab, by her beauty, causes men to experience night pollution. Scripture nowhere describes her as beautiful.

56. *Ruth Rab.* 1:4; 2:9.

57. The Midrash thereby explains why Timna's son is an enemy. At the same time, the Midrash takes a positive attitude toward accepting would-be converts in this text: "To punish the Patriarchs for the affront they had offered her, she [Timna] was made the mother of Amalek, who inflicted great injury on Israel." See *b. Sanh.* 99b; Ginzberg, *Legends of the Jews,* vol. 1, pp. 422ff.

58. *Gen. Rab.* 45:1.

59. Gen. 20:3ff.; *Gen. Rab.* 45:1. Because Abimelech, like Pharaoh, took Sarah into his palace and was punished, according to the Midrash he too gave his daughter, who is nameless, to be a handmaid to Sarah.

60. *b. Sanh.* 60a.

61. *Ruth Rab.* 1:4; 2:9; *b. Sanh.* 105b.

62. See also Ibn Ezra on Deut. 25:5; Nachmanides on Gen. 38:8; and Malbim on Ruth 4:5ff.

63. Ancient and modern scholars alike disagree over this question. Edward F. Campbell, a contemporary scholar, holds that the book of Ruth bears witness to a pre-Deuteronomic form of levirate marriage, whereas Jack Sasson agrees with Moshe Z. Segal and Robert Gordis that what is described in Ruth has nothing at all to do with the levirate customs. See Campbell, *Ruth*, 133; Jack M. Sasson, *Ruth: A New Translation with a Philological Commentary* (Baltimore: Johns Hopkins University Press, 1979), 137ff.; Robert Gordis, "Love, Marriage, and Business in the Book of Ruth: A Chapter in Hebrew Customary Law," in *A Light unto My Path: Old Testament Studies in Honor of Jacob M. Myers,* ed. H. N. Bream, R. D. Heim, and C. A. Moore (Philadelphia: Temple University Press, 1974), 248 ff.; Moshe Z. Segal, *Ruth: Introduction to the Bible,* vol. 3 (Jerusalem: Kiryat Sefer, 1955), 691 [Hebrew]; cf. Num. 27:8–11. Some scholars, following the view of Josephus (*Ant.* 5.9.4 [333–35]), have expressed the opinion that the events concerning Ruth and Boaz in Ruth 4 do describe a levirate marriage, but that this was incidental to the primary matter of the redemption of the land. That is, the duty of the *go'el* ("kinsman"), from the biblical root *ga'al* ("the restoration of an object to its primal condition"), to marry Ruth was incidental to the duties stemming from the laws concerning the redemption of property of a decedent —hence the narrative's departure in a number of details from the prescribed levirate marriage laws.

64. *b. B. Meṣ.* 47.

65. The story of Judah and Tamar (Genesis 38) is likewise a deviation from levirate marriage as described in Deut. 25:25. Nevertheless, although Judah is the woman's father-in-law rather than her brother-in-law, the situation described has more of a connection to the issue of levirate marriage than does the story of Ruth.

66. *y. Qidd.* 1:5, 60c; *Ruth Rab.* 7:11.

67. *b. B. Meṣ.* 47a.

68. *Go'el* is from the biblical root *ga'al,* "the restoration of an object to its primal condition."

5

"Remember Thy Handmaid":
On Hannah and Prayer

Prayer is a central element in most, if not all, forms of religion. "Prayer, understood as the human communication with divine and spiritual entities, has been present in most of the religions in human history."[1]

In both biblical and rabbinic Judaism, prayer is most certainly a central activity. It is based on the conviction that God exists and, moreover, hears and answers human prayer. The earliest instances of prayer in the Hebrew Bible consist of situations in which an individual petitions for help or guidance, sometimes on behalf of the community, sometimes on behalf of the self. Examples of prayer on behalf of the community include Abraham's plea that Sodom be spared (Gen. 18:23ff.) and Moses' prayer on behalf of sinful Israel (Ex. 32:31–32). A contrasting example is that of Hezekiah, who prays passionately in his own behalf to recover from a serious illness (2 Kings 20; Isaiah 38). The prayer of only one female character in the Bible is recorded—the personal prayer of Hannah. An interesting dichotomy within the rabbinic tradition regarding women's prayer is an analysis of Hannah's prayer.

Women and Prayer in the Bible

The biblical cult consisted of sacrifices, prayer, and vows. These religious practices are often described as occurring in conjunction with each other. The extent of women's participation in these activities is still much debated. According to some scholars, women were actively involved in prayer, in the bringing of sacrifices on occasions connected with ritual purification (Leviticus 12 and 15), and in participation in many sacrificial ceremonies.[2] When accompanying men to the Tabernacle and later the Temple, they participated in sacral meals.[3]

The regulations describing vows indicate that women did make religious vows, though the vows could be annulled by the fathers of the women until they married, and by their husbands afterward (Numbers 30). (Widows and divorcées were independent, and no male had control over their vows.) Women were also allowed by the Bible to take the vow of the nazirite, a sort of protomonasticism entailing abstinence from wine and the cutting of one's hair.[4] Only two characters in the Bible, Samson (Judg. 13:4–5) and Samuel (1 Sam. 1:11), are described as having taken the nazirite vow; no woman is so described.[5]

The Barren Woman and Prayer in the Bible

The barren woman was arguably the person with the most tenuous status in biblical society, for life without children seemed empty; and unless (until) she had a son, she had not fulfilled her destiny. Barrenness was regarded as a reproach, because it was believed to be a curse from God (Gen. 16:2). It was thought to be relieved by the mercy of God in response to prayer, either by the barren woman herself or by someone else on her behalf.

The Bible describes several barren women: the matriarchs (Sarah, Rebecca, Rachel), Hannah, and Samson's mother, who is unnamed in the Bible but whom the Talmud names Hazelalponit.[6] Except for Hannah, none of these biblical women is explicitly described as praying for release from her infertility. On occasion, the husband of a barren woman is described as praying on her behalf; for example, Isaac prays for his wife Rebecca (Gen. 25:21).[7] Rabbinic literature, however, fills in the empty spaces: several images of women praying, including descriptions of the matriarchs engaged in prayer, can be found in Talmud and Midrash. What we find then, in rabbinic sources, is a dialectical tension between biblical women in prayer and the parameters the rabbis set for women of their own generations. The ambivalent approach of the rabbis to women and prayer is demonstrated in their treatment of the character Hannah, a figure who elicited great interest, admiration, and comment on their part.

Prayer in the Rabbinic World

Before one can understand woman's place in the rabbinic world of prayer, a brief description of rabbinic liturgical worship is necessary. The change from sacrifice to a purely liturgical system of prayer occurred after the Second Temple was destroyed and sacrifice was no longer possible. In the wake of this catastrophic event, prayer was completely transformed.[8] The sages applied Hosea's words "render as bullocks the offerings of our lips" (14:2) to their situation.[9] Liturgical activity had already assumed a more regular character during the Second Temple period, but the crisis in national identity caused by the destruction of the Second Temple necessitated drastic changes in the form of Jewish worship. Prayer filled the vacuum caused by the destruction of the Temple cult.

The tannaitic midrash *Sipre* deduces the obligation of

prayer from the biblical verse "to love the Lord your God and serve Him with all your heart and soul" (Deut. 11:13). *'Avodah* ("service," Deut. 11:13) is service of the heart—namely, prayer—say the rabbis.[10] But the biblical requirement for prayer set no specific time or frequency of obligation. So the rabbis set the text of fixed prayer and timed it to the former schedule of Temple sacrifice, that is, three times a day.[11] By tying it to particular times of the day, the rabbis made prayer a "time-bound" commandment. Thus, whereas the command to pray is considered biblical, the details of text, time, frequency, and ritual are rabbinic. Yet within rabbinic Judaism, these details are as obligatory and binding as the biblical commandment to pray itself.

Liturgical practice after the destruction of the Second Temple was centered on the reading of the Torah and its exposition. Gradually, more prayers were introduced and specific liturgies were expanded for Sabbath, festivals, and weekdays. These services were to take place in a communal quorum of ten men, known as a *minyan*[12]—public prayer constituting, according to the rabbis, a form of prayer more desirable than solitary petitions, possibly because of the value of community.[13] Many prayers, such as the *borekhu* (the call to prayer), the *kaddish* (prayer for the dead), the *kedushah* (a sanctification), and the repetition aloud of the *'amidah* (the devotional prayer that is first "spoken" silently), were to be recited only in the presence of a *minyan*. The Torah and *haftarah* (prophetic) portions, with their accompanying blessings, were recited only during communal services.[14]

In place of the Temple, the synagogue began to take on increasing importance. Though the origins of this institution, like the service itself, are shrouded in obscurity, we know from literary and archaeological evidence that synagogues existed from at least the first century C.E. and that communal prayer services were held in them.[15] Some contemporary scholars maintain that the rabbis preferred to pray in their own study houses, the synagogue being a place for popular religious practice. The synagogue service itself developed over a period of years, particularly because it took time for these institutions to come under the sway of rabbinic authority.[16]

Eventually, rabbinic Judaism offered two chief outlets of religious expression—learning and prayer in the house of study or synagogue. These outlets were available only to men. For the male Jew in rabbinic times, prayer was at the core of daily religious life. He began his day with prayer and closed it with prayer, and most of his other day-to-day activities were interspersed with prayer and Torah study.

On Women and Prayer in Rabbinic Literature

Earlier I noted that although the Bible does not tie prayer to a specific time for performance, the classical rabbis mandated that its performance was time-bound. This ruling did not augur well for women's public liturgical participation, for women were exempt from time-bound performance. Three rabbinic texts discuss which commandments women are obligated to perform and from which commandments they are exempt (and by extension, not permitted to perform).[17] These texts lay down the following principles. First, all positive commandments (Thou shalt . . .) tied to a specific time for performance are not binding upon women. Second, positive commandments not connected to time *are* binding upon women. Third, all negative commandments (Thou shalt not), whether time-bound or not, are binding upon women.

These texts, however, equivocate, leading many to question whether there is actually one dominant principle guiding the rulings on women's obligations. For example, there are instances of positive time-bound commandments from which women are not exempt: women are obligated to eat unleavened bread on the Passover, rejoice on festivals, and assemble at the Temple once every seven years. All of these must be performed only within a particular time. Finally, there are instances of commandments that are not limited as to time but from which women are nevertheless exempt, such as the study of Torah, procreation, and the redemption of the firstborn son.[18]

Despite the difficulties in systematically categorizing commandments according to the criterion of time-boundedness,
the rabbis continue to identify prayer as such a commandment.
Thus they exempt women from regular, fixed prayer and certain other liturgical obligations.[19]

Women and Communal Prayer

Freedom from time-bound constraints was not only an
exemption but eventually became an exclusion, a prohibition. Because women were not required to fulfill the
thrice-daily communal prayer obligation, they could not be
responsible for leading public services. Under Jewish law,
only a person who is under obligation to perform a *mitzvah*
(commandment) is qualified to perform it for others.[20]
Women missed the communal bonding that characterized
male society. The communal prayer experience, which is the
privileged form of prayer in rabbinic Judaism, was virtually
closed to women.[21]

Nevertheless, the rabbis realized that women did have a
need for the spiritual experience of prayer. The Talmud states:
"[Women] are subject to the obligation of *tefillah* (prayer) because this [is supplication for Divine] mercy. You might [how-
ever] think that . . . (this refers to formal prayer) for which
there is a fixed time. Therefore we are told [that this is not
so]."[22] True, women also need to pray for God's grace but in a
fashion different from that of the public, communal liturgy
of men.

The talmudic text assumes that women fulfill their scriptural
duty of prayer by making a personal address to God, a private
prayer generally uttered in the privacy of their homes and away
from the communal worship arena—something men could and
did do. At the time of the Second Commonwealth, women
could also attend the synagogue and pray there but only as
peripheral to the communal prayer group.

Hannah's Supplication— The Paradigm of Prayer

Communal prayer performed at a specific time and place, then, constituted the heart and core of rabbinic Judaism. Women were exempt, by rabbinic interpretation, from these religious obligations. Yet despite this, the rabbis saw fit to point to the spontaneous, sincere, heartfelt petition of a barren woman—Hannah—as a paradigm of prayer. How they moved from *a* to *b* is intriguing. Also interesting is this: despite their marked gender consciousness, the rabbis never once comment on the fact that Hannah was female when discussing her brilliant aptitude for prayer.

The Hannah Story

Our first glimpse of Hannah in the Bible shows us a woman distraught over her childlessness. Hannah's sadness and sense of emptiness cannot be appeased even by her husband's rhetorical question: "Am I not more devoted to you than ten sons?" (1 Sam. 1:8). His words do not assuage; only mother-hood can alleviate her pain.[23] Hannah's story, of course, was intended to be viewed in the framework of the book of Samuel, as background for the miraculous birth and life of a great Israelite leader. Yet her powerful determination to overcome adversity places her at the forefront of the compelling narrative.

She goes up with her family to sacrifice at the shrine at Shiloh (a detail that incidentally provides scriptural evidence that women did attend these places of worship). Hannah weeps and declines to eat the sacrificial meal, and at its conclusion she goes to the sanctuary:

> In her wretchedness, she prayed to the Lord, weeping all the
> while. And she made this vow: "O Lord of Hosts, if You will look
> upon the suffering of Your maidservant and will remember me
> and not forget Your maidservant, and if You will grant Your
> maidservant a male child, I will dedicate him to the Lord for all
> the days of his life; and no razor shall ever touch his head" (1
> Sam. 1:10–11).[24]

Hannah continues to pray fervently, her lips moving, but silently. The priest Eli takes her to be drunk and turns to rebuke
her, demanding that she "sober up" in the sanctuary. Hannah
replies sincerely:

> "Oh no, my lord! I am a very unhappy woman. I have drunk no
> wine or other strong drink, but I have been pouring out my
> heart to the Lord. Do not take your maidservant for a worthless
> woman; I have only been speaking all this time out of my great
> anguish and distress" (1 Sam. 1:15–16).

Eli blesses her, saying, "Then go in peace" and "may the God
of Israel grant what you have asked of him." Thus reassured
and in an optimistic frame of mind, confident that she will
soon taste motherhood, she goes on her way.

Following the birth of her son, Hannah utters the second
prayer that figures in her story. Scripture gives the text of her
prayer, which praises God's power and ability to reverse human
fortune. The way in which the song generalizes the change in
fortune experienced by the speaker of the prayer makes her
text "usable" by others grateful for similar reversals of fortune.[25] So universal and so particular are her words that the
rabbis named it the Song of Hannah and decreed that it become part of the *haftarah* reading in the New Year service.

Hannah and the Rabbis

The fact that Hannah is depicted twice in prayer made a
deep impression on the rabbis, for no other individual female
character is ever clearly seen to pray anywhere in the Bible. The

great feeling and fervor with which she prayed to be given a son led the rabbis to regard her supplication as worthy of emulation. Hers is considered the "optimal prayer experience."[26] The Jerusalem Talmud states that one should learn to pray from Hannah. The passage elaborates in great detail the particular qualities of sincere prayer that one can learn from emulating Hannah:

> One might think that he must raise his voice and pray. [On the contrary, for] it was stated concerning Hannah, "Hannah was speaking in her heart." One might think that he may just meditate [during Prayer]. [On the contrary,] Scripture states, "Only her lips moved." What does that mean? That she spoke with her lips. . . . Said R. Yose bar Haninah, "From this verse you learn four things. (a) 'Hannah was speaking in her heart': from this you learn that Prayer requires concentration. (b) 'Only her lips moved': from this you learn that one must mouth the Prayer with one's lips. (c) 'And her voice was not heard': from this you learn that one may not raise his voice and pray. (d) 'And Eli took her to be a drunken woman': from this you learn a drunken person is forbidden to pray."[27]

From Hannah the rabbis glean four characteristics of heartfelt, worthy prayer: to pray in a low voice, with lips moving, with concentration, and not when drunk. The silence of Hannah's prayer is cited solely in the Jerusalem Talmud, to prove that despite the great distance of God from human beings, even the prayers of the humblest supplicants are heard and answered:

> See how high the Holy One, blessed be He, is above His world. Yet a person can enter a synagogue, stand behind a pillar, and pray in an undertone, and the Holy One, blessed be He, hears his prayers. As it says, "Hannah was speaking in her heart; only her lips moved, and her voice was not heard" (1 Sam. 1:13). Yet the Holy One, blessed be He, heard her prayer.[28]

The Babylonian Talmud likewise celebrates Hannah's aptitude for prayer and introduces many other aspects of her character. After listing the same lessons to be learned from Hannah's prayer as does the Jerusalem Talmud, the Babylonian Talmud introduces a further precept to be drawn from the scriptural account. From the biblical words "How long will you be

drunk?" (1 Sam. 1:10ff.), the rabbis deduce that one is obligated to reprimand a neighbor observed behaving in an unseemly manner. The passage continues by depicting Hannah as
pleading her case with God thus: "Of all the hosts and hosts
that Thou hast created in Thy world, is it so hard in Thy eyes to
give me one son?"[29] It is interesting to note that the Babylonian
Talmud attributes to Hannah the honor of giving God the
name "Ẓeva'ot" (Lord of Hosts). No one called the Lord by this
name before Hannah.

She then tries a different tactic:

> Hannah said before the Holy One, blessed be He: Sovereign of
> the Universe, if Thou wilt look, it is well, and if Thou wilt not
> look, I will go and shut myself up with someone else in the
> knowledge of my husband Elkanah, and as I shall have been
> alone they will make me drink the water of the suspected wife,
> and Thou canst not falsify Thy law, which says, *She shall be cleared
> and shall conceive seed* (Num. 5:28).

In other words, Hannah threatens to shut herself up with a
strange man. This will cause her to be suspected of adultery
and made to undergo the test for a suspected wife, but because
she will have done no wrong, she will be found innocent. Because the law states that the innocent woman "shall be cleared
and shall conceive seed," such a roundabout ruse should give
her a child.

The Babylonian Talmud continues Hannah's plaint by noting that the word "handmaid" occurs three times in the
Hannah narrative. These three references are said to refer to
the three ritual obligations binding Jewish women: the laws of
family purity, the laws of separating bread dough, and the kin-
dling of the Sabbath lights.[30] Hannah is then said to ask, "Have
I been guilty of transgressing any of these?" The implication is
that if she has not, she deserves to have a child. Hannah continues to argue her case, saying that God wisely created her with
many organs, all of which she has been able to put to use
except her breasts. "Give me a son that I may suckle with
them!" she implores.[31]

The Babylonian tradition maintains that Hannah, like Sarah,
was remembered (i.e., that God answered her prayer to be given

a child) on the New Year,[32] and that this is why the *haftarah* reading on the first day of the New Year is the story of Hannah (the Torah portion is Sarah's story).[33] The Babylonian sages once again credit her with influencing the liturgy—this time the content rather than the form. The nine times Hannah mentioned the divine name in her prayer, according to the rabbis, correspond to the nine blessings recited on the New Year.[34]

The Babylonian Talmud not only points out the qualities one can emulate in Hannah's manner of prayer, but also notes that she is the one who developed the petitional prayer. She becomes a petitioner par excellence, debating and pleading with God as do such early heroes of the Bible as Abraham and Moses. In fact, the Talmud compares the assertiveness, or almost insolence, of her manner of prayer to that of Elijah and Moses. All of them, Hannah included, were judged to be justified in their arguments and tone.[35]

The rabbis enumerate seven biblical prophetesses, including Hannah in their number.[36] The *Targum*, and the much later *Zohar* (ca. 1300) as well, attribute to her the power of prophecy. Perhaps she was considered a prophetess because her song foretold, according to the rabbis, the fall of the house of Saul and the rise of the house of David.[37] Or perhaps it was because of her power of prayer.

The rabbis also attribute to her the quality of grace, which fits with the primary meaning of her name, "to show favor" or "be gracious." To expand upon this etymology, the secondary meanings of her name—"yearn toward," "long for," "be merciful," "be compassionate," "be favorable," "incline toward," "seek or implore favor"—all suggest the phenomenon of prayer. Some meanings, such as "yearn toward," express the posture of the supplicant; others, the attitude hoped for on the part of the deity. The meaning "long for" also fits exactly Hannah's long years of yearning for a child—the impetus for her prodigious act of prayer.[38]

The grace, compassion, and forbearance suggested in the etymology of her name is shown in many of the midrashim the rabbis have woven around her: Hannah is willing not only to forgive her rival, co-wife Peninnah (who had been the mother of ten children), but she prays fervently for the survival of her rival's remaining two children, who are dying as punishment for their mother's mean-spirited teasing of then still-childless Hannah. This midrash shows both Hannah's compassion and the efficacy of her prayer:

> As things eventually turned out, when God came to remember Hannah, whenever Hannah gave birth to a child, Peninnah would be burying two of her children. By the time Hannah had given birth to four, Peninnah had buried eight. Hence when Hannah was pregnant with her fifth child, Peninnah was afraid that she would have to bury the two children that remained to her. What did Peninnah do? She went and besought Hannah, saying to her: "I beseech you, humbling myself before you. I know that I have sinned against you. But be more forbearing than I deserve, so that the two children who remain to me will stay alive." Thereupon Hannah prayed before the Holy One, blessed be He, saying to Him: "Be forbearing towards her in regard to her two children and let them stay alive." The Holy One, blessed be He, said to her: "As thou livest, they were destined to die, but since thou hast prayed in their behalf that they stay alive, I shall call them by thy name and consider them as being thine."[39]

Hannah displays similar forbearance in her attitude toward the sinful sons of Korah (Numbers 16). Her song gives hope to those who "go down into Sheol" (namely, Korah) but could come up again. She prays for the company of Korah and gives hope to the hopeless.[40]

"Remember Thy Handmaid"— The Prayers of Women

Whereas the Bible depicts only Hannah in prayer, the rabbinic sources portray other female biblical characters praying. In almost all of these stories, the strongest motive for female prayer was to end a state of childlessness. The many remarks in the Midrash and Talmud equating childlessness with a kind of death indicate the intensity and extent of the longing for children among the people of those times.

> *And [Rachel] said unto Jacob: give me children, or else I am dead*
> [Gen. 30:1]. R. Samuel said: Four are regarded as dead: the
> leper, the blind, he who is childless, and he who has become
> impoverished. He who is childless is learned from Rachel: *Or else
> I am dead.*[41]

Children were the guarantors of familial continuity and, in particular, provided security to the mother. The blessing of progeny was so highly valued that God was said to hold the key to
this gift, which is bestowed by God alone: "Three keys the Holy
One, blessed be He, has retained in His own hands and not
entrusted to the hand of any messenger, namely, the Key of
Rain, the Key of Childbirth, and the Key of the Revival of the
Dead."[42]

The problem of barrenness perturbed the sages. "Why were
our ancestors barren?" a rabbi asked.[43] This question is repeated in various rabbinic sources. One response is: "Because
the Holy One, blessed be He, longs to hear the prayer of the
righteous."[44] Yet nowhere in the Bible is Sarah, the preeminent
barren matriarch, said to pray for a child. To the contrary, she
laughs in disbelief when told of the forthcoming birth of her
son, named Isaac, meaning "laughter," for his mother's reaction to news of his arrival so late in her life (Gen. 18:12). Nevertheless, the Midrash claims her to be the only woman to speak
to God without an intermediary.[45] Not surprisingly, the Midrash
creatively puts prayer into Sarah's mouth, although her barrenness was not made the reason for her prayer. There is a biblical
incident in which Sarah is abducted while in Egypt and taken
to the palace of the Egyptian ruler (Gen. 12:15). Faced with the
prospect of imminent sexual abuse, she cries out for deliverance from Pharaoh: "The whole of that night Sarah lay pros-
trate on her face, crying, 'Sovereign of the Universe! Abraham
went forth [from his land] on Thine assurance, and I went
forth with faith; Abraham is without this prison while I am
within!' "[46] Surely this was a petitionary prayer both spontaneous and heartfelt.

Scripture describes Hagar in an activity that might be considered a form of prayer when she was cast out into the wilderness
with Ishmael. She "lifts up her voice and weeps" over her own
and her son's fate (Gen. 21:16). The rabbis took this to mean

that she prayed, and they interpolate the content of her prayer
thus: "Yesterday you promised me, 'I will greatly increase your
seed (Gen. 16:10)' and now he is dying of thirst!"[47]

In the biblical text, Isaac, Rebecca's husband, prays for an
end to his wife's barrenness (Gen. 25:21). In the very next
verse, Isaac's prayer having been answered, Rebecca is con-
fronted with twins contending mightily within her womb, and
she is moved "to inquire of the Lord."

> And the children struggled together within her [Gen. 25:22]. They
> sought to run within her. When she stood near synagogues or
> schools, Jacob struggled to come out; hence it is written, Before I
> formed thee in the belly I knew thee (Jer. 1:5). While when she passed
> idolatrous temples, Esau eagerly struggled to come out; hence it
> is written, The wicked are estranged from the womb (Ps. 58:4).[48]

The biblical expression "to inquire of the Lord" is generally
taken by scholars today to mean that she consulted an oracle.
In the stories of the rabbis, the phrase meant that Rebecca
went to inquire at the study house of Shem and Eber. According to the rabbinic legends, she received a response to her
inquiry through either an angel or the medium of Shem.[49]

Another midrash focuses on Isaac's prayer, asserting that the
word "opposite" in the biblical verse "he prayed opposite Rebecca" actually meant that Isaac himself was barren and that he
was praying in his own behalf. Another rabbi suggested that
both were barren, the corollary being that both of them
prayed. It was Isaac's prayer, however, that was answered, for
the biblical text says that God allowed himself to be entreated
"of him," rather than "of them." It is not because of his gender that Isaac's prayer, instead of Rebecca's, receives favor, but
rather because of the merit of his having been born to the
righteous Abraham and Sarah, whereas she came from Laban's
house, with no credit there.[50]

The rabbis also ascribe prayer to Leah and Rachel. Leah is
said to pray to avoid marriage to Esau.[51] She also prays to
change the gender of her sixth child from male to female. She
knew through the divine spirit that there were destined to be
twelve tribes descended from Jacob's twelve sons. (The rabbis
attribute the divine spirit [ru'ah ha-kodesh] to all the ma-

triarchs.[52]) Because Jacob's other wives had a total of four sons, if Leah herself had a seventh son, Rachel would be able to have only one son. Her prayer, therefore, showed love and concern for her sister.[53]

Rachel is said to pray out of communal concern for the continuity of her descendants. The sages note the biblical passage: "Rachel died, and was buried in the way to Ephrath (Gen. 35:19)."

> What was Jacob's reason for burying Rachel in the way to Ephrath? Jacob foresaw that the exiles would pass on from thence, therefore he buried her there so that she might pray for mercy for them. Thus it is written, *A voice is heard in Ramah . . . Rachel weeping for her children* (Jer. 31:15).[54]

This is yet another instance where the sages interpret weeping as a form of prayer or a natural accompaniment to prayer.

In midrashic lore, Tamar, too, prays. The name of the place where she stands disguised as a harlot and waiting for Judah is called Pethaḥ Enaim, the meaning of the Hebrew indicating that "she lifted up her eyes to the gate."[55]

> *And she sat at Pethaḥ Enaim.* Rabbi said: We have searched through the whole of Scripture and found no place called *Pethaḥ Enaim.* What then is the purport of *Pethaḥ Enaim?* It teaches that she lifted up her eyes to the gate (*pethaḥ*) to which all eyes (*'Enayim*) are directed and prayed: "May it be Thy will that I do not leave this house with nought."[56]

The rabbis say that she succeeded in her mission, so that her prayer is understood to have been answered.[57]

Another example of women shown in prayer in the Midrash is the story woven around the midwives Shiphrah and Puah. Having been commanded by Pharaoh to kill the Israelite males (Ex. 1:13), they pray that the children be born safely and without disfigurement, so that Israel would not think that they had tried to harm them. They declare that they want to do God's will, not Pharaoh's.[58]

Although Esther is not described as having prayed, she—together with her maids—performs an action closely connected with prayer: fasting. In the biblical account, she instructs Mordecai: "Go, gather all the Jews to be found in

Susa, and hold a fast on my behalf, and neither eat nor drink
for three days, night or day. I and my maids will also fast as you
do. Then I will go to the king, though it is against the law; and
if I perish, I perish" (Esth. 4:16). Where there is fasting, the
Midrash assumes there must also be prayer, and Esther's is
poignantly depicted as both pious and fervent:

> She took off her royal robes and ornaments and she put on
> sackcloth and loosened the hair of her head and filled it with
> dust and ashes and afflicted herself with fasting and fell on her
> face before the Lord. And she prayed, saying: "O Lord God of
> Israel who art Ruler from of old and didst create the world, help
> now Thy handmaid who has been left an orphan without father
> or mother, and is like a poor woman begging from house to
> house. So I pray for Thy mercy from one window to another in
> the palace of Ahasuerus. And now, O Lord, grant success to thy
> humble handmaid here and deliver the sheep of Thy pasture
> from these enemies who have risen against us, for nought can
> hinder Thee from saving whether with many or with few. And do
> Thou, father of orphans, stand at the right hand of this orphan
> who trusts in Thy loving-kindness, and make this man mercifully
> disposed towards me, for I am afraid of him, and cast him down
> before me, for Thou bringest low the proud."[59]

In the apocryphal and pseudepigraphal writings of the Second
Temple period, women are often depicted in prayer—for example, Eve, Judith, Asnath (the wife of Joseph), and many others—and this may well have influenced the great rabbinic
embellishment of biblical women's prayer. However, in the Talmud and Midrash there are few female characters not of biblical origin who are shown to be engaged in prayer. One story
that does appear is about R. Hilkiyah and his wife; it is reminiscent of the Midrash about Isaac and Rebecca standing in separate corners and praying.

> Rabbi Hilkiyah was a grandson of Honi the Circle-Drawer, and
> whenever the world was in need of rain the Rabbis sent a mes-
> sage to him and he prayed and rain fell. . . . He said to his wife,
> I know the scholars have come on account of rain; let us go up
> to the roof and pray, perhaps the Holy One, Blessed be He, will
> have mercy and rain will fall. . . . They went up to the roof; he

stood in one corner and she in another; at first the clouds appeared over the corner where his wife stood. . . . [The scholars asked him,] Why, Sir, did the clouds appear first in the corner where your wife stood and then in your corner? [He replied]: Because a wife stays at home and gives bread to the poor which they can at once enjoy whilst I give them money which they cannot at once enjoy. Or perhaps it may have to do with certain robbers in our neighbourhood; I prayed that they might die, but she prayed that they might repent.[60]

The Midrash shows that both husband and wife go up to the roof and position themselves at opposite corners to pray for rain. To the surprise of Hilkiyah's disciples, his wife gets her answer first. He feels it necessary to explain to the disciples why her prayers took precedence over his own. He offers two examples of her greater merit: one involving her giving food to the poor when he gave only money (which is not something they can eat right away); the other showing her having once prayed that robbers would repent rather than die, as he had prayed.

Most other rabbinic stories about contemporaneous women and prayer have to do with an enabling role. One such tale is that of Beruriah, the wife of Rabbi Meir.[61] She overhears her husband cursing some robbers and praying for their demise, whereupon Beruriah corrects him by pointing out that it is written that not "sinners" but "sin" should perish from the earth. Though the story does not say that Beruriah prays for the robbers, she does influence her husband to temper the tone of his prayer with greater mercy and compassion. There is a clear similarity between this story and that of Rabbi Hilkiyah and his wife; both women teach their husbands to revile the sin and not the sinner. Another enabler role is played by the maidservant of Rabbi Judah Ha-Nasi. When the scholar fell ill and was about to die, she observed his excruciating pain. Seeing that the well-intended prayers of his followers prevented his soul from departing, she went on to the roof to pray, saying:

"The immortals desire Rabbi [to join them] and the mortals desire Rabbi [to remain with them]; . . . may it be the will [of the Almighty] that the immortals may overpower the mortals." As the Rabbis incessantly continued their prayers for [heavenly] mercy she took up a jar and threw it down from the roof to the ground. [For a moment] they ceased praying and the soul of Rabbi departed to its eternal rest.[62]

The story of the rabbi's death illustrates once again, as did the stories about Hilkiyah's wife and Beruriah, the rabbinic belief that women are more compassionate than men, and this quality made their prayers more acceptable to God.

Conclusion

As indicated, the rabbis consistently put prayer into biblical women's mouths when the Bible had provided none. The question arises, If the rabbis generally used biblical women as models for women of their generation, then why depict them as praying, which they eventually discouraged in women of their own times?[63]

The answer may be that the prayers depicted are not formal, congregational ones and hence are nonthreatening. The rabbinic code of behavior that confined woman to the scope of the private and domestic took precedence over her prayer needs, thereby keeping her from taking part in the public realms of communal worship and economic affairs and denying her significant voice in the political arena.

Although trumpeting Hannah's aptitude for prayer and amplifying her prophetic gifts, the rabbis, surprisingly, omit mention of her femininity, in contrast to their treatment of other biblical heroines examined in this study. For authorities who relegate women to a highly circumscribed private sector of prayer, this is indeed puzzling. It may be that their exclusion of women from public prayer resulted not from regarding women as being less capable of prayer than men, but rather from their obsession with modesty and their desire to prevent the mingling of the sexes. The tensions and contradictions in their attitudes are obvious.

The manner of their handling Hannah's prayer and the

prayers of other women in rabbinic literature follows a pattern I have noted elsewhere in this study. The rabbis promulgated a culture of regulations inimical to the full expression of women's potentialities, but they also set forth currents of thought that seriously undercut and perturb the oppressive force of that dominant attitude.

Although rabbinic Judaism attaches great import to communal worship, it nonetheless also valorizes sincere, heartfelt worship wherever it is performed—whether in the home, the synagogue, or the house of study—and considers all such prayer equally effective in communicating with God. Nevertheless, the rabbis knew that God loved women's prayer. The rabbis tried to balance the imminent need for modesty with the overall desire for more prayer in the world. In all of their female biblical models, the prayer is private, direct, sincere communication with God, the ultimate form of prayer. This could possibly mean that they understood the communal prayer of men to be a reinforcement of camaraderie and the sense of community, not necessarily a higher, more spiritually pure form of prayer.

Notes

1. S. D. Gill, "Prayer," in *The Encyclopedia of Religion*, ed. Mircea Eliade (New York: Macmillan Publishing Co., 1987), 489.

2. Ismar J. Peritz, "Woman in the Ancient Hebrew Cult," *JBL* 17 (1898): 114, 129–30; Clarence J. Vos, *Woman in Old Testament Worship* (Delft, Neth.: Judels & Brinkman, 1968), 60ff.

3. We learn this from Deut. 12:12; 14:29; 15:20; 16:11, 14; 31:10–12. Even where it is specified (as in Ex. 23:17; 34:21; and Deut. 16:16) that *men* should go up to the sanctuary, these verses need not imply the exclusion of women. They suggest that these acts were mandatory for males, but that females could participate if they desired. For more on the participation of women in ritual practices, see 2 Sam. 6:19 and 1 Chron. 16:3, where David brings the ark and distributes the cultic food, and Neh. 8:2, where Nehemiah reads the law to men and women alike.

4. See Amos 2:11 and Jeremiah 35 on naziriteship and on the similar rechabite tradition.

5. See my *Sects and Separatism during the Second Jewish Commonwealth* (New York: Bloch Publishing, 1967), 19–29. Three female characters are said to have taken the nazirite vow: the proselyte Queen Helena of Adiabene (*m. Nazir* 3:6); Berenice, the sister of King Aggripa (Josephus *Wars* 2. 15. 1); and Miriam of Palmyra (*m. Nazir* 6:11). Meir I. Gruber shows that by talmudic times, ordinary women had more control over their vows than did women in biblical times; see "Women in the Cult according to the Priestly Code," in *Judaic Perspectives on Ancient Israel*, ed. Jacob Neusner, Baruch Levine, and Ernst Frerichs (Philadelphia: Fortress Press, 1987), 38.

6. *b. B. Bat.* 91a; *'Aggadot Bereshit,* vol. 4, ed. Adolph Jellinek (Jerusalem: Wahrmann Books, 1967), 73.

7. However, see below for a rabbinic interpretation of Rebecca's words: she was moved "to inquire of the Lord."

8. *b. Ta'an.* 2a.

9. *b. Yoma* 86b.

10. *Sipre Deut. 'Aykev,* end of 41. Maimonides, the great medieval halakhist, takes the *Sipre* as his authority in asserting that the requirement to pray is biblical in origin. He emphasizes, however, that the biblical requirement for prayer sets no specific obligations as to frequency beyond stipulating that one must pray daily, and no time of day is specified.

11. *m. Ber.* 4:1; *b. Ber.* 26b; cf. Maimonides, *Mishneh Torah, Sefer 'Ahavah, Hilkhot Tefillah,* chap. 1.

12. *b. Meg.* 23b.

13. *b. Ber.* 6a. *b. Ber.* 8a reads: "What is the meaning of the verse: *But as for me, let my prayer be made unto Thee, O Lord, in an acceptable time?* When is the time acceptable? When the congregation prays."

14. *m. Meg.* 4:1–4 and *b. Meg.* 5b.

15. Lee I. Levine, "The Second Temple Synagogue: The Formative Years," in *The Synagogue in Late Antiquity*, ed. Lee I. Levine (New York: JTS/ASOR, 1987), 7–32; see also his bibliography.

16. Cohen, *From the Maccabees to the Mishnah,* 221–24.

17. *m. Qidd.* 1:7; *b. Ber.* 20b; *m. Ber.* 3:3; and Maimonides, *Mishneh Torah, Sefer 'Ahavah, Hilkhot Tefillah* 1:2.

18. *b. Qidd.* 33b–34a. For detailed analysis of the subject of women's affirmative precepts, see Saul Berman, "The Status of Women in Halakhic Judaism," *Tradition* 14 (1973), reprinted in *The Jewish Woman: New Perspectives,* ed. Elizabeth Koltun (New York: Schocken Books, 1976); see also Eliezer Berkovits, *The Jewish Woman: In Time and Torah* (Hoboken, N.J.: Ktav, 1990).

19. See Berman, "The Status of Women in Halakhic Judaism." He claims that the entire rabbinic exercise was not in fact meant to display consistency in the rules but to keep women out of the public sector. Blu Greenberg enumerates various other modern scholars who have tried to attach some meaning to women's exemptions from certain commandments; see *On Women and Judaism: A View from Tradition* (Philadelphia: The Jewish Publication Society of America, 1981), 83–84. Anthropologists, too, have shown that women tend to be associated with the natural and men with the cultural; women with the private and men, the public activities. See Sherry B. Ortner, "Is Female to Male as Nature Is to Culture?" in *Woman, Culture, and Society,*

ed. M. Z. Rosaldo and L. Lamphere (Stanford, Calif.: Stanford University Press, 1974), 67–87; and Judith R. Baskin, "Introduction," in *Jewish Women in Historical Perspective*, ed. J. R. Baskin (Detroit: Wayne State University Press, 1991), 15–24.

20. *b. Roš. Haš.* 29a.

21. Greenberg, *On Women and Judaism*, 85.

22. *m. Ber.* 3:3; *b. Ber.* 20a–20b.

23. See chapter 7.

24. Hannah intended him to become a nazirite, devoted to the service of God. It is interesting to note that she makes a vow and does not need or ask for the consent of her husband. A similar detail is seen in the story of Samson, whose mother similarly dedicates her son (Judges 13).

25. The song attributed to Hannah, according to critical scholarship, was actually introduced here from some other context; see Henry Preserved Smith, *A Critical and Exegetical Commentary on the Books of Samuel*, The International Critical Commentary (Edinburgh: T. & T. Clark, 1899), 14.

26. The expression comes from Avi Weiss, *Women at Prayer: A Halakhic Analysis of Women's Prayer Groups* (Hoboken, N.J.: Ktav, 1990), 30.

27. *y. Ber.* 4:1, 7a; translated in the *Talmud of the Land of Israel*, vol. 1, *Berachot*, trans. Tzvee Zahavy, ed. Jacob Neusner (Chicago: University of Chicago Press, 1989), 149; cf. *b. Ber.* 31a and *b. Yoma* 73a–b.

28. Zahavy, *y. Ber.* 9:1, 13a.

29. The entire lengthy discussion of Hannah's prayer may be found in *b. Ber.* 31a–b.

30. Remember, these are the three special *mitzvot* associated with women and brought in the Midrash in connection with several of the women analyzed in the text, such as Eve and Tamar. *m. Šabb.* 2:6 states that for transgression of these three *mitzvot*, women die in childbirth.

31. *b. Ber.* 31b.

32. *b. Roš. Haš.* 11a; *Gen. Rab.* 83:1; *b. Yebam.* 64b; *b. Ber.* 29a.

33. *b. Meg.* 31a; Eliezer Slomowic (personal conversation) asserts that the tradition of reading the section on Hannah as the New Year *haftarah* came first and that this talmudic rationale was formulated after the fact.

34. *b. Ber.* 29a; *b. Roš. Haš.* 10a and 11a; *b. Yebam.* 64b.

35. They base their charge of insolence in the tone of her prayer on the similarity of its wording to the prayers of Elijah and Moses (the preposition used in each case to say that they prayed "to" God is *'al*, which is not normally reverential in tone); see *b. Ber.* 31b–32a. An

instance of Hannah's *not* being suitable for emulation is found in *b. Ber.* 30b (cf. *Deut. Rab.* 2:1), where it is said one should pray only in a reverential mood—which Hannah did not because of her exceptional bitterness of heart.

36. *b. Meg.* 14b.

37. *Tg. Ps.-J.* 1 Sam. 2:1–11; *Zohar,* vol. 4, trans. H. Sperling and M. Simon (London and New York: Soncino Press, 1984), Lev. 19b.

38. Brown, Driver, and Briggs, *A Hebrew and English Lexicon,* 335.

39. Quoted from *Pesikta Rabbati,* trans. William G. Braude (New Haven: Yale University Press, 1968), 767–68; *Pesiq. R.* 43:182a and *Midr. Shemuel* 5:10. The conclusion of the account solves the problem of why Hannah's song of thanksgiving says "the barren has born seven," when in fact Hannah herself is said to have eventually had only five children (1 Sam. 2:21). According to this account, the other two were Peninnah's offspring whom Hannah rescued. It should be remembered that Peninnah's vexing of Hannah is part of the biblical story, but the rabbis nonetheless tried to exonerate her midrashically. In a source contradictory to the one just quoted, we find that Peninnah had, after all, only a pious intent in provoking Hannah, intending to encourage her to effective prayer to achieve relief from her plight; see *b. B. Bat.* 16a and Braude, *Pesikta Rabbati,* 768.

40. *Gen. Rab.* 98:2 and 98:4; *Num. Rab.* 18:13–14 and 18:20; *b. Roš. Haš.* 17a.

41. *Gen. Rab.* 71:6; *b. Ned.* 64b; cf. *b. Ber.* 10b on Hezekiah.

42. *b. Ta'an.* 2a.

43. Modern scriptural commentators ask the same question and explain the barrenness of women in the Bible in diverse ways. For an interesting discussion of this issue, see Mary Callaway, *Sing, O Barren One: A Study in Comparative Midrash,* SBL Dissertation Series 91 (Atlanta: Scholars Press, 1986), 4–5, 115–23.

44. *m. Ber.* 45:4; *Cant. Rab.* 2:14; *b. Yebam.* 64b.

45. See chapter 8, " 'Deborah, Say Your Song': Female Prophecy in Talmudic Tradition."

46. *Gen. Rab.* 41:2.

47. *Gen. Rab.* 53:13.

48. *Gen. Rab.* 63:6.

49. Ibid.

50. *b. Yebam.* 64b.

51. *b. B. Bat.* 123a.

52. *Gen. Rab.* 72:6.

53. *b. Ber.* 60a and *Gen. Rab.* 72:6.

54. *Gen. Rab.* 82:10. In the Bible, Jeremiah assures Rachel that her children will return from exile (Jer. 31:16).

55. For details on Tamar and Judah, see chapter 7.

56. *Gen. Rab.* 85:7.

57. Ibid.

58. *Ex. Rab.* 1:15.

59. *Esth. Rab.* 8:6. The additions to the book of Esther found in the ancient Greek translation known as the Septuagint also provide the content of Esther's prayer, but it differs from the one in the Midrash.

60. *b. Ta'an.* 23a–b.

61. *b. Ber.* 10a.

62. *b. Ketub.* 104a.

63. True, they said women were obligated to pray, but they removed all the encouragements to prayer, such as the fixed time obligation, communal participation, and so forth.

6

"The King's Daughter Is All Glorious Within": The Estate of Daughterhood

In addition to filling roles as wives and mothers, women appear in many important places in the Bible as daughters. The word *bat* ("daughter") appears with some frequency. All things are relative, however; and as one might expect, the word *ben* ("son") appears ten times more often. This explains, perhaps, why little attention has been given to the daughter role.

The meaning of the word *bat* and the context in which it appears vary greatly. It is obviously beyond the scope of this work to deal with every occurrence of this noun.[1] But it is worth mentioning here that the word *bat* is used in the Bible to refer alternatively to actual persons; to poetic personas or characterizations adopted by speakers in poetic texts; to collectives; or to abstract qualities. As a figure of purity and moral value, *bat* was often used in the Hebrew poetry of scriptures to personify nations and peoples.[2]

Although the figurative use of daughter personas can be seen as acknowledging and dignifying female experience, when we turn to the daughter as a real person in society, we see a less glorious picture. This is true in biblical narrative and even more so in aggadic commentary. The realities of social, political, and religious life accorded the daughter a secondary place. The birth of daughters went uncelebrated, and thus unrecorded, in biblical and in later rabbinic literature, as did other events in the lives of girls apart from those associated with matrimony. Annunciation scenes occur several times in the Bible before the birth of sons, but never before the birth of daughters. Even where the exceptional name is given in the extensive listing of names, there are obvious disparities. For example, Dinah's birth is recorded in the Bible, yet no etymology of her name is given, in sharp contrast to etymologies for each of her brothers. This omission really symbolizes her diminished importance in the family (Gen. 30:21).[3]

The Lives of Daughters

The life of a young girl was dominated by considerations relating to her preparation and suitability for the state of matrimony that was her destiny. Marketability as a wife depended largely upon her virginity (Ex. 22:15–16; Deut. 22:28–29; cf. Deut. 22:22–27). Her father was therefore very concerned with preserving her virginity and honor. Indeed, the law prescribes severe punishments for different forms of loss of virginity, which were sometimes applied to the girl, sometimes to the violator, and sometimes to both (Deut. 22:13–29).[4] The father's right to sell (Ex. 21:7–11) or give his daughter in marriage[5] and to annul her vows (Num. 30:4–6) bespeaks his virtual control over her body, mind, and destiny.[6]

When a daughter married, authority over her was transferred to her husband, as the word *ba'al* ("husband/master") attests. In a patriarchal society, where the weakest position belonged to the daughter, a married woman could enhance her importance and value by producing progeny, thereby assuring family continuity in behalf of her husband's family line.[7]

These attitudes regarding the relative importance of sons over daughters and the singular roles set before them carried over to rabbinic times as well. Numerous statements in Talmud and Midrash bear this out. For example: "As soon as a male comes into the world, peace comes into the world. . . . A female comes with nothing with her."[8]

Or consider this statement, in which the Talmud preserves a

statement also found in Ben Sira, describing the worries a daughter brings to her father at every stage of her life:

> A daughter is a vain treasure to her father: through anxiety on her account, he cannot sleep at night. As a minor, lest she be seduced; in her majority, lest she play the harlot; as an adult, lest she be not married; if she marries, lest she bear no children; if she grows old, lest she engage in witchcraft![9]

Though this latter quotation can be seen as disparaging and infantalizing women, one can also look at it from the perspective of genuine fatherly concern. And in this regard, it points up a far graver lacuna, both in biblical and rabbinic sources. Mothers play no role in the daughter stories, and they are never shown interceding in behalf of their daughters, as they are often seen to do in behalf of their sons.[10] Where was Dinah's mother in that calamity? How pained was Tamar's mother when Amnon raped her daughter?

Let us turn our attention to several of the daughter stories in the Bible and their exegetical treatment. Most of these stories involve some extraordinary event—a scandal or tragedy—that was the apparent reason the story warranted inclusion in the biblical record. In some of these, midrashic commentary offers an intriguing countercurrent in defending the daughters against patriarchal powers, in some cases even empowering the daughters to act in their own defense. The rabbis at times contravened their own patriarchal assumptions and biases in attempting to assist these hapless characters. We will see this in the stories of Dinah, Tamar, and the daughters of Lot and Zelophehad, in which themes of incest, rape, and inheritance are played out.

The Enigma of Lot's Daughters

The story of Lot and his daughters is disturbing and complicated. Angels visit Lot in Sodom to warn him of its impending destruction. Townspeople, having heard that Lot had guests, surround Lot's house and demand that he surrender his visitors to their cruel pleasures. Lot offers instead his daughters to satisfy their sexual lust. The angels intervene and save the situation by striking the mob with blindness and rescuing Lot's daughters. Ultimately, Sodom is destroyed, as the angels had foretold. Lot's daughters, thinking that they and their father are the sole human survivors, seduce their father with the intent of continuing the human race.

Not least among this story's difficulties is Lot's willingness to surrender his virgin daughters to an unruly mob bent on rapine. Then there is the matter of the incestuous intercourse the young women initiate with their father.

The rabbinic retelling of the Lot episodes discusses his character at great length, beginning with his self-aggrandizing act of separating from his uncle Abraham. The rabbis identify lasciviousness and lust for material wealth as his motives. Moreover, they note, in parting from Abraham, Lot also separated himself from the God of Abraham.[11] The rabbinic consensus is that having gone to live among the wicked Sodomites and having left the community of the righteous, Lot fell into evildoing himself. On the other hand, some sages do praise Lot for the hospitality he extended to the guests, an ethical value he learned from Abraham (Gen. 18:2) and continued to practice once he settled in Sodom (Gen. 19:1).[12] These contrasting rabbinic evaluations of Lot set the stage for the next episode.

The willingness of a father to hand over his own daughters to be raped rather than allow the homosexual rape of a stranger who happens to be a guest in his home is a baffling problem to moderns and, I believe, to the sages of the Talmud as well. Lot's behavior recalls the story in Judges 19 in which the people of the city surround the house of an old man who was providing hospitality to a traveler and his concubine. There, too, the threatening mob demands that the man be surrendered for their sexual abuse. Lot, when faced with a similar demand, said: "Look, I have two daughters who have not known a man. Let me bring them out to you, and you may do to them as you please; but do not do anything to these men, since they have come under the shelter of my roof" (Gen.

19:8). The old man of Judges makes an almost identical statement.[13]

Some traditional biblical scholars have explained the behavior of Lot and the old man as a choice between allowing the commission of the supposedly lesser evil of rape and facilitating the greater sin of homosexuality (Lev. 18:22; 20:13). Some other scholars explain that the ancients may have placed the Middle Eastern values of hospitality and the protection of one's guests above the preservation of one's own family and interests.[14]

But nowhere in classical rabbinic literature is there a discussion of the daughters' feelings about the matter, and nowhere is there a condemnation of Lot. We might ask ourselves why the sages of talmudic times were so reluctant to discuss what must have appeared to them as immoral behavior on Lot's part. True, hospitality was an important value in rabbinic ethics— this value had not changed from Lot's time—but clearly, the rabbis put sexual morality before hospitality. Moreover, classical rabbinic literature tends to discuss all aspects of life and is normally not reticent regarding sexual matters. Yet it remains silent on this important issue.

Three possible explanations come to mind here: (1) the rabbis' silence may reflect deep revulsion on their part, a sentiment that comes to full expression only centuries later in the writings of the medieval commentators; (2) they, too, in judging this moral dilemma, saw homosexuality as the greater evil and therefore saw no point in castigating Lot in his no-win choice; (3) the Talmud does describe in great detail the depraved social, religious, and moral practices that prevailed in Sodom.[15] It is in the context of these descriptions that the rabbis hint at Lot's degeneracy. Such moral laxity was infectious, the rabbis believed: "Woe to the wicked and woe to his neighbor,"[16] they declared. His daughters, growing up in this immoral environment, were presumably also infected by these evil influences.

The earliest source to discuss the plight of the virgin daughters is the *Tanḥuma* (ninth century c.e.),[17] which comments that normally a father would sacrifice himself to protect his wife and daughters, whereas Lot was willing to hand them over.

This is the midrashic source on which all later medieval commentators base their discussion, including Ramban, Rabbenu Bachia, and Abarbanel, who consequently indict Lot for his indecent behavior.

The sages' general readiness to grapple with all kinds of problems, including sexual matters, is evidenced by their willingness to discuss forthrightly the incest between Lot and his daughters. It is interesting to note that their evaluation of the incestuous intercourse incident is refreshingly fair and free of androcentric prejudice. Quite the contrary, although they indict neither party unequivocally, they lay more of the blame on Lot than on his daughters.

> To these [the daughters], whose intention was to do right, [applies] *the just do walk in them,* whereas to him [Lot] whose intention it was to commit the transgression [applies], *but transgressors do stumble therein!*[18]

After a brief discussion of the important question of who lusted after whom, the rabbis bring up the following verse: "He who isolates himself pursues his desires" (Prov. 18:1). The sages associate Lot's having separated himself from Abraham—the one source of positive influence in his life—with his becoming caught up in desire, which eventually brought him into sin with his daughters.[19]

In the belief that the world was coming to an end, Lot's daughters seduced their father, ostensibly in order to produce further generations. But could the two stories—namely, of the daughters' being surrendered to the mob and their seduction of their father—be linked? Could the young women have had a different motive (or a compound motive), entailing revenge on the father who placed duties of host ahead of duties of father and willingly gave them over to be violated? Were they exacting retribution in turn by degrading him in incestuous intercourse?

Whatever the case, the rabbis subject Lot to further criticism, saying that the first time his elder daughter misled him, made him drunk, and seduced him, he was innocent by reason of his intoxication. The second time, however, he should have known better and resisted the seduction.

> *And the firstborn said unto the younger: Our father is old, and there is*
> *not a man in the earth . . .* (Gen. 19:31). They thought that the
> whole world was destroyed, as in the generation of the Flood.
> *Come, let us make our father drink wine . . . that we may preserve seed*
> *of our father . . . and they made their father drink wine . . . and he*
> *knew not when she lay down, and when she arose—u-vequmah* ["and
> when she arose"]: this word [*u-vequmah*] is dotted, intimating
> that he did not indeed know of her lying down, but he did know
> of her arising. . . . We would not know whether Lot lusted after
> his daughters or they lusted after him, but that it says, *He that*
> *separateth himself seeketh desire* (Prov. 18:1), whence it follows that
> Lot desired his daughters.[20]

The rabbis base their explanation on the fact that the word
u-vequmah ("when she got up") is written with certain diacritical marks (it is "dotted," as the Midrash says) above it in the
verse "and he knew not when she lay down, and when she got
up" (Gen. 19:33). The rabbis say that the diacritical marks
mean that although Lot did not know of her lying down, he did
indeed know of her arising.[21] The sages thus hold him culpable
for failing to resist the second seduction and for his willing
participation.

Not only do the sages apply more lenient standards in judging the daughters; they in fact praise them as the progenitors of
two nations.[22] They maintain that God tolerated the behavior of
the elder daughter even though she brazenly proclaimed her
son as being "from my father" (which was the meaning of the
name Moab that she gave the child).

> *And the firstborn bore a son, and called his name Moab* (Gen. 19:37).
> . . . the firstborn disgraced her father and called his name
> Moab, which means, "by my father" (*me-'ab*). . . . The younger
> spared her father's honor, for *She called his name Ben-Ammi*, de-
> claring, He is a son (*ben*) of one who was with me (*'immi*).[23]

The rationale for the sages' tolerance was that often from evil
comes good; for though the action itself was evil, they accept
that the motivation had been to continue the race, a good and
justified end. So worthy was this motivation, according to the
sages, that Ruth, a descendant of the Moabite line, has the
honor of being ancestress to the Messiah.[24] The merit discerned by the rabbis in the other daughter, who named her son

Ben-Ammi ("The Son of My People"), was that she displayed modesty; thus, the pious Naamah, a wife of Solomon, sprang from her:

> But the Holy One, blessed be He, said . . . "The idea you have in your mind is not the idea I have in My mind. Two doves have I to bring forth from them; Ruth the Moabitess and Naamah the Ammonitess."[25]

Dinah Went Out

Rape was a serious problem, as suggested by the penalties and punishments in the biblical law codes (Ex. 22:15–16; Deut. 22:22–29). These references indicate that rape occurred often in the biblical world and that it was considered an outrage—but not so much against the individual as against the family or clan. The two cases of rape described in detail in the Bible indicate that such heinous crimes could be perpetrated even against the daughters of leaders of the highest echelons of society: Dinah, the daughter of Jacob, the patriarchal founder of Israel; and Tamar, a princess, the daughter of King David. Though the victims have much in common, there are differences in the attitude of the rabbis toward them.[26]

The biblical story of Dinah is concisely told in Genesis 34:

> Now Dinah, the daughter whom Leah had borne to Jacob, went out to visit the daughters of the land. Shechem son of Hamor the Hivite, chief of the country, saw her, and took her and lay with her by force. Being strongly drawn to Dinah daughter of Jacob, and in love with the maiden, he spoke to the maiden tenderly. So Shechem said to his father Hamor, "Get me this girl as a wife" (Gen. 34:1–4).

Nuptial negotiations ensue. Jacob's sons agree to enter into a treaty with Hamor and his people to live among them only if the townsmen will all submit to circumcision. Hamor's people undergo the procedure; but while they are painfully recuperating, Dinah's full brothers Simeon and Levi come and slay them

all. Simeon and Levi remove Dinah from the house of Shechem. Jacob is furious about their actions, to which the brothers reply, "Should our sister be treated like a whore?"

The Bible presents meager information about Dinah herself.
Her life seemed to have a dark cloud over it before the rape,
and even more so after it. Unlike Tamar, she was not said to be
beautiful; perhaps she was like her mother Leah, who was physically flawed. Dinah herself seems not to have been a favorite of
her father, possibly because she was a girl or perhaps because
she was born to his unloved wife Leah.

The Midrash offers a story about Dinah's birth, explaining
her name thus: Dinah originally had been destined to be a
male; but Leah, knowing that Jacob was destined to have a total
of twelve sons, prayed that the child she was carrying would be
a girl so that, of the twelve promised sons, two would be born to
her sister. Leah then called her daughter "Dinah" because of
the "judgment" she had passed on herself, by giving up the son
she might have had, and thus on the daughter she bore instead.[27] Her name connoting "judgment" seems appropriate in
the context of events that befell her, for many have passed
harsh judgment on her.

The sages blame Dinah's tragedy on her own actions: she
was violated because "she went out" (Gen. 34:1).[28] This phrase
"she went out" is repeated again and again in *Genesis Rabbah*
and other rabbinic sources. We will quote just two samples to
illustrate:

> *And Dinah the daughter of Leah went out.* . . . This may be com-
> pared to one who was holding a pound of meat in his hand, and
> as soon as he exposed it a bird swooped down and snatched it
> away. Similarly, *And Dinah the daughter of Leah went out,* and forth-
> with, *And Shechem the son of Hamor saw her.* . . . *And he took her and
> lay with her*—in a natural way; *And humbled* [i.e., *violated*] *her*—
> unnaturally.[29]

> *And Jacob said to Simeon and Levi: Ye have troubled me* (Gen. 34:30).
> . . . [Simeon and Levi answered:] "The vat was muddied, and
> we have purified it" [i.e., our honor was stained, and we have
> cleansed it]. *And they said: Should one deal with our sister as with a
> harlot* (Gen. 34:31)? "Will they treat us as common property,"

they exclaimed. What caused all this? The fact that *"Dinah went out."*[30]

Dinah was, in their words, a gadabout, leaving her tent to look around at the life of the women about her.[31] In the ancient world, this was regarded as incorrect, even wanton, behavior—a defiance of the regime of modesty.

Three separate midrashim discuss the shortcomings of biblical women.[32] In each one of these, Dinah is described as a gadabout. To add to the insult, they add, "Like mother, like daughter" (Ezek. 16:44), suggesting that Dinah learned this immodest behavior from her mother Leah: " 'And Leah *went out* to meet him,' which means that she *went out* to meet him adorned like a harlot; therefore 'And Dinah the daughter of Leah *went out.*' "[33] Elsewhere, however, the sages defend Leah, saying that when she went out to meet Jacob to tell him that she had hired him for that night by giving to Rachel the mandrakes of her son (Gen. 30:14–18), she did so in order to produce the tribes of Israel and not for sexual gratification.[34]

As always, rabbinic views are never monolithic. In contrast to the disparaging remarks about Dinah, certain midrashim defend her behavior. Some rabbis go so far as to blame Jacob for the violation of Dinah. Jacob, some say, was arrogant;[35] others, that he had failed to fulfill a vow;[36] still others, that he had been unkind to his brother Esau in failing to give Dinah to him in marriage.[37]

The Holy One . . . reproved him: "Thou hast withheld kindness from thy brother; when she married Job, didst thou not convert him?[38] Thou wouldst not give her in marriage to one who is circumcised [Esau]; lo! she is married to one who is uncircumcised. Thou wouldst not give her in legitimate wedlock; lo! she is taken in an illegitimate fashion"; thus it is written, *And Dinah went out.*[39]

This line of midrashic discourse is in accordance with the rabbinic view that minor children suffer and even die for the sins of their parents.[40] This again blames Jacob, for it supposes that Dinah was a minor, based on the use of the word *yaldah,* which appears but once in the story: "Get me this girl (*yaldah*) to wife" (Gen. 34:4). This theory, though not developed in great detail by the rabbis, places the blame on the father and makes Dinah an immature, innocent victim.

The indifference shown by her father Jacob seems puzzling but may explain why the rabbis appear rather harsh toward Dinah in considering her case. In contrast to her father's indifference is the concern shown by Simeon and Levi—her brothers from the same mother—who avenged her violation. But, as if to confirm Jacob's lack of compassion for Dinah, scripture teaches that Simeon and Levi incurred the wrath of their father, who never forgot their belligerence and cursed them from his deathbed (Gen. 49:5–8).[41]

The medieval author of *Pirqe de Rabbi Eliezar* adds his voice to earlier midrashists who try to defend Dinah's actions by blaming someone else for the event. Rabbi Eliezer lays the blame on Shechem, saying that he enticed Dinah to leave her home by having women play beautiful music to draw her out.

> The daughter of Jacob used to stay in her tent and *did not go out*. What did Shechem the son of Hamor do? He brought girl musicians playing on timbrels. Dinah went out to see the players.[42]

In another source, Shechem is described as having "bitten" Dinah, and in this way the author suggests that Shechem was as deceptive as the seductive snake in the Garden of Eden.[43]

One final midrash adds an interesting epilogue to Dinah's sad story. It appears as comment to the last biblical reference to her in a genealogical list (Gen. 46:15). According to this aggadic tradition, and in keeping with the pattern we have seen of finding a good genealogical outcome to such violations, Dinah's union with Shechem produced Asnath, who became the wife of Joseph.[44] The sages further endeavored to soften Dinah's story by providing her with a husband. Some married her off to Job,[45] others to her brother Simeon.[46]

Nevertheless, despite some aggadic efforts to sweeten her life, Dinah bears most of the midrashic blame for her violation. Very often when her name came up, it would elicit a sneering "because Dinah went out."

Tamar: The Rape of a Princess

Like all biblical narrative, the Tamar text is brief but to the point and does not deviate to discuss irrelevant issues.[47] The opening verses set the scene by naming the three most important characters in the story: Absalom, Tamar, and Amnon. They all share the same father, King David. Tamar is described as the beautiful sister of Absalom. Her half-brother Amnon is infatuated with her. To help carry out Amnon's designs on her, Amnon's friend Jonadab advises him to feign illness so that his father, King David, will come to visit him. Jonadab tells Amnon to ask his father to send Tamar to prepare food for him. Jonadab's plan works, and Tamar is summoned to Amnon's quarters. The stage is then set. Tamar arrives with the meal she has prepared; and, though she tries to stave off the attack, she is unsuccessful. She leaves, disgraced and humiliated by her brother; and once again, as in the case of Dinah, it is not the victim's father but her brother from the same mother, Absalom, who comes to her rescue (2 Sam. 13:1–22).

The rabbinic commentary on the Tamar episode revolves around two specific themes. The sages are perturbed by the possibility of a marriage between half-siblings that was suggested in Tamar's speech: "Please, speak to the king; he will not refuse me to you" (2 Sam. 13:13). In their concern about the legal issues here, the aggadists overlooked the most obvious interpretation of her words in that desperate situation—as a ruse to gain time and put him off.[48] True, there is a biblical precedent for such marriage between half-siblings; for example, Sarah, who was the daughter of her husband Abraham's father but not of his mother (Gen. 11:29; 20:12).[49] But the sages believed that such marriages, although permissible prior to the giving of the Torah at Sinai, were no longer allowed during the monarchic time in which the narrative was set (Lev. 18:9; 20:17; Deut. 27:22). How then did they eliminate the discrepancy between Tamar's statement and biblical law? By resorting to the midrashic interpretation that Tamar's mother,

Maacah, the daughter of King Geshur, had been taken captive in war by David—and that she had conceived Tamar before converting to Judaism. Tamar would therefore be permitted to marry Amnon according to Jewish law, because she was a non-Jew.[50]

The second problem that evoked comment by the rabbis was the transformation of Amnon's passion from love to hatred. Whereas Shechem's desire for Dinah had in it an element of love, the rape of Tamar is characterized more by lust on the part of Amnon and ends with him loathing her. What motivated the change? Why does love—or even lust—turn to loathing? Modern theory about the nature of rape places its roots not in love or lust but in violence and hatred[51]—a view this story in certain respects anticipates. The rabbis seemed to have shared the view that Amnon's behavior was violent and loathsome, and they discuss at length what they consider to be Tamar's understandable desire for revenge. Thus they empower Tamar to punish Amnon by physically maiming him in such a way as to impair his virility,[52] which would further explain why he comes to hate her so passionately.

The sages' empowerment of Tamar in her revenge displays a greater empathy for her than they feel for Dinah. They are cognizant of the fact that she went innocently to her brother's home, at the behest of her own father, and that she tried to safeguard her virginity but was overpowered by her attacker.

Thus the sages hold Tamar in higher regard than Dinah because in their eyes Tamar was not a gadabout. Moreover, she made public her shame; and, according to rabbinic opinion, thereby helped prevent violence to others. The biblical text states: "And Tamar put ashes on her head and rent her garment of many colors" (2 Sam. 13:19). This action evoked the rabbinic comment "in that hour Tamar set up a great fence [about chastity]."[53] The sages say that Tamar's contemporaries heard her cries, exclaiming that if such a crime could be done to the daughter of a king, how much more vulnerable were the daughters of ordinary men. They credit Tamar's response to her violation as bringing about the introduction of the worthy institution of *yihud,* the laws that prohibit private meetings between the sexes.[54]

As we observed earlier, nothing is given of the mother-daughter relationship in such traumatic events, and what is told concerning fathers and daughters leaves much to be desired. There is no direct communication with Tamar and even less evident warmth.[55] David visited his sick son in person but sent a message to direct his daughter to go to her brother. When she is raped, the king, her father, does not visit or comfort her, even though she is not merely suffering from some illness but instead has suffered a devastating violation.[56] Unlike Jacob's silence regarding his daughter's rape, at least here David becomes angry when he hears about it. Yet he does nothing to punish Amnon, which would have been some way of communicating to her his empathy and outrage.

One interesting reference to the Tamar story occurs in the Mishnah. It appears in a discussion in which a contrast is drawn between love of a man for a woman versus love (friendship) between two men:

> All love which depends on some material cause, if the material cause ceases, the love ceases. Love which does not depend on some material cause, never fails forever. What love is that which depends on some material cause? This is the love of Amnon and Tamar. And that which does not depend on some material cause? This is the love of David and Jonathan.[57]

The verses contrast love that depends on self-gratification, carnal love, to another love that is unselfish and seeks only the good of the one who is loved. This analysis views the love of a man for a woman as changing with outward appearance or outward fortune, whereas love between two men is timeless and endures forever. The passage appears to offer a negative evaluation of the male-female relationship in contrast to male friendship, which is described in glowing colors. Such an extreme attitude would be rather unusual in rabbinics, which usually emphasizes marriage as the highest human state. Perhaps one has to understand the mishnaic reference as the closest the rabbis could get to a condemnation of the use of women as sex objects.

The Daughters of Zelophehad: A Success Story

At the outset, I claimed that the daughter characters who figure significantly in the Bible generally warranted inclusion because their lives were connected with some scandal or calamity. The daughters of Zelophehad actually fit this pattern after all, because initially they were bereft of an inheritance and a place in Israel. Such breaks in family heritage were regarded as a very great calamity.[58] The daughters of Zelophehad formulated a plan to obtain their father's inheritance and thereby continue the family estate. Their initiative constituted a unique success story for women, which some have called the first feminist revolution in recorded history.

The situation faced by the daughters of Zelophehad was difficult and pitiful. Their father has died in the desert, leaving no son to inherit his land. Despite the fact that there was no precedent for female inheritance, the five sisters—Mahlah, Noah, Hoglah, Milcah, and Tirzah—decide to put their case directly before Moses to ask that he allow them to inherit their father's land. Moses listens and then consults God, who declares that the claim of the daughters of Zelophehad is just and that they should be given a fair share of their father's inheritance along with his brothers (that is, their uncles). More striking, the ruling is generalized to show that henceforth, in cases where there is no son, daughters would inherit.

> And the Lord said to Moses, "The plea of Zelophehad's daughters is just: you should give them a hereditary holding among their father's kinsmen; transfer their father's share to them. Further . . . if a man dies without leaving a son, you shall transfer his property to his daughter" (Num. 27:6–8).

The second part of this narrative appears in Numbers 36, which addresses the male relatives' concern that the land should not leave their tribe. Moses then promulgates an additional law to protect the integrity of the tribal land holdings:

female inheritors were not to be allowed to marry out of their tribe. The book of Joshua records the allotment of territory to the daughters of Zelophehad as part of the general description of land distribution to the tribes (Josh. 17:3).

The audaciousness of the daughters of Zelophehad is unparalleled in scripture, in keeping with the name Zelophehad, which means "protection from fear."[59] The sages of the Talmud, following their scriptural exemplar, praise rather than criticize them for their bold behavior. Rabbis vie with each other in the effort to praise them. I will examine some of these rabbinic texts and pay particular attention to the varied social attitudes displayed in them.

The Talmud states that the law of inheritance concerning women was intended to be promulgated through Moses; but, because Moses had been arrogant, the women were found worthy to have it pronounced at their behest.[60] *Sipre* adds the remark: "Happy is the one to whose words God consents."[61] Typically, a later source offers an alternate view, holding that Moses knew the law pertaining to the daughters' situation, but he did not know whether their father was worthy of having his line continued, that is, whether the sin for which he had died had been forgiven.[62] This medieval version avoids criticizing a great figure of the stature of Moses.

The midrashic sources come up with a remarkable statement in describing the daughters' consultation regarding how to approach Moses. It is unique in midrashic literature in both tone and value:

> They [the daughters] said: "The compassion of God is not as the compassion of men. The compassion of men extends to men more than to women, but not thus is the compassion of God; His compassion extends equally to men and women and to all, even as it is said, 'The Lord is good to all, and His mercies are over all his works' " (Ps. 145:9).[63]

This midrash is fascinating because in it men, through words that they place in the mouths of women, strongly criticize the mores of the society that they themselves dominate. Only God is to be trusted to love impartially all of God's creations. Men display neither understanding nor compassion for women's problems; only God listens, understands, and assists. The rabbinic sources imply that it is not the religious laws per se that demean women, but rather the male monopoly on interpretation that creates the problem.

Rabbinic praise of daughters of Zelophehad knows no bounds. The sages taught, "The daughters of Zelophehad were wise (*hakhmaniyyot*), they were exegetes (*darshaniyyot*), and they were virtuous (*zidqaniyyot*)."[64] This is exceptional praise for women in any literature, and certainly rabbinic literature. The daughters are called wise by the rabbis because they spoke at an appropriate moment. Moses was teaching the law of levirate marriage, which deals with maintaining family inheritance—"if brethren dwell together . . . " (Deut. 25:5)—when the women approached him. They said to Moses: " 'If we have the status of a son let us inherit as a son, if not let our mother be subject to the levirate marriage.' "[65] Moses was apparently impressed by their argument and immediately placed their case before God.

The use of the term *hakhmaniyyot* is unusual. Whereas biblical literature provides evidence for the activities of "wise women" (*'ishah hakhamah*—2 Sam. 14:2 and 20:16), the term is not often used in relation to women in the Talmud, because the title *hakham* ("wise man") became a term restricted solely to the male elite of wise teachers. One exception uses the term to refute the idea that a woman could be wise in anything but a limited, technical sense:

> A wise woman asked R. Eliezer: Since with regard to the offense with the golden calf all were evenly associated, why was not the penalty of death the same?—He answered her: There is no wisdom in woman except with the distaff. Thus also does Scripture say: *And all the women that were wise-hearted did spin with their hands.*[66]

The rabbis claimed that they themselves were *hakhamim*. As the Babylonian Talmud states, "Since the day when the temple was destroyed, prophecy has been taken from the prophets and given to the wise."[67] The daughters of Zelophehad, however, were viewed in the context of the prophets or the biblical wise woman, invoking divine authority for their teachings. Though the terms describing the attributes of these daughters here are used in an adjectival rather than a nominal sense, they nevertheless indicate that women were at least sometimes believed capable of possessing the qualities necessary to be leaders and teachers.

They were called virtuous by the rabbis, for they were willing to marry only such men as were worthy of them, to wait a long time to marry, and to marry only when they found the proper spouse. Thus the sages comment that Moses separated from his spouse because he had been commanded to do so by God;[68] whereas the daughters had not been so commanded, but wisely postponed marriage anyway. The sages claim that the youngest of the daughters was over forty, but a miracle happened and they all bore children, confirming the correctness of their having waited to find appropriate spouses.[69]

Further, rabbinic sources praise the sagacious manner in which they defend their father. The women argued he was not among the followers of Korah who murmured against God, nor was he among the spies who brought back a negative report; rather, he died for a personal sin (which would not disqualify him from inheriting the land). Their argument is one reason why, elsewhere, the sages identify him as the man accused of gathering wood on the Sabbath (Num. 15:32), which was a personal rather than national transgression.[70]

The rabbis credit the women with being exegetes because their argument indicates knowledge of the legal source material. The daughters said that they would not have spoken up if their father had a son or even if a son of his had a daughter. They impressed the sages with the erudition entailed in knowing that a son's daughter had preference over a decedent's daughter.[71]

The positive outlook of the daughters is likewise lauded by the sages. They contrast the daughters' loving attitude toward the land with the negative and indifferent one expressed by the men. The women said, "Give us an inheritance in the land" (Num. 27:4), whereas the men said, "Give us a leader and let us return to Egypt" (Num. 14:4).[72] The rabbis credit the daughters of Zelophehad for serving as model par excellence for other women of that generation who refrained from participating with the men in the making of the golden calf:

Then drew near the daughters of Zelophehad (Num. 27:1). In that generation the women built up the fences which the men broke down. Thus you find that Aaron told them: *Break off the gold rings, which are in the ears of your wives* (Ex. 32:2), but the women refused and checked their husbands; as is proved by the fact that it says, *And all the* [male] *people broke off the golden rings which were in their ears* (Ex. 32:3), the women not participating with them in making the Calf. It was the same in the case of the spies, who uttered an evil report: *And the men . . . when they returned, made all the congregation to murmur against him* (Num. 14:36), and against this congregation the decree [not to enter the Land] was issued, because they had said: *We are not able to go up* (Num. 13:31). The women, however, were not with them in their counsel, as may be inferred from the fact that it is written in an earlier passage of our section, *For the Lord had said of them: They shall surely die in the wilderness. And there was not left a man of them, save Caleb the son of Jephunneh* (Num. 26:65). Thus the text speaks of *a man* but not of "a woman." This was because the men had been unwilling to enter the Land. The women, however, drew near to ask for an inheritance in the Land. Consequently the present section was written down next to that dealing with the death of the generation of the wilderness, for it was there that the men broke down the fences and the women built them up.[73]

This unique biblical case history, with its measured rebellion, gives us a paradigm for women demanding their rights and thereby bringing about a reinterpretation of the law. Rabbinic acceptance and praise both for the women's assertiveness and their supposed erudition is unparalleled in rabbinic sources.

Jephthah's Daughter: Victim?
Or Heroine of Her Own Life?

The narrative of Jephthah's daughter is one of the saddest in the Bible. It has some obvious parallels to the *Aqedah* story (the binding of Isaac), though its ending is tragic rather than purposeful. However, the aspect of the story that concerns us here is how the role of the daughter in the story is changed in the rabbis' retelling.

The story appears in Judges 11–12:7, and there it is told as the story of Jephthah. Though it concerns her awful fate, the daughter is never even given a name in the biblical account. Jephthah is presented as a rash, arrogant person, disparaged by his half-brothers for being the son of a harlot. They expel him from their home, which embitters him, and he becomes a leader of outcasts. When the Ammonites attack Israel, Jephthah's brethren ask him to come back and lead them in war. He reminds them of how they had abused him and demands that they unequivocally make him head of the tribe, which they agree to do. He makes a rash vow before setting out for battle: "If you deliver the Ammonites into my hands, then whatever comes out of the door of my house to meet me on my safe return from the Ammonites shall be the Lord's and shall be offered by me as a burnt offering" (Judg. 11:30–31).

The Bible passes over the battle quickly, noting that the Ammonites were defeated, and moves on to Jephthah's homecoming, where the terrible consequences of his vow unfold. It is his daughter who comes out of his house, for it was the custom in those times for women to greet victorious warriors with timbrels and dancing (cf. Ex. 15:20–21; 1 Sam. 18:6–7). He cries out, saying, "Alas, daughter! You have brought me low; you have become my troubler! For I have uttered a vow to the Lord and I cannot retract" (Judg. 11:35). His phrasing has an extraordinarily egocentric quality; his own loss is highlighted rather than the terrible consequences that will result for her. He blames his daughter instead of acknowledging his own foolishness.[74]

The daughter nonetheless responds loyally, praising his victory and expressing humble submission to her fate: "Do to me as you have vowed." The text notes that she was his one and only child. She requests from her father only two months in which to weep upon the mountains and mourn her early death, which would mean that she would never marry (Judg. 11:34).[75] The biblical language, which is ambiguous, especially concerning the fulfillment of the vow, has prompted generations of Bible scholars to discuss what really happened to Jephthah's daughter.

Altogether, the rabbis view Jephthah unkindly, emphasizing

his negative traits. Only once do they praise him, and grudgingly at that. Having found that Jephthah was mentioned together with the great and noble Samuel in scripture (1 Sam. 12:11), the sages said that "Jephthah in his generation is like Samuel in his generation."[76] They undercut any glory this might seem to confer on him by saying that this somehow meant that even the most insignificant man, when appointed to an important position, must be treated with the respect equal to his office. In sum, the statement implies that Jephthah's generation was not deserving of a better judge, and so offers an unfavorable assessment of Jephthah.

Unlike Ben Sira, Josephus, and the New Testament, which praise Jephthah for his physical strength and valor, the talmudic and midrashic sages harp on his weaknesses of character; namely, that he was rash, arrogant, and ignorant.[77] According to the rabbis, Jephthah attracted vain men (Judg. 11:3) and thus personified for them the proverb that a sterile date palm associates with fruitless trees.

Rabbinic interpretation of the actual events revolves around three issues: the rashness of the vow; how it was finally executed; and the daughter's relative passivity/activity in her fate.

> Four asked improperly: three were granted their request in a fitting manner, and the fourth, in an unfitting manner.... They are Eliezer, Caleb, Saul, and Jephthah. ... Jephthah asked in an unfitting manner and God answered him in an unfitting manner. He asked in an unfitting manner, as it says, *And Jephthah vowed a vow unto the Lord, and said: Then it shall be, that whatsoever cometh forth . . . it shall be the Lord's and I will offer it up for a burnt-offering* (Judg. 11:30f.). Said the Holy One, blessed be He, to him: "Then had a camel or an ass or a dog come forth, thou wouldst have offered it up for a burnt-offering!" What did the Lord do? He answered him unfittingly and prepared his daughter for him, as it says, *And Jephthah came . . . and, behold, his daughter came out to meet him* (Judg. 11:34).[78]

In this midrash, the sages continue by blaming Jephthah, who should have known that his vow was not valid or binding. They further blame Pinchas, the High Priest, for failure to annul the vow out of arrogance and pride. Jephthah arrogantly had asked: "Am I, the chief of Israel's leaders to go to Pinchas?"

Pinchas the High Priest, too, was derelict in his duty, saying: "Why should I go to him when he needs me!" Between the failings of the two of them, the maiden perished.[79]

Both, according to the sages, were punished for the blood of Jephthah's daughter. They describe a most horrible death for the judge. Quoting the scriptural verse "Then died Jephthah the Gileadite, and was buried in the cities of Gilead," they comment that it does not say "in the city of Gilead." This indicates that his death was horrible, his limbs dropping off; wherever he went, a limb would drop off him and be buried there on the spot. Likewise, Pinchas strangely incurs their wrath, because he did not act in keeping with his stature as a High Priest and leader of Israel. They claim, basing their interpretation on scripture, that his spiritual inspiration departed from him.[80]

This earliest midrash falls into the "sacrificialist" camp, that in the end she was indeed sacrificed.[81] By implying rather than overtly describing her end, the rabbis show their great compassion for her and their great horror at the turn of events. Jephthah is condemned as one of those who took an improper vow and then regretted it. He had merely to pay a certain sum to the sacred treasury of the Sanctuary in order to be free of his vow. Another opinion holds that even this was unnecessary, for the vow was never valid in the first place.

A late midrash in *Tanḥuma* (ca. ninth century C.E.) illustrates strikingly how much the rabbis continued to be disturbed by the horrible situation of the daughter. Consequently, in that retelling of the story they endeavor to empower her to save herself.[82]

Synthesizing various midrashim, the *Tanḥuma* points to the account of the daughter inquiring of her father, "Is it written in the Torah (Leviticus 1) that human beings should be brought as burnt offerings?" He answers: "My daughter, my vow was, 'whatever comes forth from my house.' " She replies, "But Jacob too vowed that he would give to the Lord the tenth part of all that the Lord gave him (Gen. 28:22). Did he sacrifice any of his sons?" All these pleas were to no avail. Jephthah remains resolved in his decision to sacrifice her to fulfill his vow. She observes that he is refusing to listen to her, and, as the Bible records, asks him to allow her two months' respite.

In this midrash, one can see the exegetical mind at work. The commentators noted the discrepancy of language and used it as a scriptural peg upon which to hang their interpretation. Jephthah's daughter spoke about going *down* to the mountains, whereas normally people go *up* to the mountains. The rabbis interpret her peculiar phrasing as indicating that she really intended to go down to the Sanhedrin to consult them about the validity of the vow. In this way they convert her two months of passively awaiting her fate into a period of activity in which she can use her own ingenuity and initiative to try to save herself.

In most rabbinic literature on the Jephthah theme heretofore, the father is the focal point of the story. It is the father's vow that holds the interest of the rabbis, and the daughter is discussed only in the context of the vow. In the *Tanḥuma*, for the first time there is an account bringing together some aggadic materials in which the daughter becomes an active participant in the story, not merely a passive victim. This exegetical move resonates with the modern feminist interpretations, like those of Trible[83] and Fuchs,[84] who attempt to restore a role to the daughter in the unfolding tragedy.

Nevertheless, in the end her efforts were unavailing, and she was sacrificed. The father's wickedness has been too powerful to go unpunished and thus cancels out her efforts. The Sanhedrin was struck with forgetfulness about the law and unable to invalidate the fateful vow. In this way God punished Jephthah for his slaughter of forty-two thousand Ephraimites (they had complained that he had not called them to participate in the triumphant war over the Ammonites; Judg. 12:1–7). Once again, as in the story of Dinah, a daughter suffers for the sin of the father.

Only in the medieval period, beginning with Kimhi (1160–1235 C.E.), do rabbinic sources espouse the nonsacrificialist view, claiming that she became a celibate, leading a secluded life. Kimhi bases this view on the fact that it is never clearly stated in the Bible that Jephthah carried out the sacrifice of his daughter—only that he fulfilled his vow and that his daughter went into seclusion. Kimhi's interpretation influenced other medieval exegetes, both Jews and Christians. Or perhaps his seclusion reflects the influence upon him of Christian monasticism of the day.[85]

There is one other early source that is worth mentioning here, and that is a Jewish pseudepigraphic work of the first century c.e. Like rabbinic tradition, the *Biblical Antiquities* of Pseudo-Philo holds the poor daughter blameless, a victim of her father's rashness. "I have seen that the virgin is wise in contrast to her father and perceptive in contrast to all the wise men." Significantly, these words are said to be God's own.

In addition, Pseudo-Philo is the only source that gives her a name, Seila, which means "loaned" or "dedicated" to the Lord (1 Sam. 1:28).[86] Given the rabbinic propensity for giving names to women who go unnamed in the Bible, such as the mother of Abraham, Lot's wife and daughter, the mother of David, the mother of Samson—the fact that the sages do not use this pseudepigraphic source raises two possibilities: (1) they were unaware of the tradition,[87] or (2) the name was avoided because it would be hard to connect with her story, except ironically. She was valued ("asked for"—*s'l*) by her father,[88] but in the end he discards her to carry out his foolish vow.

The story of Jephthah's daughter does not seem to pivot around her gender as do those of the other biblical women we have examined. Had Jephthah had a son, he might have made the very same vow. But the story has captured the attention of many modern feminists, in part, I believe, because they have perceived that the powerlessness of daughters in biblical times is what led to her sacrifice being carried out. Thus, the later rabbinic retelling that empowers the daughter to some extent is a valuable contribution to the contemporary discussion.

Conclusion

What yardstick of values did the rabbis use in creating their midrashic interpretations of the female characters in the daughter narratives? Earlier I stated that modesty was the overriding value. And indeed, we can see, for example, that Dinah was denigrated largely because "she went out." Conversely, Tamar, who was also raped, was lauded for her modesty.

But modesty was not the only standard the rabbis applied. Tamar was also empowered to avenge herself against her rapist, striking a blow at his genitals. The daughters of Zelophehad, who went outside the private female domain and acted boldly and assertively, were praised highly for their initiative. True, the rabbis took their cue from the scriptural text; still, they could have taken some exegetical latitude but did not.

Finally, over the course of centuries, the rabbis respond to the horror they felt at the fate of Jephthah's poor daughter by attributing actions to her suggested nowhere in the scriptural account: going to the Sanhedrin; arguing with her father; choosing monasticism over death. If all things were to be seen in the context of modesty, the rabbis could have said of her as well: "And she ran out"; but wisely, they did not.

In some ways, the rabbis treated these aggadic materials much as they would legal case studies, noting all details and drawing from the text evidence of guilt or innocence. But there the similarities stop. In contrast to their legal rulings, which appear quite strict, their aggadic treatment of the daughter narratives is most compassionate. A way is often found to soften the harsh circumstances of the daughter in the face of patriarchal disabilities. Sometimes this is done through justification of the daughters' actions, at other times through an explicit expression of sympathy, and at yet other times through enhancing the powers of the daughters themselves.

Notes

1. A. Even-Shoshan, *A New Concordance of the Old Testament* (Jerusalem: Kiryat Sefer Publishing House, 1985); Robert Young, *Young's Analytical Concordance to the Bible* (Grand Rapids: Wm. B. Eerdmans, 1970; repr. 1978), s.v. "daughter" and "son."

2. For example, see Barbara Bakke Kaiser's recent analysis of three poems of suffering, which demonstrates that female experience was often used as a metaphor through which a poet expressed joy or agony over Jerusalem's fate or gave voice to other happy or painful experiences of the nation. See B. B. Kaiser, "Poet as 'Female Impersonator': The Image of Daughter Zion as Speaker in Biblical Poems of Suffering," *Journal of Religion* 67 (1987): 164–82. She uses the word *bat* in a precise, carefully defined sense, quoting William Lanahan's definition given in a study of the book of Lamentations. On the word *bat*, see also *Encyclopaedia Judaica*, 16, 161, s.v. "virgin, virginity."

3. The Midrash supplies an imaginative explanation for Dinah's name, which is discussed below in this chapter.

4. A discussion of how matters changed in the days of the rabbis may be found in Valler, *Women and Womanhood in the Stories of the Babylonian Talmud*, 39–55.

5. Rabbinic law, on the other hand, limited the father's power over the daughter by prohibiting him from giving her in marriage without her consent, once the signs of puberty became evident, legally defined as the age of twelve years and one day; see *b. Ḥul.* 26b; *Encyclopedia Talmudit*, 2, 377–79, s.v. "bogeret" [Hebrew].

6. The language used in Ex. 21:7 is *mkr*, meaning "to sell." However, the actual meaning is to give her in marriage to pay off his debt.

7. Esther Fuchs, "The Literary Characterization of Mothers and

Sexual Politics in the Hebrew Bible," *Semeia* 46 (1989): 151–66; Rachel Adler, "A Mother in Israel: Aspects of the Mother Role in Jewish Myth," in *Beyond Androcentrism: New Essays on Women and Religion,* ed. R. M. Gross (Missoula, Mont.: Scholars Press, 1977), 237–55; Carol Meyers, *Discovering Eve: Ancient Israelite Women in Context* (Oxford: Oxford University Press, 1988).

8. *b. Nid.* 31b. The Hebrew for male, *zakor,* was construed by the rabbis by fanciful exegesis as being composed of the consonants of the words *zeh kar,* "this is provision." The Hebrew for female, *nekevah,* is also given a fanciful etymology connecting it with the phrase *nekiyyah ba'ah,* "she comes clean (naked, empty-handed)."

9. *b. Sanh.* 100b; cf. Ben Sira 42:9–14; 7:24–25; Warren C. Trenchard, *Ben Sira's View of Women,* Brown Judaic Studies 38 (Chico, Calif.: Scholars Press, 1982); Patrick W. Skehan and Alexander A. Di Lella, *The Wisdom of Ben Sira,* The Anchor Bible (New York: Doubleday & Co., 1987); Moshe Z. Segal, *The Complete Book of Ben Sira* (Jerusalem: Mosad Bialik, 1956) [Hebrew]. Segal often makes cogent comparisons with rabbinic literature.

10. As, for example: Sarah and Isaac; Rebecca and Jacob.

11. The rabbinic explanation derives from a pun on the Hebrew root *kdm: mikedem* ("from the east") and is read as *miKadmon* ("from the 'Ancient One' "); see *Gen. Rab.* 41:7.

12. *Gen. Rab.* 51:6 presents an unfavorable view of Lot. For more negative citations, see Ginzberg, *Legends of the Jews,* vol. 1 nn. 171 and 176; but positive views can be found in *Gen. Rab.* 49:13; *Pirqe R. El.* 25; cf. Wisdom 10:6; 19:17; 1 Clem. 11:1; 2 Peter 2:7–8.

13. "Since this man has entered my house, do not perpetrate this outrage. Look, here is my virgin daughter, and his concubine. Let me bring them out to you. Have your pleasure of them . . . but don't do that outrageous thing to this man" (Judg. 19:23–24).

14. Roland de Vaux, *Ancient Israel,* vol. 1 (New York: McGraw-Hill; repr. 1965), 10; E. A. Speiser, *Genesis,* The Anchor Bible (Garden City, N.Y.: Doubleday & Co., 1964), 143; and Nahum A. Sarna, *Understanding Genesis* (New York: Jewish Theological Seminary/McGraw-Hill, 1966), 150.

15. *t. Sota* 3:12; *Sipre Deut.* 43; *b. Sanh.* 109a; *Lev. Rab.* 5:2; Ginzberg, *Legends of the Jews,* vol. 5 n. 155 on Abraham.

16. *m. Neg.* 12:6.

17. *Tanhuma, Vayera* 12.

18. *b. Nazir* 23a.

19. *b. Nazir* 23a–b.

20. *Gen. Rab.* 51:8–9.

21. *Gen. Rab.* 51:8.

22. Modern scholars offer different explanations for the origins of the Moabite and Ammonite peoples; see John Skinner, ed., *A Critical and Exegetical Commentary on Genesis,* The International Critical Commentary (Edinburgh: T. & T. Clark, 1969), 314.

23. *Gen. Rab.* 51:11; *b. Nazir* 23b; *b. Hor.* 10b.

24. *b. Nazir* 23b–24a; *b. B. Qam.* 38b.

25. *b. B. Qam.* 38b; *b. Yebam.* 63a and 77a.

26. It is particularly relevant to mention in this context David Noel Freedman's paper, which claims that the relationship of the two stories is so significant that he believes they emanate from the same author. See D. N. Freedman, "Dina and Schechem, Tamar and Amnon," *Austin Seminary Bulletin* 105 (1990): 51–63. Freedman adduces detailed, persuasive evidence—in themes, vocabulary, and so on—for common authorship. There is much substance in this article, and he concludes that the aim of the stories was to teach that violation of virgins would have serious repercussions beyond those prescribed in the law codes. I differ with Freedman on one point: his article reflects a modern sense of outrage at rape, and he imposes that standard on a text written from the perspective of an androcentric world.

27. *b. Ber.* 60a; a variant explanation for the name "Dinah" is given in *Gen. Rab.* 72:6, claiming that the matriarchs assembled to pray, saying, "We have sufficient (*dayyenu*) males; let [Rachel] be remembered." See further chapter 5 on Hannah.

28. Meir Sternberg, an Israeli critic, implicitly agrees with the rabbis regarding the importance of recurrent verbs in the Dinah story, like "take," "give," and "go out"; see Danna N. Fewell and David M. Gunn, "Tipping the Balance: Sternberg's Reader and the Rape of Dinah," *JBL* 110 (1991): 193–211. The verb "to go out" is played on richly by the rabbis in *Midrash Genesis Rabbah.* Dinah is also described as a gadabout in *Pseudo-Philo* 8:7f. and *Tg. Job* on 2:9.

29. *Gen. Rab.* 80:5.

30. *Gen. Rab.* 80:12.

31. *Gen. Rab.* 80:5.

32. *Gen. Rab.* 18:2; 45:5; 80:5.

33. *Gen. Rab.* 80:1.

34. *Gen. Rab.* 72:5. As in the tales of Lot's daughters, and even more so Tamar, continuity of the chosen people is an end that always justifies the means.

35. *Gen. Rab.* 79:8; 80:4.

36. *b. Šabb.* 32b; *Lev. Rab.* 37:1.

37. *Gen. Rab.* 80:4.

38. There is a midrashic opinion that Dinah married Job, who was not an Israelite.

39. *Gen. Rab.* 80:4.

40. *b. Šabb.* 32b.

41. Clinton Bailey sees the cultural impetus toward vengeance as a more dominant motivating factor than love in this situation; see "How Desert Culture Helps Us Understand the Bible: Bedouin Law Explains Reaction to Rape of Dinah," *Bible Review* 7 (1991): 14–21, 38. The Bible indicates in the stories of Dinah, Tamar, and the Song of Songs that the brothers play a more protective role than does the father. This seems in keeping with the traditions of the ancient Near East, as described by Rivkah Harris, "Independent Women in Ancient Mesopotamia?" in *Women's Earliest Records: From Ancient Egypt and Western Asia,* ed. B. S. Lesko (Atlanta: Scholars Press, 1989), 153.

42. *Pirqe R. El.* 38. (The translation is mine.) There is a general tendency in this work to glorify biblical figures, even female ones.

43. *'Abot R. Nat. b* 3:14.

44. *Gen. Rab.* 57:4; 80:11; *Pirqe R. El.* 38; Victor Aptowitzer, "Asenath, the Wife of Joseph: A Haggadic Literary-Historical Study," *Hebrew Union College Annual* 1 (1924): 239–306. An alternate view has her giving birth to the Saul listed in Simeon's genealogy (Gen. 46:10); *Gen. Rab.* 80:11.

45. *Gen. Rab.* 80:4. The rabbis accomplish this match by connecting the Hebrew word *nevalah,* meaning "disgraceful," from the biblical narrative about Dinah (Gen. 34:7) with its occurrence in Job 2:10, where it is applied to his wife, whom they thus identify as Dinah; *Gen. Rab.* 57:4.

46. *Gen. Rab.* 80:11.

47. A full literary analysis is presented in Shimon Bar-Efrat, "The Narrative of Amnon and Tamar," in his book *Narrative Art in the Bible* (Sheffield, Eng.: The Almond Press, 1989).

48. This is the most commonly offered interpretation by modern scholars; see Ganse Little, "II Samuel, Exposition," in *The Interpreter's Bible,* vol. 2 (Nashville: Abingdon Press, 1953), 1113.

49. On this theme of sister marriage, see Skinner, *Genesis,* 237.

50. *b. Sanh.* 21a; *b. Yebam.* 23a.

51. E.g., Little, *The Interpreter's Bible,* 2, 1113.

52. *b. Sanh.* 21a.

53. Ibid.

54. Ibid.

55. Ben Sira 7:24–25; 23:3–5 (second century B.C.E.) depicts the

lack of warmth and closeness in father and daughter relationships; Trenchard, *Ben Sira's View of Women*, 129–65.

56. Phyllis Trible, *Texts of Terror: Literary-Feminist Readings of Biblical Narratives*, Overtures to Biblical Theology (Philadelphia: Fortress Press, 1984), 53–54.

57. *m. 'Abot* 5:19 [my translation].

58. In fact, the levirate marriage had been instituted to solve the problem of a deceased man who left no progeny; it ensured that his name would not be erased from Israel (Deut. 25:5).

59. *The Interpreter's Dictionary of the Bible*, 4, s.v. "Zelophehad."

60. *b. Sanh.* 8a; *Tanhuma Pinchas* 8; S. Wertheimer, ed., "Midrash Rabbi Akiva," in *Batei Midrashot*, vol. 2 (Jerusalem: Ketav Yad Yosef; repr. 1982), 486.

61. *Sipre Num., Pinchas* 133; Rashi on Num. 27:7.

62. *Zohar* 3:157a.

63. *Sipre Num., Pinchas* 133; translated in Montefiore and Loewe, *A Rabbinic Anthology*, 510.

64. *b. B. Bat.* 119b.

65. *Sipre Num., Pinchas* 133; *Num. Rab.* 21:11.

66. *b. Yoma* 66b. *Hakhamah* is also a term for a midwife.

67. *b. B. Bat.* 12a. There are different opinions offered on this important subject of prophecy. Nevertheless, it shows that the wise man became the leader figure in rabbinic Judaism; see Travers V. Herford, *Talmud and Apocrypha* (New York: Ktav, 1971), 71–72.

68. *Num. Rab.* 21:11.

69. *b. B. Bat.* 119a–b; *Yalqut Shimoni, Pinchas.*

70. *b. Šabb.* 96b; *b. B. Bat.* 119a.

71. See *b. B. Bat.* 115b for a discussion of this complicated issue of inheritance.

72. *Sipre Num., Pinchas* 133.

73. *Num. Rab.* 21:10; *Tanhuma Pequde* 7.

74. Trible, *Texts of Terror,* 100–2.

75. David Marcus discusses the possibility that Jephthah may have had other children. I reject this conclusion, because the absence of other children heightens the tragedy; see his *Jephthah and His Vow* (Lubbock, Tex.: Texas Tech Press, 1986), 28.

76. *b. Roš. Hoš.* 25b.

77. Ben Sira 46:11–12; Josephus, *Ant.* 5.7.10 [264]; Heb. 11:32–34; cf. *b. B. Qam.* 92b.

78. *Gen. Rab.* 60:3.

79. Ibid.

80. Ibid.

81. On the subject of sacrificialist and nonsacrificialist traditions about Jephthah's daughter, see Marcus, *Jephthah and His Vow,* 9f.

82. *Tanhuma Behuqqotai* 5 (toward the end).

83. Trible, *Texts of Terror,* 108.

84. Esther Fuchs, "Marginalization, Ambiguity, Silencing: The Story of Jephthah's Daughter," *Journal of Feminist Studies in Religion* 5 (1989): 36.

85. Marcus, *Jephthah and His Vow,* 8–9.

86. Cheryl Anne Brown, *No Longer Be Silent: First Century Jewish Portraits of Biblical Women,* Gender and the Biblical Tradition (Louisville, Ky.: Westminster/John Knox Press, 1992), 100–101; and Daniel J. Harrington, "Pseudo-Philo," in *The Old Testament Pseudepigrapha,* vol. 2, ed. James H. Charlesworth (Garden City, N.Y.: Doubleday & Co., 1985), 353. Pseudo-Philo displays a keen interest in naming women to the biblical genealogical lists.

87. In *b. B. Bat.* 91a some unnamed biblical women are provided with names by the rabbis, but not Jephthah's daughter.

88. It should be noted that even the radical extent to which Pseudo-Philo favorably develops the character of Seila is mitigated, as Esther Fuchs remarks ("Marginalization, Ambiguity, Silencing," 45), by the elaborate biblical dramatization of the father's anguish as a strategy to limit the horror of his behavior.

7

Hope for the Harlot: The Estate of the Marginalized Woman

As one would imagine, harlotry ran afoul of everything that Jewish tradition and culture stood for. The social practice of prostitution challenged all of the normative institutions so carefully constructed over the course of many centuries: marriage and family; a well-defined framework of modest behavior, particularly, though not exclusively, for women; and strict codes of sexual morality. Rabbinic law set out certain codes of proper female demeanor and behavior that were designed to restrain the anarchic possibilities of uncontrolled sexuality. Women were obliged to be modest and to remain safely within the sphere of domesticity, finding social status as wives and (especially) mothers. The occurrence of harlotry in ancient Israel was something that the rabbis had to explain and somehow encompass within their moral framework—a challenging problem to be sure. The biblical figures of Rahab and Tamar, as viewed in the aggadic traditions of the Talmud and Midrash, are good examples of how the rabbis came to terms with this disturbing phenomenon. Other, nonbiblical harlot tales in rabbinic literature will help us to understand their evaluation of the biblical harlot-heroine.

Scholars have studied the subject of prostitution and the role and place of prostitutes in ancient Israel.[1] There is ample evidence in scripture for the existence of prostitution as a professional–commercial institution. There is also reference to cultic or sacred prostitution, although this form of harlotry is generally characterized as a foreign intrusion into Israelite Temple practice. Though scripture documents the persistent practice of commercial prostitution, scripture never countenances it. Commercial prostitution was not criminalized, but it was strongly condemned. In contrast to several other ancient literatures where the professional harlot or sacred prostitute was occasionally introduced as a civilizing force, in Judaism harlotry was always seen as a corrupting force.[2] Professional harlotry is addressed numerous times in Proverbs, always with an explicit warning of the dangerous challenge it poses to family morality.[3]

Nevertheless, despite the emphasis on family and on modesty, despite a highly censorious attitude in scripture, prostitution did exist. One theory about what might have impelled some women in ancient Israel to engage in commercial harlotry proceeds from the following (and to my mind dubious) assumption. Women were active in Israelite religious life, and one form of devotion other than prayer that was heavily practiced by women was the making of religious vows. Vows often entailed certain monetary or material obligations. When a woman was unable to override her husband's opposition to a vow she had undertaken—which happened often—and having no financial independence, she would resort to prostitution to earn the means of fulfilling the terms of her vow. Though she acted as a commercial prostitute, turning over her earnings to the Temple gave the activity a sacred overtone.[4]

This theory seems to me to be too contrived. In a society where adultery was punishable by death, women who achieved the respectable status of matrimony would hardly jeopardize their status in this way. It would seem that women of ancient Israel entered this oldest profession for the same social and economic reasons as prostitutes have for thousands of years.

One of the ways scriptures communicated negative value to its own and to succeeding generations was its wide use of the word *prostitute* (*zonah*) in a figurative sense.[5] Often, especially in the later prophetic books, the root *zanah* is used metaphorically to criticize Israel for the sinfulness of forsaking God and "playing the harlot" with foreign cults. Paradoxically, one scholar observes, the metaphor is used not to indict women, but is addressed to men, who are responsible for a backsliding society:

> Its female orientation does not single out women for condemnation; it is used rather as a rhetorical device to expose men's sin. By appealing to the common stereotypes and interests of a primarily male audience, Hosea turns their accusation against them. It is easy for patriarchal society to see the guilt of a "fallen woman"; Hosea says, "You (male Israel) are that woman!"[6]

This rhetorical trope is not, however, the focus of this study. Rather, my interest here is the rabbis' view of the institution of prostitution and their interpretation of harlot characters in scripture. Harlotry was considered a sin in rabbinic literature, yet it was openly acknowledged. The rabbis said that "ten measures of harlotry went down into the world—nine were taken by Arabia and one by the rest of the world."[7] Beyond obvious criticism of the neighboring peoples, the adage indicates that the rabbis, although trying to censure and minimize the occurrence of harlotry among the Israelites, at the same time cannot help but acknowledge its existence.

Yet, when confronting what they saw as aberrant human behavior, the sages are more condemnatory in theory than in practice. The rabbis believed that individual marginalized women could be transformed and reinstated as useful individuals in society. Even more astonishing, in midrashic interpretation such women would become the progenitors of important people in Israel's future. But let us first examine the sages' attitudes toward the temptations of harlotry.

Harlot Tales

These aggadic stories intend to convey how bad things can get when a man gets tangled up with harlots.

> For a certain student once left his *tefillin* [phylacteries] in a hole adjoining the public way, and a harlot passed by and took them,

and she came to the Beth ha-Midrash and said: See what So-and-so gave me for my hire, and when the student heard it, he went to the top of a roof and threw himself down and killed himself. Thereupon they ordained that a man should hold them [*tefillin*] in his garment and in his hand and then go in.[8]

This story relates how a young student left his *tefillin* outside a public privy. A passing prostitute happened on them; and, though the story does not tell us how she identified their owner, she used them to humiliate him. The young man is so mortified that—though the narrative holds that he had done nothing untoward—he commits suicide. This disciple seems to have taken to heart the teaching that "the Holy One, blessed be He, is long-suffering for everything except immorality"[9]—a harsh scrupulousness against harlotry indeed. The tale indicates the high standards the rabbis held for themselves as students of Torah.

Another account is that of a well-known rabbi, Eleazar b. Dordia, who had been so addicted to harlotry that he would travel great distances to experience a new practitioner.

It was said of R. Eleazar b. Dordia that he did not leave out any harlot in the world without coming to her. Once, on hearing that there was a certain harlot in one of the towns by the sea who accepted a purse of *denarii* for her hire, he took a purse of *denarii* and crossed seven rivers for her sake.[10]

As the harlot is lying with him, she teases him by saying, "As this blown breath will not return to its place, so will Eleazar b. Dordia never be received in repentance." He is utterly shaken by this remark and leaves on a pilgrimage of *teshuvah* (repentance). His quest ends in his death but gains for him forgiveness. A heavenly voice, it is said, was then heard to proclaim that R. Eleazar b. Dordia was destined for the life of the world to come. Eleazar b. Dordia, though he perishes, is forgiven for his sins, for *teshuvah* can erase sin.

Additional talmudic tales reinforce the point that Torah will keep a man from succumbing to the blandishments of the prostitute. Two rabbis come to a fork in the road, one path leading to a place of idol worship and the other to a place of harlotry. One rabbi wanted to choose the way of idol worship, believing that the inclination for this transgression had already been abolished, because Jews were no longer tempted by paganism. The other rabbi preferred to confront the temptation of harlotry head-on and receive thereby the reward for resisting the lure of sin. When they approached the place of the harlots, the women withdrew; the resulting lesson is that Torah protects against lewdness.[11] This idea is reinforced in 'Abot de Rabbi Nathan: "Torah is an antidote to harlotry." Rabbinic literature often emphasizes that Torah will keep a person from succumbing to sin, as the quoted adage from 'Abot de Rabbi Nathan illustrates.[12] Among similar temptation stories, two feature R. Meir and R. Akiva, respectively, showing how their learning protects these great sages from Satan, who has come to trouble them in the guise of a woman.[13]

Another story shows how a rabbi who abandons his Torah falls into evil ways:

> A Voice from Heaven went forth and said: *Return, ye backsliding children* [Jer. 3:22]–except Aḥer [i.e., R. Elisha b. Abuyah]. [Thereupon] he said: Since I have been driven forth from yonder world, let me go forth and enjoy this world. So Aḥer went forth into evil courses. He went forth, found a harlot and demanded her. She said to him: Art thou not Elisha b. Abuyah? [But] when he tore a radish out of its bed on the Sabbath and gave it to her, she said: It is another [Aḥer].[14]

A young student, renowned for his piety and especially concerned with observing the precept of the ẓiẓit (plural, ẓiẓiot; the ritual fringe men are commanded to wear upon their garments), heard about a certain harlot and decided to seek her out. He forwarded her fee in advance and went to her home, where she had decked out her couch to receive him.[15] At the moment he was to sin, however, the four fringes of his garment struck him across the face, and he pulled back from the brink of temptation.

> It was taught: . . . There is not a single precept in the Torah, even the lightest, whose reward is not enjoyed in this world; and as to its reward in the future world I know not how great it is. Go and learn this from the precept ẓiẓit (fringes). Once a man, who was very scrupulous about the precept of ẓiẓit, heard of a certain

harlot in one of the towns by the sea who accepted four hundred gold [*denars*] for her hire. He sent her four hundred gold [*denars*] and appointed a day with her. When the day arrived he came and waited at her door. . . . "That man who sent you four hundred gold . . . is here and waiting." . . . When he came in she prepared for him seven beds. . . . [A]ll of a sudden the four fringes [of his garment] struck him across the face; whereupon he slipped off and sat upon the ground.[16]

Astonished, the harlot asked what fault he found in her. He replied that he had simply remembered that the *ẓiẓiot* taught one to fear the Lord. So impressed was she that she thereupon went to his master, converted to Judaism, and decked out her bed for him lawfully; in other words, the pair ended up marrying properly.

Among other things, this latter story shows that the harlot could easily be converted and accepted in rabbinic society. More than that! Harlots who repent are, in the rabbis' aggadic elaboration, forgiven and shown to live on and eventually to produce legitimate, even righteous, offspring—indeed, to become the progenitors of heroes of Israel. Thus rabbinic literature held out hope for the harlot, who could be rehabilitated and integrated into respectable society.

Biblical "Harlots": Rahab and Tamar

We turn now to consider Rahab, the one harlot who appears by name in the Bible, and Tamar, a biblical figure whose disguising of herself as a harlot is a key plot element in her story. According to scripture, one of Tamar's twin sons, Zerah, had a cord of crimson tied about his wrist as a sign that he was the firstborn. The rabbis don't pick up this connection; but, if I may conjecture, perhaps this crimson cord ties the story of Tamar with that of Rahab, who employed a crimson cord in her rescue of her family. Both of these women had unusual stories. Rahab's is the story of an actual harlot who is so impressed by the valor of the conquering Israelites that she joins the people of Israel in their destiny and becomes the mother of priests and prophets. Tamar's story, though played out on the small canvas of a single family, is no less dramatic, and her actions are certainly no less resourceful and courageous. She was allowed to waste away in her so-called widowhood, which was not really widowhood, for she was still bound by her husband's family, not having been released by the levirate custom. She is an example of a woman who empowers herself to change her woeful destiny. According to rabbinic sources, all her actions are done for the sake of the continuity of the Jewish people through the Holy Spirit working in her. These two women become paradigms of courage and symbols of self-directed, destiny-changing action. Though these women operated for a time in the marginalized space of the harlot, the rabbis found hope for their redemption through the courage and selflessness of their own actions. The Bible refers without censure to the stratagem of harlotry employed by Tamar and to the professional harlotry of Rahab. Not only do the rabbis not condemn these two women, but they rehabilitate them so thoroughly through midrashic exegesis that both women are transformed into exceptional figures—virtually heroines of the nation.

The Rehabilitation of Rahab

Rahab's story is given in the book of Joshua (2:1–24; 6:22–25). A woman of Jericho, she is described as an *'ishah zonah,* a harlot woman. According to scripture, she lives within the wall of the city, that is, in the disreputable outskirts. This suggests that she kept a house easily available to men going in and out of the city, in the outlying quarters away from the daily life of the respectable inhabitants of the town. The spies sent by Joshua lodge at her house, and when the king sends for them with harm's intent, she hides them. Thus she betrays her own people in favor of the Israelites. Her motivation is not clear, but it seems to be that she acts to protect her father, mother, brothers—"all her father's household"—in exchange for helping the spies to escape. Rahab and her household are in fact saved when the Israelites return, and the reader of scriptures looks upon her with great favor.

Indeed, she is described favorably in the Talmud, so much so that the rabbis' tradition marries her to Joshua, the conquering hero. In the Midrash she becomes a progenitor of priests and prophets.[17] What motivated the rabbis to refashion a biblical harlot into a mother of the righteous? Although there was an attempt on the part of some commentators to "clean up" Rahab's story, as is typical in midrashic literature, there are rabbinic sources that maintain that she was most definitely a harlot. These "tough-minded" rabbis nonetheless come to terms with her profession and contribute to the exegetical project of attributing to her outstanding qualities. Little by little Rahab is rehabilitated or transformed in rabbinic exegesis from harlot to proselyte and, ultimately, to a suitable wife for a hero of the nation.

One sanitizing version offered by some commentators is that she was an innkeeper.[18] The root of the word *zonah* (*zn*) is shared with the word *zon*, "to feed," and is the key to transforming her into an innkeeper. Another sage suggests that she kept the perfumery.[19] Josephus also depicts her as an innkeeper.[20]

Several talmudic traditions hold that Rahab had played the harlot throughout the forty years that the Israelites wandered in the desert. (She took up harlotry at the age of ten.) Her sinful way of life becomes, with sharp exegetical irony, the means of her redemption. Consorting as she had with *all* the kings and rulers of the age, she learned of the successful exploits of the Israelites, and this moves her to convert to their religion. "How did she know [of the incident at the Red Sea (Josh. 2:10)]? . . . Because, as a master said, 'There was no prince or ruler who had not possessed Rahab the harlot.' "[21] The rabbis go so far as to suggest that she was a better proselyte than both Jethro and Naaman—that she acknowledged God more completely than they did, declaring that He was God on both heaven and on earth.[22]

The rabbis have it that she married Joshua, and they ascribe to her many righteous descendants—priests and prophets—

including the prophets Huldah, Jeremiah, and the priest Hilkiah. The sages state that Joshua had no sons, only daughters. This midrash comes to explain how a proselyte could come to be an ancestor of priests, for priesthood is transmitted through the male line: men from priestly lines married into her line of descendants.[23] Once again, as we saw in the above aggadic narrative about the harlot and the *ziziot*, a positive attitude is shown toward harlots who become proselytes. Perhaps it was the paradigm of Rahab that set this pattern for the rabbis.

There is only scant instance of rabbinic chastisement directed at Joshua for taking a harlot and proselyte as wife.[24] Generally the attitude is more positive, however. One midrash suggests that Rahab did not come to Israel sheerly of her own volition, but with the encouragement of a righteous Israelite, by whom is meant Joshua.[25] But some give her the full credit. Borrowing imagery from the Song of Songs, the rabbis describe Rahab as a dove who freely flocked to join the ranks of Israel.

> Sovereign of the Universe, because Thou bringest light into the world Thy name is magnified in the world. And what is the light? Redemption. For when Thou bringest us light, many proselytes come and join us, as for instance Jethro and Rahab. Jethro heard the news and came, Rahab heard and came.[26]

> When a certain kind of dove is being fed, the other doves smell the food and flock to her cote. So when the Elder sits and expounds, many strangers at that time become proselytes, like Jethro who heard and came, or Rahab who heard and came.[27]

Once she becomes a proselyte, we observe, she is no longer called a harlot (Rahab the harlot). Several midrashim, then, transform Rahab into a righteous person. One important midrash even lists her as a woman of valor together with twenty-one other women, including the four matriarchs, Ruth, Jael, the mother of Samson, and others.[28]

As was noted earlier, both beauty and modesty are qualities the sages often attribute to female characters whose stories they embroider. When describing Rahab, however, the question of modesty does not come up. In consideration of her past career, that subject was probably thought better left alone.[29] Moreover, her beauty or attractiveness is given in rather suggestive terms.

According to the sages, the very sound of her name evoked sexual excitement.[30]

> The Rabbis taught: there have been four women surpassing beauty in this world—Sarah, Rahab, Abigail, and Esther. . . . Rahab inspired lust by her name. . . . [Another opinion says]: Whosoever says, "Rahab, Rahab" at once has an issue. [Another sage said]: I say Rahab, Rahab and nothing happens to me![31]

They interpret her name, whose etymology means "broad" or "open," as implying sexual looseness, indicating that they construed it as meaning "wide-open."[32]

Nonetheless, the rabbinic sources find redemption for her from her fallen condition in noting that she sinned with three things—namely, the commandments for women concerning the rituals of dough, *niddah* (the laws of menstruation), and lighting of candles; but she is forgiven for these because of three acts that she performed—namely, the actions involving the rope, the window, and the wall—all important objects figuring in her protection of the spies.[33] This midrash, like other commentaries exonerating her, shows that adoption of Israelite law and custom can be considered as an act of repentance and can bring salvation for any person—man or woman—no matter the gravity of one's past sin. As noted above, "Torah is an antidote to harlotry" and a preventive against sin.

Tamar: A Woman's Vindication

Although the story of Rahab chronologically follows that of Tamar of Genesis (not to be confused with Tamar of Samuel), I chose to deal with Rahab first because Rahab is unequivocally a prostitute, whereas Tamar's "involvement" in harlotry is more complicated. The portion in Genesis (chapter 38) describing the liaison between Judah and Tamar is a mystery.[34] Why did Tamar, a decent widow, have to resort to the ruse of prostitution in order to attain her rightful status in society?

In the biblical story, Tamar had been married successively to two sons of Judah, both of whom died, leaving her childless. Er was punished with death for a sin that is not specified; his brother Onan married Er's widow according to the levirate law; but he, too, commits a sin. This sin is spelled out—in fact, bears his name, onanism. It is the act of spilling his seed on the ground, thereby thwarting procreation. In this act, he refuses to carry on his brother's name.

Judah sends Tamar home to wait for Shelah, his third son, to grow up. As time passes it becomes evident to Tamar that Judah has no intention of marrying her to his third son and that she is doomed to the ignominy of childless widowhood.

She takes matters into her own hands and exchanges her widow's garb for that of a harlot. The biblical text is puzzling on this point, saying that "she covered her face with a veil, and, wrapping herself up, sat down at the entrance to Enaim, which is on the road to Timnah," and later, "when Judah saw her, he took her for a harlot; for she had covered her face" (Gen. 38:15).[35] She waits, then, for her father-in-law, who is said not to recognize her and who solicits her for a sexual act. They agree on a price (a kid from his flock), and Tamar carefully obtains from him a surety in advance, asking for items that will serve as identification: his signet, cord, and staff. They conclude their agreed transaction, and Tamar thus conceives a child. Afterward she resumes her widow's garb. When Judah later sends the kid in payment for his act, he is told that there is no harlot in that place. Three months later he is informed that his daughter-in-law had "played the harlot . . . [and was] with child by harlotry." Judah calls for her to be brought forward to be burnt, whereupon Tamar shows the three items and says to him "I am with child by the man to whom these belong." Judah acknowledges them as his own and declares that Tamar was more righteous than himself, because he had withheld from her his son.

It must be assumed that many women would have found themselves in the unfortunate position of being widowed and childless, but few would have had the courage to take matters into their own hands as Tamar did. This indicates that Tamar, in keeping with her name, which means "date tree," was strong and sturdy. The date tree was also a symbol of fertility, an irony, given her barrenness in two marriages.[36] Tamar actively takes steps to change her destiny, by an act that defies the patriarchal order, in the interest of allowing her, ultimately, to fulfill herself according to its terms.

Although Tamar was a widow, her childlessness meant that she did not possess the independence of the widow with children. A widow with children could feel the security of knowing she would be looked after, because her children would inherit their father's estate and could be assumed to provide for their mother. A childless widow, in contrast, received no estate. Under the laws of levirate marriage, the childless widow was at the mercy of the brother-in-law who was supposed to marry her, but who might refuse, leaving her in an untenable and insecure position. Widows were not as desirable for marriage as were virgins. Tamar took a great risk in her bold solution to her predicament, for she was regarded in society as a married woman and therefore subject to the death penalty for adultery.

Tamar is trapped in the customs of biblical society. She is neither an independent widow nor a dependent wife. She is an abandoned woman who is barren, so she devises a plan that, at the risk of her life, will enable her to bear a child, the only means for her to attain status in society and security in life. As the Midrash states: "Who secures the woman's position in her home? Her children."[37] A wife did not inherit from her husband, and Tamar acts according to a logic dictated by this patriarchal fact. The patriarchal laws of marriage and inheritance make it more urgent for her to acquire a child than to find a husband, and this she shrewdly contrives to accomplish.

We will consider one more item—the matter of deception—before turning to rabbinic analysis. Deception is a key feature in the Tamar narrative but is not unique to her story. In fact, women figure prominently in several narratives turning on the use of deception: Sarah's brother-sister ruse staves off the death of Abraham at the hands of King Abimelech (Gen. 20:1–18); Rebecca sends off Jacob to his father all decked out as Esau (Gen. 27:8–16); Rachel deceives her father by hiding the household gods (Gen. 31:34); the midwives in Egypt fail to kill the Israelite newborns (Ex. 1:15–21); Michal the daughter of Saul deceives her father and helps David escape (1 Sam. 19:11–

17); Jael kills Sisera by deception, as she welcomes him to her tent (Judg. 4:17–24).

It has been suggested that women, being the weaker party, have often resorted to deception to oppose the stronger party;[38] however, men too used these sorts of ploys to advantage, even on occasions when they are not the weaker party, as in the stories of Ehud and the King of Moab (Judg. 3:12–31); Joshua and the Gibeonites (Josh. 9:3–16); Jacob and Laban, and so on.[39] Women, however, are not only noted for their frequent recourse to deceptive stratagems; they are characterized as frivolous and indecisive when they resort to ruse, whereas when men use these methods, they are credited with political astuteness and presence of mind.[40] Awareness of this issue of deception has come to light as a result of modern, feminist scholarship and does not figure in rabbinic retelling of these stories.

The rabbinic retelling does not construe Tamar as either deceptive or a harlot.[41] To the contrary, in the rabbis' version she is transformed into a woman of exceptional modesty, a quality they generally grant to female characters of whom they approve. But they do ask about the veil, which on the surface is an act of deception.[42] Their answer? Her wearing the veil did not mislead Judah. In fact, she was customarily so modest, the rabbis say, that she never uncovered her face and would not have needed to veil herself to ensure that Judah not recognize her.

As further proof that the veil was not deception, but rather valor, the sages draw a parallel between Tamar and another biblical heroine (albeit a woman whose deception was acknowledged and justified), her great-grandmother-in-law, Rebecca. Both wore veils; both gave birth to twins.

> Two covered themselves with a veil and gave birth to twins, Rebecca and Tamar. Rebecca: *And she took her veil, and covered herself* (Gen. 24:65); Tamar: *and covered herself with her veil, and wrapped herself* (Gen. 38:14).[43]

Linking Tamar with the matriarch Rebecca gives her prominence and importance. Although Rebecca had twins, only one of whom (Jacob) was regarded by the tradition as great,

Tamar's twin boys both remained in the fold and one of them—Perez—was the forerunner of the Messiah.

On this issue we again observe the interweaving of *halakhah* and *aggadah*. In their exegetical musing on this textual puzzle, the rabbis prescribe that men should see the female members of their family so that they do not run the risk of someday committing the same sinful act as did Judah.[44] Altogether, the rabbinic tradition rescues Tamar from the taint of a highly questionable sexual ruse by ascribing to her a profound sense of modesty and piety.

The rabbis comment on the scriptural scene of her standing and waiting for Judah at the entrance to Einayim (Gen. 38:14). They interpret the name of the place in a manner that elevates Tamar's character, saying that she sat there piously raising her eyes (*'einayim*) in prayer so that the right course of events should occur and that what she had seen through *ruaḥ hakodesh* (the power of prophecy) should come to pass.[45] The rabbis attribute piety to Tamar and place the *ruaḥ hakodesh* behind the whole incident. They turn her for the moment into a prophetess who foresaw that through her would come kings and princes of the messianic line. Tamar is truly exonerated in aggadic tradition. The signs of the signet, cord, and staff are said to represent royalty, the Sanhedrin, and the messiahship, the implication being that she will give birth to this lineage.[46]

The sages heap further praise on her. The fact that she did not reveal the name of her father-in-law as the "culprit" and embarrass him publicly, at the risk of herself being burned as an adulteress, is held up as an act of selfless courage: "It is better that he should cast himself into a fiery furnace than put his fellow to shame in public."[47] Her selfless heroism is held up to future generations as praiseworthy and exemplary.

The rabbis' great concern lest individuals be shamed in public led them to prohibit certain passages of the Bible from being read out loud in synagogue, for this would cast an unflattering light on some of the biblical ancestors. According to the Mishnah, certain passages could be read aloud in the synagogue but were not to be translated, and some were not to be read in public at all.[48] Among those that could be read but not translated are Genesis 35:22, which describes Reuben's sin with his father's concubine Bilhah; the story of David's adultery with Bathsheba (2 Sam. 11:2–17); and Amnon's incest with his sister Tamar (2 Sam. 13:1–4).

The story of Judah and Tamar is brought up in this discussion, yet—to our surprise—the decision is that their story may be both read and translated. Why should this have been the case? The Talmud doesn't tell us why, but a contemporary theory offers a possible explanation. All of these biblical incidents deal with improper, sometimes illicit, sexual activity. The first three are destructive of the social fabric, leading, in the case of Reuben, to distrust and resentment; in the case of David, to the death of Uriah; and, in the case of Amnon, to his own death and bitter family strife. In contrast, the union of Judah and Tamar does not mar the social fabric, but repairs it. Therefore the rabbis set the tale of Tamar apart from the other three incidents and acknowledge its socially constructive message. For this reason, the rabbis regarded Tamar in a favorable light and permit her story to be read publicly.[49]

There is a tendency in the Talmud to exonerate those seen as heroes even when they are guilty of foibles and misdeeds. Therefore men like David and Judah are subject to little censure for their peccadilloes. It is interesting that Judah is criticized less for the incident with Tamar than for marrying a Canaanite woman.[50] This Canaanite woman is described in pseudepigraphic sources as hating Tamar and influencing the spiteful actions of her sons against her, which lead in turn to their deaths.[51]

Still, some questions remained about adultery, a grave sin in Judaism. The rabbis compare Tamar to another adulterer, Zimri ben Salu (Num. 25:14). Although both Tamar and Zimri committed adultery, Tamar committed adultery and gave rise to kings and prophets, whereas Zimri's adultery resulted in the deaths of many tens of thousands of Israelites. The Talmud continues with a discussion in which Rav Nachman states that a transgression performed out of good intention is better than a precept performed out of evil intention.[52] This is the one time the rabbis call Tamar's act adulterous, but they immediately exonerate her and go on to discuss her in the terms of an exemplary heroine.

Conclusion

Our analysis of rabbinic attitudes toward prostitutes has shown a surprising degree of tolerance, not toward the institution but toward the women themselves and their potential for rehabilitation. The perspective is always male, however. These stories never enter the head or heart of the woman involved. Nevertheless, the image is a variegated one. Each instance presents its own moral message, and that message is not always the same. The story of the student who commits suicide at the mere hint of impropriety indicates the harshest of attitudes toward immorality, whereas the student who converts his paramour reflects a far more lenient one. Though Rahab and Tamar operated for a time in the marginalized space of the harlot, they became paradigms of courage and symbols of self-directed, destiny-changing action. The rabbis found hope for the women's redemption through the courage and selflessness of their own actions. The sages were not always as magnanimous toward the less idealized women of their own generation.

Rabbinic belief in the power of *teshuvah,* even for prostitutes, should not be confused with modern-day notions of fairness toward women. A story shocking modern sensibilities is that of Beruriah's sister, who is cast into a brothel by her Roman captors. At Beruriah's insistence, her famous husband R. Meir goes to rescue the girl. Arriving in disguise as a client, he tests her virtue to determine if she is worthy of rescue. She deflects his advances by trying to convince him of her unsuitability as a consort, and Meir is convinced that she has retained her honor. This tale is disturbing for several reasons. First, it indicates that only the "good girl" is worthy of being saved. It further identifies the rape victim with her fate, suggesting that she somehow had control over what happened to her. The tendency to blame the victim may be tied to the idea of divine punishment for sins and the justness of one's fate. As Rachel Adler astutely observes: "Women are assumed to be solely responsible for sexual behavior, even when pressured, deceived, or entrapped by men. Chastity is the measure of women's worth, and there are no extenuating circumstances."[53] If the power of repentance was placed entirely in the hands of the sinful woman, so was the blame for her sinful actions.

Notes

1. *The Interpreter's Bible*, 3, 931–34, s.v. "Prostitution"; *The Encyclopaedia Judaica*, 13, 1243–47, s.v. "prostitution"; *The Encyclopedia of Religion*, 6, 309–13, s.v. "hierodouleia"; Phyllis Bird, " 'To Play the Harlot': An Inquiry into an Old Testament Metaphor," in *Gender and Difference in Ancient Israel*, ed. Peggy L. Day (Minneapolis: Fortress Press, 1989), 75–94, and "The Harlot as Heroine: Narrative Art and Social Presupposition in Three Old Testament Texts," *Semeia* 46 (1989): 119–39; Mary K. Wakeman, "Sacred Marriage," *JSOT* 22 (1982): 21–31; Michael C. Astour, "Tamar the Hierodule: An Essay in the Method of Vestigial Motifs," *JBL* 85 (1966): 185–96; Camp, *Wisdom and the Feminine*, 112–20.

2. Numerous examples of the civilizing effect of a harlot can be seen in other literatures parallel to biblical times. The Gilgamesh Epic, for example, one of the oldest works from ancient Mesopotamia, offers a positive image of a prostitute. In it, a harlot introduces Enkidu, a mythical man-beast, to the culture and ways of the world. She is thus portrayed not as a corrupting force but a civilizing one. See "The Epic of Gilgamesh," in *Ancient Near Eastern Texts*, ed. James B. Pritchard (Princeton, N.J.: Princeton University Press, 1955), 75. The old Indian myth of Rsysrnga offers a parallel story about a harlot. In both stories, the courtesan can be understood allegorically, as representing human culture and therefore able to transform a semiwild creature into a civilized human being; see further *The Encyclopedia of Religion*, 6, 310, s.v. "hierodouleia."

3. Prov. 2:16–22; 5:3–23; 6:24–30; 7:5ff.; and, esp., 7:10–23.

4. For more on women's vows, see Karel Van der Toorn, "Female Prostitution in Payment of Vows in Ancient Israel," *JBL* 108 (1989):

193–205; and Gruber, "Women in the Cult according to the Priestly Code," 38.

5. Erlandsson, for example, discusses the meaning of the word *zanah* and shows that in the Hebrew Bible it is used just as frequently in its figurative meaning. See S. Erlandsson, *The Theological Dictionary of the Old Testament*, vol. 4, ed. G. J. Botterweck and H. Ringgren (Grand Rapids: Wm. B. Eerdmans, 1978), 104, s.v. "zanah." The term *zonah* is found in the following texts relating to the period of the monarchy or later. The meaning varies according to the content of the text, whether literal or figurative: Lev. 21:7–14; Deut. 23:19; 1 Kings 3:16; 22:38; Isa. 1:21; 23:15–16; Jer. 3:3; 5:7; Ezek. 16:30–41; 23:44; Hos. 4:14; Joel 4:3; Micah 1:7; Nahum 3:4.

6. Bird, " 'To Play the Harlot,' " 89.

7. *b. Qidd.* 49b.

8. *b. Ber.* 23.

9. *Gen. Rab.* 26:5.

10. *b. 'Abod. Zar.* 17a.

11. *b. 'Abod. Zar.* 17a–b.

12. *'Abot R. Nat. a.* 20:1.

13. *b. Qidd.* 80a. As pointed out by Rachel Adler, Beruriah was not granted similar dispensation by being saved from sexual temptation through her Torah learning; see Adler's "The Virgin in the Brothel," 26.

14. *b. Hag.* 15a.

15. See Prov. 7:17.

16. *Sipre Num.* 115 and *b. Menah.* 44a.

17. Cf. Matt. 1:5, where Rahab is said to be the mother of Boaz, and hence an ancestor of King David and, supposedly, also Jesus as well.

18. *Tg. Onq.* on Josh. 2:1 and other sources translate the word *zonah* from the root in Hebrew, "to feed," thus describing her as an innkeeper; see A. Sperber, *The Former Prophets (Targum Jonathan)*, vol. 2 of *The Bible in Aramaic* (Leiden, Neth.: E. J. Brill, 1959), 2.

19. *Ruth Rab.* 2:1.

20. Josephus, *Ant.* 5.1.2[7–8].

21. *b. Zebah.* 116 a–b.

22. *Deut. Rab.* 2:26; *Sipre Deut.* 78; and Ephraim E. Urbach, *The Sages: Their Concepts and Beliefs* (Jerusalem: Magnes Press, 1975), 21 and 553.

23. *Ruth Rab.* 2:1; *Num. Rab.* 8 (end); 16:1; *b. Meg.* 14b; cf. Matt. 1:5.

24. Ginzberg, *Legends of the Jews*, 6, 173 n. 19.

25. *Eccl. Rab.* 8:10.

26. *Cant. Rab.* 1, 3, 3.

27. *Cant. Rab.* 1, 15, 2; 4, 1, 2.

28. *Midrash Mishle* 31:21.

29. It is important to keep this in mind when we turn to the question of whether Tamar was considered a harlot by the rabbis: Tamar *is* credited by them as conducting herself with especially strong modesty.

30. See *b. Meg.* 15a, in which the voice of Jael is said to be so alluring that merely hearing it was a sexual provocation to men.

31. *b. Meg.* 15a.

32. *b. Meg.* 14a–15a; cf. *b. Ta'an.* 5b.

33. *Mekilta, Yitro* 57 and *b. Zebaḥ.* 116b.

34. It has given rise to considerable scholarship in the effort to understand the meaning of this story in its socioreligious setting; e.g., Susan Niditch, "The Wronged Woman Righted: An Analysis of Genesis 38," *Harvard Theological Review* 72 (1979): 143.

35. The text is puzzling in that covering oneself is usually considered proper, modest behavior, not shameless and loose. But perhaps this was necessary to explain how Judah could find her impossible to recognize.

36. Ps. 92:12; Mordecai A. Friedman, "Tamar, a Symbol of Life: The 'Killer Wife' Superstition in the Bible and Jewish Tradition," *AJS Review* 15 (1990): 23–26.

37. *Gen. Rab.* 71:5.

38. Robert C. Culley, "Structural Analysis: Is It Done with Mirrors?" *Interpretation* 28 (1974): 174–81.

39. Esther Fuchs, " 'For I Have the Way of Women': Deception, Gender, and Ideology in Biblical Narrative," *Semeia* 42 (1988): 68–83; Johanna W. H. Bos, "Out of the Shadows: Genesis 38; Judges 4:17–22; Ruth 3," *Semeia* 42 (1988): 37–67.

40. Fuchs (" 'For I Have the Way of Women' ") cogently makes this point.

41. This is in contrast to some contemporary feminist scholarship; see Bird, " 'To Play the Harlot,' " 75–94, and "The Harlot as Heroine," 119–39.

42. The fact that Tamar covered herself with a veil has posed difficulties for many interpreters. In the ancient world, harlots did not cover themselves, for a veil was the symbol of a woman belonging to and being under the protection and authority of one man. Some scholars maintain that the sacred prostitute did cover her head and that this would explain this puzzling feature in the biblical narrative. This does not seem to be a satisfactory explanation, however, because Tamar is described in the text as disguising herself with a veil and a wrap as a *zonah* (a commercial prostitute, v. 14). She also stations

herself in an open place, which would be the mode of the common commercial prostitute, although later in the biblical text she is referred to as a *kedesha* (a sacred or cultic prostitute, v. 21). As mentioned above (note 35), the veiling may have been a plot necessity to explain how she could remain incognito to her father-in-law. See Astour, "Tamar the Hierodule"; Wakeman, "Sacred Marriage"; and Joan G. Westenholz, "Tamar, Qedeša, Qadištu, and Sacred Prostitution in Mesopotamia," *Harvard Theological Review* 82 (1989): 245–65.

43. *Gen. Rab.* 85:7; cf. *b. Soṭa.* 10a.

44. *Gen. Rab.* 85:8; *b. Soṭa* 10b; and *b. Meg.* 10b.

45. *Gen. Rab.* 85:7.

46. *Gen. Rab.* 85:9.

47. *b. Ber.* 43b; *b. Pesaḥ.* 10b; cf. *m. 'Abot* 3:12.

48. *m. Meg.* 4:10.

49. Niditch, "The Wronged Woman Righted," 149.

50. Some rabbis found it difficult to accept that Judah would marry a Canaanite woman and explained the word as meaning that she was the daughter of a merchant (Gen. 38:2); *b. Pesaḥ.* 50a; *Tg. Onq.* to Gen. 38:2 translates *ka'anani* as *tagrah,* which means "merchant"; cf. Prov. 31:24.

51. *Testament of the Twelve Patriarchs, Judah,* chapters 8 and 10–12 and *Jubilees* 41; see Kee, "Testaments of the Twelve Patriarchs," in *The Old Testament Pseudepigrapha,* vol. 1, 797–98; Orville S. Wintermute, "Jubilees," in *The Old Testament Pseudepigrapha,* vol. 2, ed. James H. Charlesworth (Garden City, N.Y.: Doubleday & Co., 1983), 130.

52. *b. Nazir* 23a and *b. Hor.* 10b.

53. Adler, "The Virgin in the Brothel," 103.

8

"Deborah, Say Your Song": Female Prophecy in Talmudic Tradition[1]

Many of the women of the Bible are recorded in connection with traditional female roles as daughter, wife, mother, and even harlot. A few characters break the mold and emerge as women of independent power. The ambivalence of rabbinic literature in its treatment of these figures is most revealing.

A definitive statement in the Talmud declares there to have been seven female prophetesses:

> Our rabbis taught: "Forty-eight prophets and seven prophetesses prophesied to Israel. . . . Seven prophetesses. Who were these?—Sarah, Miriam, Deborah, Hannah, Abigail, Huldah and Esther."[2]

The female prophetesses are enumerated by name, but surprisingly, the names of the forty-eight male prophets are not given. The only other female figures to whom the prophetic spirit is attributed by the rabbis are the matriarchs, of whom only Sarah appears in the previous list.[3] In the Hebrew Bible itself, the word *nevi'ah* ("prophetess") is applied to five specific women, three of whom—Miriam, Deborah, and Huldah—appear on the sages' list. Nodiah, the false prophetess of Nehemiah's day (Neh. 6:14), and the anonymous prophetess in Isaiah 8:3 are the two omitted from the rabbinic list.

The primary attribute of a prophet in the Jewish tradition is to serve as a channel of communication between the human

and the divine worlds. The Hebrew for (male) prophet, *navi',*
means "to call, announce," and thus to speak the word of God.
Does the *nevi'ah,* the feminine counterpart of the *navi',* function according to the sages in the same way? This chapter will
help answer this question.

"She Discerns by the Spirit of God"

Sarah's prophetic excellence is described by R. Isaac by
means of an exegetical analysis of the name *Yiskah,* which appears in a biblical account relating to Sarah:

> Abram and Nahor took to themselves wives, the name of
> Abram's wife being Sarai and that of Nahor's wife Milcah, the
> daughter of Haran, the father of Milcah and of *Yiskah* [Gen.
> 11:29].

Upon this verse, R. Isaac comments:

> Yiskah is Sarah; and why was she called Yiskah? Because she
> discerned (*sakhetah*) by means of the Holy Spirit.[4]

Nowhere does scripture say that Sarah had the power of prophecy; this is a midrashic tradition. Conversely, Abraham is called
a *navi'* in the Bible (Gen. 20:7). Some scholars suggest that the
word *nevi'ah* was used in the book of Isaiah to mean the wife of
a prophet; that is, Isaiah's wife was called this only because her
husband was a prophet (Isa. 8:3). However, a survey of Israel's
historical sources would indicate that, in general, the wife was
not given the feminine title of the husband's profession in biblical times. Certainly, the sages believed that Sarah was herself a
prophetess who, as the Talmud says, "discerned by means of
the Holy Spirit."

The sages are eager to see Sarah as a prophetess. They proceed to claim, without explicit scriptural backing, that not only
was she a prophetess, but her spirit of prophecy was even
greater than Abraham's.[5] A scriptural peg is found by R. Isaac,
who cites as proof of Sarah's prophetic ability the words of the

Lord to Abraham: "In all that Sarah tells thee, hearken to her voice" (Gen. 21:12).[6]

A further tradition about Sarah's spiritual uniqueness is found in a midrash that claimed she was the only woman in the Bible with whom God spoke: "The Holy One, blessed be He, never spoke directly with a woman save with that righteous woman [i.e., Sarah]."[7] This midrash implies that with the other prophetesses God used an intermediary.

The sages show a continuing fascination with the word *yis-kah*. Some build upon it to highlight her beauty rather than her prophetic powers. The word *yiskah* is derived from a root meaning "to look." They interpret this as meaning that all gazed at her beauty, which she retained throughout her days, even into her old age.[8] Rabbi Hisda explained the verse "After I have waxed old, I have youth" (Gen. 18:12) as meaning that once the flesh was worn and the wrinkles multiplied, Sarah was rejuvenated and her original beauty restored.[9] In the opinion of the sages, the phrasing of the biblical text (Gen. 23:1) giving Sarah a 127-year life span once again emphasizes her beauty. In scripture, the word *year* is inserted after each figure in the number of her age; this the sages take as showing that she was as beautiful at one hundred as at the age of twenty.[10]

Criticism of Sarah's behavior by the rabbis pales in comparison with the praise they shower on her. Nevertheless, the sages make even Sarah, the founding mother, subject to the frailties of the female sex. In a well-known midrash, Sarah represents a general female tendency to eavesdrop:

> The Rabbis said: Women are said to possess four traits: they are greedy, eavesdroppers, slothful, and envious . . . eavesdroppers: "And Sarah heard in the tent door" . . . R. Joshua b. Nehemiah said: "She is also a complainer." . . . "And Sarai said unto Abram: My complaint be upon you."[11]

One commentator, commenting on Kohelet's verse "A man in a thousand I found but a woman in a thousand not", gives Abraham and Sarah as the examples.[12]

A rather serious sin is attributed to Sarah in *Genesis Rabbah* and other later sources. They claim that because Sarah laughed in disbelief rather than accepting in faith that she would bear a child in her old age suggests that she lacked faith. The Midrash states:

> In an act of [God's] turning toward her, He heard her laugh within herself: "Is it possible that these bowels can yet bring forth a child, these shriveled breasts give suck? And though I should be able to bear, yet is not my lord Abraham old?"[13]

The Midrash known as *Bereshit Rabbati* claims that her lack of faith in God's promise at this important moment caused her to die young. Originally she was destined like Abraham to live 175 years, but display of disbelief in God's word led to forty-eight years of her span of life to be taken away.[14] Although Abraham also laughed (Gen. 17:17), he was not rebuked for it, either in the Bible or by the rabbis.[15]

Moreover, though the sages ascribe higher prophetic powers to Sarah than to Abraham, in reality it is empty praise, for she had little opportunity to influence the immediate world around her. One midrash, however, describes not only Abraham but also Sarah being involved in making proselytes. The Midrash writes in comment on the verse: "the souls that they made in Haran" (Gen. 12:5):

> It refers . . . to the proselytes (which they had made)? Then let it say, "That they had *converted*"; why "that they had *made*"? That is to teach you that he who brings a Gentile near (to God) is as though he created him. Now let it say, "that *he* had made"; why "that *they* had made"? Said R. Hunia: "Abraham converted the men and Sarah the women."[16]

More significantly, Sarah is totally ignored in scripture during the trauma of the *Aqedah*, the binding of Isaac, and the sages were quite aware of this. Some midrashim ask, "Where was Sarah when Abraham went to sacrifice Isaac?" Why wasn't Sarah—the only woman prophetess to speak with God, a woman superior to her husband in prophecy, one who died by a kiss of God[17]—not even consulted by her husband at the important moment of the great trial?

Later legends connect Sarah's death with the *Aqedah*. One midrash relates that Satan, disguised as an old man, tells Sarah that her son is being taken by his father to be sacrificed:

> The Satan being annoyed that he could not frustrate God's plan concerning the sacrifice of Isaac, turned his attention to Sarah. He said to her, "your old husband has seized the boy, and sacrificed him. The boy wailed and wept but could not escape from his father." Sarah began to cry bitterly and ultimately died of her grief.[18]

Another midrash relates that Satan, disguised as an old man, tells her that her son Isaac has been sacrificed. In this instance she is depicted more positively, because when Satan tells her that Isaac was sacrificed, she cries but is comforted that he was offered for a holy cause at the behest of God. The Satan subsequently returns in human form to tell her that Isaac lives. However, the shock of the experience causes her instant death.[19]

Another legend describes Abraham as vacillating over whether to tell Sarah of his intentions to sacrifice their son. This account places the words "women are lightheaded" in Abraham's mouth, implying that the wife would hinder rather than help him fulfill God's command.[20]

These latter midrashim come to answer the question, What happened to Sarah's prophetic powers in such an hour as this? Some of the answers intentionally or otherwise contrast female frailty against male stability, which apparently can withstand all difficulties. Once again the Midrash slips in the idea that women are not responsible and that they are inferior to men in tenacity of purpose and piety—even an exceptional woman like Sarah.[21] The *aggadah* invents for her what it regards as a (typically feminine) weakheaded response to the lofty event and criticizes her for showing the intense love of a mother for her son. When all is said and done, the impression remains that her greatest merit is in supporting, not leading or acting in her own person.

"Sing unto the Lord"

Revisiting Miriam's story, in light of talmudic and midrashic exegetical elaboration and imagination, we find new aspects to her character. Following scriptural lead, the rabbis regarded Miriam as a prophetess, and though scripture does not attribute any specific prophecies to her, the rabbis attributed some to her. In *Midrash Rabbah* and elsewhere she is depicted as engineering the remarriage of her parents and dancing at their wedding.[22] The Midrash on Exodus identifies Miriam with the character Puah, one of the midwives credited with saving the Hebrew infants in defiance of Pharaoh's command. They offer a variety of explanations why she is thus called, connecting the name Puah with *hofi'ah*, "lift up," saying that on a number of occasions she lifted her face in defiance:

> [She was called Puah] because she dared to reprove her father, Amram, who was at that time the head of the Sanhedrin, and when Pharaoh decreed that *if it be a son, then ye shall kill him,* Amram said it was useless for the Israelites to have children. Further he ceased to have sexual relations with his wife Jochebed and even divorced his wife, though she was already three months pregnant. Whereupon all the Israelites arose and divorced their wives. Then said his daughter to him: "Your decree is more severe than that of Pharaoh; for Pharaoh decreed only concerning the male children, and you decree upon males and females alike. Besides, Pharaoh being wicked, there is some doubt whether his decree will be fulfilled or not, but you are righteous and your decree will be fulfilled." So he took his wife back and was followed by all the Israelites, who also took their wives back. Hence she was called Puah, because she dared to reprove her father.[23]

In rabbinic tradition, Miriam prophesies the birth of Moses and foretells his brilliant career as redeemer:

> And Miriam the prophetess . . . said: "My mother will bear a son who will be the savior of Israel." When Moses was born the whole house was filled with light: and her father arose and kissed her upon her head saying, "My daughter, thy prophecy has been fulfilled."[24]

The meaning of her name is linked with the time of bondage in Egypt. The name Miriam has been variously interpreted in modern scholarship.[25] Rabbinic tradition has its own explanation, teaching that the name Miriam means "bitterness" and

rcflects her deep involvement as leader during the bitter time
of slavery.

> Why, in fact, was she named Miriam? Because, as R. Isaac said,
> Miriam means "bitterness" (*mrr*), as in the verse: "And they
> made their lives bitter (*mrr*)" (Ex. 1:14).[26]

The talmudic and midrashic sources most frequently describe Miriam and her brothers as leaders and redeemers of
their people from Egypt. "R. Jose the son of R. Judah says:
'Three good leaders (*parnasim*) had arisen to Israel, namely,
Moses, Aaron, and Miriam. For their sake three good things
were conferred upon Israel, namely the well, the pillar of
cloud, and the manna." When they died, these good things
disappeared.[27] Like the patriarchs, Miriam and her brothers are
described as dying by the kiss of God, and their corpses "are
not exposed to ravage," signs of their favor with God.[28]

The sages' most serious difficulty with the figure of Miriam
was her apparent celibacy.[29] Nowhere does the Bible state or
even hint that Miriam was married. In contrast to scripture's
two other prophetesses, both of whom are presented as the
wives of named persons, Miriam is simply introduced as the
sister of Aaron and Moses.[30] Rabbinic sources undertake to sup-
ply her with a husband and son, Caleb and Hur, respectively.
Thus Miriam becomes the ancestress of Bezalel. This match is
necessary not only to sustain the rabbis' image of women as
being made for marriage, but also to show that she was re-
warded for her efforts as a midwife; for in scripture, God promised to give the midwives who disobeyed Pharaoh's orders
households of their own (Ex. 1:21). Rabbinic tradition maintains that these midwives, named in the Bible as Shiphrah and
Puah, were actually Jochebed and Miriam, and that their descendants were given the gifts of priesthood and kingship.[31]

As shown in our discussion of Sarah, rabbinic literature
places a high value on physical and spiritual female beauty.
Though the biblical text never describes Miriam as beautiful,
the Midrash fills this lacuna. In scripture, after Miriam's sin of
slandering her brother, she was stricken with a terrible skin
disease in punishment. The Midrash narrates that Miriam con-
tracted a grievous sickness from which everyone thought she

would die, yet she recovered. God restored her youth, bestowing unusual beauty upon her so that renewed happiness awaited her husband, who had been deprived of conjugal life during her illness.[32] As one of the heroines of the nation, Miriam was given by the rabbis a pleasing appearance and an acceptable status as wife and mother.

Though the sages are discomfited by women leaders, the case of Miriam begs the rule. The one instance of rebuke against her comes in connection with her criticism of Moses, which is used as an example of women's talking too much.[33] In general, however, they portray Miriam as a fearless leader who stands up and defends Israel against destruction by her enemies. She was a prophetess who foretold redemption for her people and, as her name Puah indicated, she spoke up fearlessly for Israel against friend and foe. Although the sages try to add to the scriptural account a picture of Miriam as wife and mother, the image of Miriam that nonetheless finally emerges is of a woman and leader in her own right—one of the biblical elite with whom God conversed and finally parted, as the Midrash comments, with a divine kiss. Josephus and Philo, who lived before the sages, already manifest great respect for Miriam. Her leadership activities are praised rather than criticized.[34] The sages, like Josephus and Philo, are influenced by the incontrovertible material in the biblical text.

"Awake, Sing!"

Two outstanding women leaders mentioned in the Bible are Deborah and Huldah. Indeed, as we noted above, the rabbis acknowledge them as prophetesses. But their public careers discomfited the rabbis, who had no such immediate models and no established methodological principles for dealing with women of this caliber. Through their treatment of Deborah, in particular, we can see how they adjusted or altered the reality to meet their own preconceptions about powerful women. They do this largely through three approaches: defining her husband, attributing to her the unlovely quality of hubris (leaders often overstep that border, an invitation to midrashic transformation), and redefining her functions.

The Bible introduces Deborah as a prophetess who is married to a man named Lappidoth. Thus the rabbis turn to discover what type of person Deborah's husband was. Their investigation is more fanciful than factual, and this type of rabbinic scrutiny concerning a woman's husband is not found in connection with any other female figure whose husband is mentioned in scripture. The rabbinic mind tends to define women as belonging to men, not vice versa. So the Midrash proceeds to discuss what is meant by the words *'eshet Lappidoth,* literally, a "woman of flames," as well as "the wife of Lappidoth." Some sages said that Deborah's husband was an ignorant man and that she made wicks for the Sanctuary on his behalf so that he might achieve merit and gain a share in the world to come.[35]

Other exegetical sources discuss whether Barak, the leader of the army, was her husband. If he was her husband, why did she have to send for him? The Midrash comments on the biblical verses as follows:

> She summoned Barak son of Abinoam, of Kedesh in Naphtali, and said to him, "The Lord, the God of Israel, has commanded: 'Go, march up to Mount Tabor . . . ' " (Judg. 4:6–7). What connection was there between Deborah and Barak and between Barak and Deborah, since, to begin with, they lived some distance from each other; Deborah in her place (Mount Ephraim), and Barak in his place (Kedesh in Naphtali)? The answer is that Barak ministered to the elders during the life of Joshua and after Joshua continued to minister to them. Therefore it came about that he was fetched and joined in marriage to Deborah (who as an elder in Israel was worthy of his ministering to her).[36]

Kimhi, a medieval exegete, suggested that just as Moses separated himself from his wife when he became a prophet, so Deborah, when she became a prophetess, separated from her husband; therefore they lived apart and she had to send for him.[37] Other sages attempt to show that Barak and Lappidoth were not identical, because Barak was a learned person, unlike the ignorant Lappidoth.

Another midrashic tradition gives Deborah's husband three different names:

> In fact he had three names—Barak, Lappidoth, and Michael: Barak, because his face had the livid look of lightning; Lappidoth, because he used to make wicks which he took to the Holy Place in Shiloh; and Michael, which was his given name.[38]

The names Barak and Lappidoth are explained in this midrashic text, but not Michael, which is elsewhere explained as one who humbles himself.[39] The *Yalqut Shimoni* connects the name with the Hebrew root *mwkh*, translating "he made himself humble and therefore his name is Michael." Or perhaps this midrash is intended as a dig at Deborah, whose husband exhibits humility, a quality that is the reverse of the arrogance attributed to her? The rabbinic connection between Barak and Lappidoth might have emerged from the semantic similarity between the terms *barak* and *lappidoth*, both associated with fire or light.[40]

Now we turn to the unsettling matter of rabbinic tradition attributing arrogance to Deborah. In the words of Rav Nachman, a fourth-century Amora:

> Haughtiness does not befit women. There were two haughty [arrogant] women and their names are hateful, one being called a hornet, *ziborata* (Deborah), and the other a weasel, *kurkushta* (Huldah). Of the hornet it is written, "And she sent and called Barak, instead of going to him." Of the weasel it is written, "Say to the man," instead of, "say to the king."[41]

The larger context in which this passage appears implies that R. Nachman was suggesting that the names (given in the passage in Aramaic) are ugly and are indicative of the personalities of these women. Traditionally, names in the Bible and Talmud are taken very seriously, for they are regarded both as a key to the person named and as a guide to his or her personality. Elijah, for instance, is, according to scholars, called by the name "YHWH is God" to demonstrate that every fiber of his being was devoted to worship.[42] Although theophoric names are rare for women in scripture, women are often given animal names without any suggestion that such names are negative—however, not in this midrash.[43]

Deborah's arrogance comes up in another passage, this time from the Talmud.[44] "Rav Judah said in Rav's name: 'Whoever is boastful, if he is a sage, his wisdom departs from him: if he is a prophet, his prophecy departs from him.' " Rabbi Hillel claims that this can be demonstrated from the experience of Deborah, who boasted: "The rulers ceased in Israel, they ceased, until I arose, Deborah, I arose a mother in Israel." Her words are followed by "Awake, awake, Deborah, awake, awake, utter a song" (Judg. 5:12). Rabbinic exegesis explains that because Deborah boasted that she was a mother in Israel she was punished and the Holy Spirit was taken from her. "Awake, utter a song" was taken as an indication that the song had left her. How could the rabbis have faulted her for referring to herself as "a mother in Israel"? The sages do not say how she should have referred to herself and why that statement would merit the loss of prophecy. Clearly, there was more going on than meets the eye.

Deborah's career as judge disturbs the halakhic guidelines of the sages. For one thing, they could not accept a woman in this powerful leadership role. Regarding her role as judge, they discuss the matter at length, and a consensus is reached that she was only a prophetess appointed by God's word, but not a judge. From this interpretation of Deborah as prophetess rather than judge comes the basis for the rabbinic disqualification of women to act as judges.[45] A late midrash, *Tanna Debe Eliyahu*, took a far more liberal stance toward women fulfilling a nontraditional role. Apparently surprised to find Deborah acting as prophetess, leader, and judge, this midrash comments that the spirit of the Lord rests upon individuals according to their deeds and not because of race or gender. The Midrash states:

> What was the special character of Deborah that she, too, judged Israel and prophesied . . . ? In regard to her deeds, I call heaven and earth to witness that whether it be a heathen or a Jew, whether it be a man or a woman, a manservant or a maidservant, the holy spirit will suffuse each of them in keeping with the deeds he or she performs.[46]

The issue of modesty also arises in connection with Deborah's role as judge. As mentioned elsewhere in our discussion of

King David's daughter Tamar, the rabbis formulated the law of *yihud*, according to which a man and a woman were not permitted to be alone together in closed quarters, something a judge must do in investigating testimony. To solve the problem of modesty, the rabbis point out that she held court under a palm tree, ensuring that she was not left alone with a man in the course of fulfilling her duties.[47] This model approves of her modestly teaching and counseling outdoors to avoid being secluded with men. As it says in Judges:

> Deborah, wife of Lappidoth, was a prophetess; she led Israel at that time. She used to sit under the Palm of Deborah, between Ramah and Bethel in the hill country of Ephraim, and the Israelites would come to her for decisions (Judg. 4:4).

Summing up the discussion about Deborah, it is beyond doubt that scripture shows her as a full-fledged prophetess, teaching and leading the people of Israel in a time of crisis. The song attributed by tradition to Deborah (Judges 5) is considered by many scholars as one of the greatest ancient Hebrew poems. Although the rabbis acknowledge Deborah's greatness as prophetess, they had difficulties in coming to terms with the idea of a woman acting as a leader of such stature and authority. By analyzing this great biblical figure in terms of the "unwomanly" trait of arrogance, the rabbis diminish her towering image as a leader. Surprisingly, not one sage comes to her defense or suggests a different interpretation. This is not in keeping with the typical talmudic discussion, in which both pro and con arguments are given. Why did no one give the contrary view that scripture offers no evidence to indicate that she was arrogant?

"Say unto the Man"

The relatively unknown figure of Huldah is nevertheless unique in scripture (2 Kings 22). It can be safely stated that among the very few prophetesses mentioned in the Bible,[48] she alone appears as a woman sought out by the king for advice in an hour of crisis. When an unknown Scroll of the Law (now believed by scholars to have been the book of Deuteronomy) is discovered in the Temple, King Josiah is fearful because the people had been inadvertently disobeying the precepts contained within it. The king commands the priests to seek out Huldah and discern God's will in the matter. Huldah relates that great destruction will come in retribution for their previous disobedience; but, because of Josiah's sincere repentance, the punishment will not come during his reign.

With Huldah, too, gender questions were raised by the rabbis. The sages discuss why Huldah was chosen for delivering this particular prophecy rather than her male "relative" and contemporary, Jeremiah. They suggest that he was out of the city when the event took place; therefore Josiah turned to Huldah for advice. By describing Huldah as a relative of Jeremiah, the sages suggest that he allowed her to engage in the activity as if Huldah were under his tutelage. Further, these exegetes suggest that the tragic forebodings of the Deuteronomic scroll called for a compassionate interpretation more common to women. The rabbinic adage suggests that Huldah's female quality of compassion rather than the male quality of "intelligence" resulted in her calling.[49]

This is not to suggest, however, that all rabbinic sources reject women in leadership roles. The *Targum* looks favorably upon Huldah's public role and explains the word *bamishneh* as a place of study where she instructed men in the study of the law.[50] The image of Huldah instructing men in matters usually considered solely within the male purview should not be underestimated.

"The Lord Raises the Horn of His Anointed"

The figure of Hannah has been discussed at length above. Thus, only a brief comment here is warranted. It is difficult to understand why the sages decided to transform Hannah into a biblical prophetess. Hannah, unlike Deborah and Huldah, displays no real leadership tendencies; rather, she is a barren woman who longs for children. It is possible that Hannah was chosen as a candidate for prophecy because in her song she foretells, according to the rabbis, the fall of the house of Saul and the rise of the house of David.[51] The *Zohar* claims that Hannah's and Deborah's songs are the greatest ever written, unmatched by any attributed to men.[52]

"Hear the Word of Your Handmaid"

Abigail was one of the wives of King David. She first appears in 1 Samuel 25:3 as the intelligent, beautiful wife of the wealthy but wicked sheep farmer Nabal. Nabal refuses sanctuary to David and his followers, who are fleeing from Saul. David and his men prepare to attack, but one of Nabal's shepherds explains to Abigail what is happening. She takes action. Without her husband's knowledge, Abigail prepares a large stock of provisions and brings them to David. She pleads for David's sufferance, and he, quite pleased, grants it and peacefully goes his way. Shortly thereafter, Nabal dies, and David sends for Abigail to be his wife.

Abigail's biblical actions have been variously interpreted as either those of a model wife or a shrewd woman.[53] The rabbis attributed to her a prophecy dealing with an event in the life of David. According to the rabbis, David was aroused by Abigail, but she stopped him by revealing that she was in her *menses;* therefore intercourse was forbidden. In the biblical story, Abigail says in her conversation with David: "Do not let *this* be a cause of stumbling" (1 Sam. 25:31). The rabbis infer from the word "this" that something else (other than she) would be his stumbling block, namely, the incident of Bathsheba. The rabbis indicate that she foresaw this prophetically.[54]

To my view, however, Abigail's behavior in the Bible recalls the image of a biblical wise woman more than that of a prophetess.[55] She shows great skill and wisdom in her handling of

David and in saving her husband's life and household. This raises the question of why the sages designated her a prophetess rather than a wise woman.

The relationship between what is meant by a "prophet" and what is meant by a "sage" or "wise person" in rabbinic theology is a large subject. For our purposes, let us point out that the Talmud states that when the spirit of prophecy departed from Israel, it went into the *hakhamin,* the sages.[56] The sage becomes more favored than the prophet. The rabbinic source *Seder Olam* states that before the time of the sages, the prophets prophesied through the medium of the Holy Spirit, but: "From now on incline your ear and listen to the words of the wise sages."[57] The title *hakham* (wise man) came to be more a *learned* man than wise, per se; and the term was restricted solely to the male elite of teachers and sages. In one place the sages do apply the Aramaic term *hakhmiya* to Miriam, but in this instance it means midwife, one wise in the skills of midwifery.[58] In another place, the Talmud describes the daughters of Zelophehad as *hakhmaniyot,*[59] although a parallel version calls them *hakhamot.*[60] Adjectival use of the word (*hakhmaniyah,* "a wise person") does not confer the same titular status on the bearer as would the nominal use—*hakhamot* ("the Wise"). Because the talmudic teachers take the title of "the Wise" for their elite class of male scholars and teachers, they do not normally apply it to women, not even biblical women who are treated with greater respect than women of their own time. It is possibly because of this that, although Abigail emerges in the Bible as a wise woman, the sages express their admiration for her activities by imputing to her prophecy for having foretold the tragic events that would befall David and Bathsheba.

"She Put on Royal Robes"

The story of Esther opens with Ahasuerus, one of the most powerful rulers of the ancient world, holding a munificent banquet. With drunken enthusiasm he commands Queen Vashti to be brought forth so that he may display her beauty before the party attendees. Vashti's refusal and subsequent dethroning, which engender the whole story of Esther, results in an empirewide search for a replacement queen. Esther, the lovely orphan girl who had been raised by her uncle Mordecai, is selected to be the new queen. Mordecai apparently holds a position in the royal court and comes to offend the high official Haman by not bowing down to him, as was Haman's due.[61] As a result, Haman plots revenge against all Jews throughout the realm. A royal decree is issued, and the doom of the Jews seems certain.

Mordecai prevails upon Esther to intercede on behalf of her people before the king. Esther, whose true identity as a Jew is unknown at court, is reluctant to expose herself but ultimately agrees. Commanding that the Jews fast for her, she risks her own life by defying Persian protocol and appearing before the king uninvited. She finds favor with the king, however, who grants her an audience. Thereupon, she requests that he come with Haman to a special banquet that will be prepared for the three of them. At the party, Ahasuerus is charmed and offers to grant whatever Esther desires. She asks only that he and Haman return for a second banquet the following night. At the second banquet, she reveals that Haman's machinations would undo her along with the rest of the Jews, for she too was a Jew. Incensed, the king orders Haman's execution and allows the Jews to defend themselves, because the original order against them cannot be rescinded. Mordecai, Esther, and the Jews emerge victorious, and the holiday of Purim is proclaimed, the events being recorded in a book.

What moved the rabbis to crown Queen Esther with prophecy? After all, there is no hint of this in the text. Moreover, the book she supposedly penned is surprisingly secular in tone, not once mentioning the name of God.[62] Yet the Talmud ordains her as prophetess, basing itself on this verse: "Now it came to pass on the third day that Esther clothed herself in royalty" (Esth. 5:1). "Surely it should say, 'royal apparel'? What it shows is that the holy spirit clothed her."[63]

In keeping with the rabbis' religious values, they first transformed Esther into a pious Jewess observing the tenets of her faith in the manner of Daniel and his friends: "Daniel resolved not to defile himself with the king's food or the wine he drank, so he sought permission of the chief officer not to defile himself" (Dan. 1:8). Although the biblical account makes no such claim, the rabbis assert that Esther observed Jewish law in the king's palace. Not only did she keep the Sabbath; she would not eat of the king's food, but, like Daniel and Judith, remained faithful to the laws of *kashrut.*

> [In reference to] the seven maidens who were given to her (Esth. 2:9), Rava said: "[They were seven so that] she could count the days of the week by them [and keep track of which day was the Sabbath]." "And he changed her and her maidens" (Esth. 2:9). Rav said: "[This means that] he gave her Jewish food to eat."[64]

Nevertheless, this prophetess's sexuality, even more than her spirituality, pervades talmudic and midrashic sources. The biblical book of Esther mentions her great beauty in three different verses (Esth. 1:11; 2:3, 7). Her physical beauty makes her the object of a king's desire, and it leads to her ability to save her nation. The rabbinic material on Esther's sexual appeal and appearance fills numerous pages and is very erotic in tone. To the rabbis, Esther was one of the four most beautiful women ever created: "Our rabbis taught: There have been four women of surpassing beauty in the world—Sarah, Rahab, Abigail, and Esther." Like her ancestress Sarah, she remained eternally young.[65]

Perhaps the rabbis understood Esther's prophetic ability to mean her leadership. Talmudic sources inform us that Esther sent a letter to the sages requesting that they perpetuate her name, book, and festival for all generations.[66] This talmudic reference echoes the biblical account of her leadership aspirations (Esth. 9:29f.). At first the sages refused her request, saying a commemoration of her festival would lead to hatred against the Jews. But she refuses to give up her demand, mentioning that she was already recorded in the annals of the Persians and wants to be remembered by her own people. Eventually they yield. In this midrash it may have been the rabbis themselves who were transformed. Required to confront the model of a woman in an unusual capacity, they come to accept and value her actions.

Why they accepted her leadership uncritically, in contrast to how they treated Deborah's, may have something to do with the legal issues of judges and courts that the rabbis were dealing with at that time. Deborah as judge presented more of a threat than did Esther. Esther, after all was said and done, was still the wife very much under control of her kingly husband. She stood in contrast to so-called "arrogant" Deborah, who summoned Barak to come to her from afar. Queen Esther waited, with both strength and temerity, to be recognized and summoned into her husband's presence. Perhaps that is why so much is elaborated on her physical beauty. The dual role that she played—savior of her people and tiptoeing wife—enabled the midrashists to heap glory upon her.

Conclusion

Based on the material presented here, the following conclusions can be drawn concerning the rabbinic sages' views on biblical prophetesses. They attributed a variety of functions to those they designated as prophetesses. Prophecy was comprised of religious instruction and occasional predictions. The earliest individuals who were called prophets in ancient times were persons endowed with the gift of song; in later times, such individuals were consulted to discern the word of God.[67] Although the talmudic scholars do not divide the prophetesses into two types in this way, their understanding of the nature of prophecy is implicitly informed by both of these meanings. Sarah was a prophetess because she spoke with God and gave advice to Abraham. Miriam qualified as a prophetess because she predicted the career of her brother Moses and was instrumental in leading the people from slavery to freedom.

Deborah and Huldah seem to be included on the rabbis' list of prophetesses because the Bible itself so categorized them; but the rabbis do not discuss the prophetic activities of these characters, and they sharply criticize rather than praise their personal demeanor. The sages seem to have difficulty in coming to terms with powerful women who were leaders of the people and who overshadowed their male contemporaries. In this, Deborah and Huldah were unlike Miriam, for Miriam was on a par with Aaron but of less significance than Moses, and therefore posed less of a problem in the minds of the sages. In contrast to Deborah and Huldah, who are paradigms of prophetic leadership, Hannah and Abigail did not particularly discomfit the rabbis, most probably because neither entered the male realm of public leadership. Hannah's prophetic function was manifested in her song, in which she prayed and predicted future events in the life of the nation. Abigail also foretold the future in a way that aided her husband.

The rabbis saw in Esther a spirit of prophecy, which strengthened her and enabled her to wield power to save her people. Unlike the other six women, Esther did not speak with God, sing a song, foretell the future, teach (like Huldah), or lead (like Deborah). No doubt the word *prophetess* was applied to her because she was an important woman, a queen, who delivered her people from oppression.

The material presented here, it must be stressed, exemplifies rabbinic attitudes toward an elite group of female figures, the biblical prophetesses. Although the sages tend to describe their activities with great respect and interest, nevertheless, in some instances they attribute to even the finest of these biblical women negative characteristics ascribed to the female gender as a whole. This is best illustrated by the midrashim that accuse Sarah of being an eavesdropper, Miriam of being a talebearer, and other characters of being guilty of various other feminine failings.[68] This shows that the rabbis, despite their obvious admiration for the biblical prophetesses, could not entirely separate their general attitudes regarding the proper role of women from their response to these powerful, competent women.

In fairness, we should reiterate that there was no monolithic view among the sages regarding woman leaders any more than there was on other topics. In their treatment of men, their aggadic brushstrokes were also sometimes white, sometimes black.

Notes

1. This chapter is based on a paper originally published as "Biblical Prophetesses through Rabbinic Lenses," *Judaism 40* (1991): 171–83.

2. *b. Meg.* 14b.

3. *Gen. Rab.* 67:9; *Midrash Tehillim* 105, 14.

4. *b. Meg.* 14a; see also *b. Sanh.* 69b.

5. *Ex. Rab.* 1:1.

6. *b. Meg.* 14a; *Gen. Rab.* 47:1.

7. *Gen. Rab.* 20:6.

8. *Gen. Rab.* 40:4; *b. Sanh.* 69b.

9. *b. B. Meṣ.* 87a.

10. Rashi on Gen. 23:1. The tradition of Sarah's beauty existed even before the sages, as is witnessed by the *Genesis Apocryphon* found among the Dead Sea Scrolls. Joseph A. Fitzmyer, *The Genesis Apocryphon of Qumran Cave I* (Rome: Pontifical Institute, 1966), col. 20:2ff.

11. *Gen. Rab.* 45:5; cf. 18:2.

12. *Eccl. Rab.* 7:49. For more unflattering comments concerning Sarah, see Ginzberg, *Legends of the Jews,* 5, 236 n. 142.

13. *Gen. Rab.* 48:16–20.

14. Chanoch Albeck, ed., *Bereshit Rabbati, Va'era* (Jerusalem: n.p., 1940), 18:12–13.

15. *Tg. Onq.* on Gen. 17:17; cf. *Tg. Onq.* on Gen. 18:12. One should compare the disparity of treatment between biblical heroes and heroines, such as Aaron and Miriam, Adam and Eve, and so forth.

16. *Gen. Rab.* 39:14.

17. The *Zohar* tradition is that Sarah, like the patriarchs and other great figures, died by the kiss of God. *Zohar,* vol. 2, 125b.

18. *Pirqe R. El.* chap. 32.

19. *Sefer Ha-Yashar, Vayera.*

20. *b. Šabb.* 33a.

21. Ibid.; *b. Qidd.* 80b; cf. Rashi on *b. 'Abod. Zar.* 18b.

22. *b. B. Bat.* 120.

23. *Ex. Rab.* 1:13.

24. *Ex. Rab.* 1:13; *b. Sota* 12b. A different version is given by Pseudo-Philo; see Harrington, "Pseudo-Philo," 2, 297.

25. A recent study by Burns gives a detailed analysis of the name Miriam in light of the latest research: Rita J. Burns, *Has the Lord Indeed Spoken Only through Moses?* SBL Dissertation Series 84 (Chico, Calif.: Scholars Press, 1987), 87ff.

26. *Ex. Rab.* 26:1; *Midrash Pesiqta Rabbati,* ed. M. Friedmann (Vienna: n.p., 1880; Israel: n.p., repr. 1888), 5:50b.

27. *b. Ta'an.* 9a.

28. *b. Mo'ed Qat.* 28a; *b. B. Bat.* 17a.

29. This is in sharp contrast to a Christian interpretation of Miriam, in which she is viewed as a typology of Mary, the virgin mother of Christ. See R. Le Deaut, "Miryam, soeur de Moise, et Marie, mère du Messie," *Biblica* 45 (1964): 198ff.

30. In Ex. 15:21, only Miriam is mentioned; in Num. 12:1–15 and Micah 6:4, all of the siblings are mentioned.

31. *Ex. Rab.* 1:16–17.

32. *b. Sota* 12a; *Ex. Rab.* 1:17.

33. *Gen. Rab.* 45:5. This is part of the list of women's negative attributes that appears in rabbinic literature in several versions (*Gen. Rab.* 18:2; 45:5; and 80:5), each of which lists different biblical women as examples.

34. Josephus, *Ant.* 4.4.6 [78]; Philo, *Moses* 1.180; *Agr.* 80f.; Sly, *Philo's Perception of Women,* 119–22. Nevertheless, Josephus omits other important information about Miriam.

35. *b. Meg.* 14b; cf. *Midrash Eliahu Rabba (Tanna Debe Eliyahu),* chap. 9, edited by M. Friedmann [Ish-Shalom] (1904; reprint, Jerusalem: Wahrmann Books, 1960), 48ff.

36. Ibid.

37. David Kimhi (1160?–1235?) on Judg. 4:6.

38. Ibid. *Midrash Eliahu Rabba* 9.

39. *Yalqut Shimoni* (Jerusalem: Lewin/Epstein, 1941–42), Judg. 4:1.

40. *Midrash Eliahu Rabba,* chap. 10, p. 50.

41. *b. Meg.* 14b.

42. Leila L. Bronner, *The Stories of Elijah and Elisha* (Leiden, Neth.: E. J. Brill, 1968), 23.

43. It is interesting to note that Josephus (*Ant.* 5.5.2 [200]) states

that the people sought help from a prophetess whose name was Deborah, which meant "a bee" in Hebrew. Though he attributes no sinister connotations to the name, in light of the later rabbinic comment it is of interest that he mentions it at all. It is amusing to note that Semonides of Amorgos, who lived in the seventh century B.C.E., in his unflattering description of the creation of woman, enumerates seven animals from which woman was made. He claims that only the one made of the bee is a good wife. This early Hellenic tradition had obviously not reached the sages. See further *The Encyclopaedia Judaica*, vol. 12 (Jerusalem: Keter Publishing House, 1972), 803ff.; and J. P. Sullivan, *Women in Classical Literature* (Los Angeles: UCLA, 1988), 5–7.

44. *b. Pesaḥ.* 66a.

45. *Tosafot Nid.* 50a.

46. *Midrash Eliahu Rabba,* chap. (9)10, p. 152; cf. Gal. 3:28.

47. *b. Meg.* 14b.

48. As pointed out above, these are Miriam, Deborah, Huldah, Nodiah, the false prophetess of Neh. 6:14, and the anonymous prophetess in Isa. 8:3.

49. *b. Meg.* 14b.

50. *Tg. Ps.-J.* on 2 Kings 22.

51. *b. Meg.* 14a.

52. *Zohar,* vol. 4, Lev. 19b.

53. *The Anchor Bible Dictionary,* vol. 1 (New York: Doubleday & Co., 1992), 15–16, s.v. "Abigail."

54. *b. Meg.* 14b.

55. Bronner, "The Changing Face of Woman from Bible to Talmud," n. 2.

56. *b. B. Bat.* 12a; *b. Soṭa* 48b.

57. *Midrash Seder Olam,* vol. 6, ed. M. K. Mirsky (Brooklyn, N.Y., 1988), 140.

58. Gross, *Ozar HaAgadah,* s.v. "Hakham."

59. *b. B. Bat.* 120a.

60. *Sipre Num., Pinchas* 133; and *Num. Rab., Pinchas* 21:11.

61. Cf. Esth. 2:21 and Dan. 2:49.

62. *b. B. Bat.* 15a attributes the authorship of Esther to the Men of the Great Assembly.

63. *b. Meg.* 14b.

64. *b. Meg.* 13a.

65. *b. Meg.* 15a.

66. *b. Meg.* 7a. The biblical book makes reference to a similar letter sent to all the Jews in Esth. 9:29f.

67. Brown, Driver, and Briggs, *A Hebrew and English Lexicon,* 612.

68. *Gen. Rab.* 18:2; 45:5; 80:5.

Conclusion: Complexity and Contradiction in the Rabbinic Construction of Woman

It is often thought that because the rabbis held an androcentric worldview, they were unrelentingly repressive and unreceptive toward women and their daily condition. Yet, by assuming that the rabbis merely stereotyped women, we in turn stereotype the rabbis. As a result of my analysis, I have presented a more balanced picture than one might have anticipated.

There is no question that the society in which the sages lived was male dominated. Still, the aggadic discourse of the rabbis gave women greater rights and protections within their limited domestic realm. Moreover, biblical models were treated with respect and comparative open-mindedness by the sages relative to their time. The biblical female represented a particular type of woman. She had to be viewed as a paradigm—for good or for evil—because she was a part of scripture. As such, she was larger than life and was viewed rather differently than was the average woman of the rabbis' own milieu. Biblical women were object lessons that taught contemporary women how to behave. In their narrative retellings about biblical women, these teachers stressed—and sometimes created—those attributes that they wanted women of their own day to emulate.

Nevertheless, there remain a number of disturbing dilemmas concerning the rabbinic approach to women. Despite their sometimes surprisingly open-minded views, the rabbinic vision for women was, and in traditional circles still is, constricted. Although the sages were able to recognize virtue and heroism in female

characters, even ascribing to them certain admirable qualities nowhere explicit in the biblical narratives, their retellings are also rife
with contradictions and stereotypes of feminine characteristics. I
have demonstrated a repeated pattern whereby the rabbis initially
note traits of weakness and threatening sexuality on the part of
women in biblical stories. They then formulate canons of female
behavior designed to restrain the explosive, anarchic energies of
woman's intrinsic seductiveness, which must be controlled by strict
codes of modesty and in the valorized roles of matrimony and
motherhood. These rules, encoded in the value of modesty, relegate women to the private sphere of home and family responsibility, and remove them from learning and leadership, the keys to
power and prominence in rabbinic Judaism.

At times it is difficult for a woman to be faithful to laws based on
principles that are inappropriate in the social context of our times.
Rabbinic hierarchical values prevent women today from participating equally in public life. Although modesty may have had a protective benefit for women in antiquity, in today's world, modesty
standards have changed. The question poses itself, Should this traditional Jewish value be reinterpreted? Should we reexamine basic
Jewish values, such as modesty, family, and marriage? The difficulty
is in eliminating inequity and one-sidedness, but not sacrificing
what is important and eternal in Judaism.

I have taken pains to recognize and present what the aggadic
traditions of Talmud and Midrash actually say about women, rather
than what in retrospect we might like them to have said, so that the
process of reinterpretation and recuperation can proceed on an
honest and authentic ground. The reconsideration and reinterpretation of texts is an exciting project, and I hope that this study
might be taken as part of a larger trend toward looking at the
women of the Bible and Talmud afresh, and that it encourages
further studies in the emerging tradition of depatriarchalizing interpretation.* Therefore, the task for women and men is to forge
ahead with a new undertaking. Without giving up our personal
religious identifications and love for sacred and quasisacred texts,
we must reclaim biblical women with our *own* midrash and rein-
state them as paradigms for our modern lives.

*Trible, "Depatriarchalizing in Biblical Interpretation," 218, 234–35.

Bibliography

Adler, Rachel. "A Mother in Israel: Aspects of the Mother Role in Jewish Myth." In *Beyond Androcentrism: New Essays on Women and Religion,* edited by R. M. Gross. Missoula, Mont.: Scholars Press, 1977.

————. "The Virgin in the Brothel: The Legend of Beruriah." *Tikkun* 3 (1988): 28–31, 102–5. Reprinted in *Vox Benedictina* 7 (1990): 7–29.

Aggadot Bereshit. Vol. 4. Edited by Adolph Jellinek. Jerusalem: Wahrmann Books, 1967.

Alter, Robert. *The Art of the Biblical Narrative.* New York: Basic Books, 1981.

Amaru, Betsy Halpern. "Portraits of Biblical Women in Josephus' *Antiquities.*" *JJS* 39 (1988): 143–70.

The Anchor Bible Dictionary. Vol. 1. New York: Doubleday & Co., 1992.

Aptowitzer, Victor. "Asenath, the Wife of Joseph: A Haggadic Literary-Historical Study." *Hebrew Union College Annual* 1 (1924): 239–306.

Archer, Léonie J. "The 'Evil Woman' in Apocryphal and Pseudepigraphical Writings." In *Proceedings of the Ninth World Congress of Jewish Studies.* Division A: *The Period of the Bible.* Jerusalem: WUJS, 1986.

Arthur, Marylin B. "The Origins of the Western Attitude Toward Women." In *Women in the Ancient World: The Arethusa Papers,* edited by J. Peradatto and J. P. Sullivan. Albany: SUNY Press, 1984.

Astour, Michael C. "Tamar the Hierodule: An Essay in the Method of Vestigial Motifs." *JBL* 85 (1966): 185–96.

Babylonian Talmud. Edited by I. Epstein. London: Soncino Press, 1952.

Babylonian Talmud. Venice edition. New York: Yam Ha-Talmud/ Shulsinger Bros., 1948.

Bailey, Clinton. "How Desert Culture Helps Us Understand the Bible: Bedouin Law Explains Reaction to Rape of Dinah." *Bible Review* 7 (1991): 14–21, 38.

Bar-Efrat, Shimon. "The Narrative of Amnon and Tamar." In *Narrative Art in the Bible.* Sheffield, Eng.: The Almond Press, 1989.

Barr, James. "The Symbolism of Names in the Old Testament." *The Bulletin of the John Rylands Library* 62 (1969): 1–29.

Baskin, Judith R. "Introduction." In *Jewish Women in Historical Perspective,* edited by Judith R. Baskin. Detroit: Wayne State University Press, 1991.

Bereshit Rabbati. Edited by Chanoch Albeck. Jerusalem: n.p., 1940.

Berkovits, Eliezer. *The Jewish Woman: In Time and Torah.* Hoboken, N.J.: Ktav, 1990.

Berman, Saul. "The Status of Women in Halakhic Judaism." *Tradition* 14 (1973). Reprinted in *The Jewish Woman: New Perspectives,* edited by Elizabeth Koltun. New York: Schocken Books, 1976.

Biale, Rachel. *Women and Jewish Law: An Exploration of Women's Issues in Halakhic Sources.* New York: Schocken Books, 1984.

Bialik, Hayim Nahman. *Halachah and Aggadah.* Translated by Leon Simon. London: pamphlet published by the Education Department of the Zionist Federation of Great Britain and Ireland, 1944.

Bialik, Hayim N., and Y. H. Ravnitzky. *Sefer Ha-Aggadah.* Tel Aviv: Dvir, 1955.

Biblia Hebraica Stuggartensia. Edited by R. Kittel et al. Reprint. Stuttgart: Deutsche Bibelgesellschaft, 1984.

Bird, Phyllis. "The Harlot as Heroine: Narrative Art and Social Presupposition in Three Old Testament Texts." *Semeia* 46 (1989): 119–39.

———. " 'To Play the Harlot': An Inquiry into an Old Testament Metaphor." In *Gender and Difference in Ancient Israel,* edited by Peggy L. Day. Minneapolis: Fortress Press, 1989.

Bloch, Renee. "Midrash" and "Methodological Note for the Study of Rabbinic Literature." Reprinted in *Approaches to Ancient Judaism: Theory and Practice,* edited by William Scott Green. Missoula, Mont.: Scholars Press, 1978.

Bos, Johanna W. H. "Out of the Shadows: Genesis 38; Judges 4:17–22; Ruth 3." *Semeia* 42 (1988): 37–67.

Botterweck, G. J., and H. Ringgren, eds. Vol 1, *The Theological Dictionary of the Old Testament.* Grand Rapids: Wm. B. Eerdmans, 1970–72.

Boyarin, Daniel. *Carnal Israel: Reading Sex in Talmudic Culture.* Berkeley: University of California Press, 1993.

_____. "Reading Androcentrism against the Grain: Women, Sex and Torah Study." *Poetics Today* 12 (1991): 29–52.

Bronner, Leila L. "Biblical Prophetesses through Rabbinic Lenses." *Judaism* 40 (1991): 171–83.

_____. "The Changing Face of Woman from Bible to Talmud." *Shofar* 7 (1989): 34–47.

_____. "From Veil to Wig: Jewish Women's Hair Covering." *Judaism* 42 (Fall 1993): 465–77.

_____. "Gynomorphic Imagery in Exilic Isaiah." *Dor Le Dor* [*The Jewish Quarterly*] 12 (1983/84): 71–76.

_____. *Sects and Separatism during the Second Jewish Commonwealth.* New York: Bloch Publishing Co., 1967.

_____. *The Stories of Elijah and Elisha.* Leiden, Neth.: E. J. Brill, 1968.

Brooten, Bernadette J. *Women Leaders in the Ancient Synagogue: Inscriptional Evidence and Background Issues.* Brown Judaic Studies 36. Chico, Calif.: Scholars Press, 1982.

Brown, Cheryl Anne. *No Longer Be Silent: First Century Jewish Portraits of Biblical Women.* Gender and the Biblical Tradition. Louisville, Ky.: Westminster/John Knox Press, 1992.

Brown, F., S. R. Driver, and C. A. Briggs. *A Hebrew and English Lexicon of the Old Testament.* Reprint. Oxford: Clarendon Press, 1951.

Burns, Rita J. *Has the Lord Indeed Spoken Only through Moses? A Study of the Biblical Portrait of Miriam.* SBL Dissertation Series 84. Chico, Calif.: Scholars Press, 1987.

Callaway, Mary. *Sing, O Barren One: A Study in Comparative Midrash.* SBL Dissertation Series 91. Atlanta: Scholars Press, 1986.

Camp, Claudia V. *Wisdom and the Feminine in the Book of Proverbs.* Bible and Literature Series 11. Decatur, Ga.: The Almond Press, 1985.

Campbell, Edward F., Jr. *Ruth.* The Anchor Bible. Vol. 7. Garden City, N.Y.: Doubleday & Co., 1975.

Charles, R. H. *The Apocrypha and Pseudepigrapha of the Old Testament in English.* 2 vols. Oxford: Clarendon Press, 1913; repr. 1979–83.

Charlesworth, James H., ed. *The Old Testament Pseudepigrapha.* 2 vols. Garden City, N.Y.: Doubleday & Co., 1983–85.

Cohen, Shaye J. D. *From the Maccabees to the Mishnah.* Library of Early Christianity. Philadelphia: Westminster Press, 1987.

_____. "Women in the Synagogues of Antiquity." *Conservative Judaism* 34 (1980): 23–29.

Culley, Robert C. "Structural Analysis: Is It Done with Mirrors?" *Interpretation* 28 (1974): 165–81.

de Vaux, Roland. *Ancient Israel.* Vol. 1. New York: McGraw-Hill; repr. 1965.

The Encyclopaedia Judaica. Vol. 16. Jerusalem: Keter Publishing House, 1971.

The Encyclopedia of Religion. Edited by Mircea Eliade. 16 vols. New York: Macmillan Publishing Co., 1987.

Encyclopedia Talmudit. Vol. 2. Jerusalem: Yad Harav Herzog Press, 1982.

"Epic of Gilgamesh." In *Ancient Near Eastern Texts,* edited by James B. Pritchard. Princeton, N.J.: Princeton University Press, 1955.

Epstein, Louis M. *Sex Laws and Customs in Judaism.* Revised edition. Hoboken, N.J.: Ktav, 1987.

Erlandsson, S. "Zanah." In *The Theological Dictionary of the Old Testament.* Vol. 4, edited by G. J. Botterweck and H. Ringgren. Grand Rapids: Wm. B. Eerdmans, 1978.

Eskenazi, Tamara C. "Out from the Shadows: Biblical Woman in the Post-Exilic Era." *JSOT* 54 (1992): 25–43.

Even-Shoshan, A. *A New Concordance of the Old Testament.* Jerusalem: Kiryat Sefer Publishing House, 1985.

Fewell, Danna N., and David M. Gunn. "Tipping the Balance: Sternberg's Reader and the Rape of Dinah." *JBL* 110 (1991): 193–211.

Finkelstein, Louis. *Halachah and Agadah.* New York: The Jewish Theological Seminary of America, 1960.

Fitzmyer, Joseph A. *The Genesis Apocryphon of Qumran Cave I.* Rome: Pontifical Institute, 1966.

Freedman, David Noel. "Dina and Schechem, Tamar and Amnon." *Austin Seminary Bulletin* 105 (1990): 51–63.

Freedman, R. David. "Woman: A Power Equal to Man." *BAR* 9 (1983): 56–58.

Friedman, Mordecai A. "Tamar, a Symbol of Life: The 'Killer Wife' Superstition in the Bible and Jewish Tradition." *AJS Review* 15 (1990): 23–61.

Friedman, Theodore. "The Shifting Role of Women, from Bible to Talmud." *Judaism* 36 (1987): 479–87.

Fuchs, Esther. " 'For I Have the Way of Women': Deception, Gender, and Ideology in Biblical Narrative." *Semeia* 42 (1988): 68–83.

———. "The Literacy Characterization of Mothers and Sexual Politics in the Hebrew Bible." *Semeia* 46 (1989): 151–66.

———. "Marginalization, Ambiguity, Silencing: The Story of Jephthah's Daughter." *Journal of Feminist Studies in Religion* 5 (1989): 35–45.

Gill, S. D. "Prayer." In *The Encyclopedia of Religion,* edited by Mircea Eliade. New York: Macmillan Publishing Co., 1987.

Ginzberg, Louis. *The Legends of the Jews.* 7 vols. Philadelphia: The Jewish Publication Society of America, 1942–47.

Goldfeld, Anne. "Women as Sources of Torah in the Rabbinic Tradition." In *The Jewish Woman,* edited by Elizabeth Koltun. New York: Schocken Books, 1976.

Goodblatt, David M. "The Beruriah Traditions." In *Persons and Institutions in Early Rabbinic Judaism,* edited by William Scott Green. Brown Judaic Studies 3. Missoula, Mont.: Scholars Press, 1977.

Gordis, Robert. "Love, Marriage, and Business in the Book of Ruth: A Chapter in Hebrew Customary Law." In *Light unto My Path: Old Testament Studies in Honor of Jacob M. Myers,* edited by H. N. Bream, R. D. Heim, and C. A. Moore. Philadelphia: Temple University Press, 1974.

Greenberg, Blu. *On Women and Judaism: A View from Tradition.* Philadelphia: The Jewish Publication Society of America, 1981.

Gross, Moshe D. *Ozar HaAgadah.* 3 vols. Jerusalem: Mosad HaRav Kook, 1960–86 [Hebrew].

Gruber, Meir I. "Women in the Cult according to the Priestly Code." In *Judaic Perspectives on Ancient Israel,* edited by Jacob Neusner, Baruch Levine, and Ernst Frerichs. Philadelphia: Fortress Press, 1987.

Hackett, Jo Ann. "Women's Studies and the Hebrew Bible." In *The Future of Biblical Studies: The Hebrew Scriptures,* edited by Richard Elliott Friedman and H. G. M. Williamson. SBL Semeia Studies. Atlanta: Scholars Press, 1987.

Harper's Bible Dictionary. San Francisco: Harper & Row, 1985.

Harrington, Daniel J. "Pseudo-Philo." In *The Old Testament Pseudepigrapha.* Vol. 2, edited by James H. Charlesworth. Garden City, N.Y.: Doubleday & Co., 1985.

Harris, Rivkah. "Independent Women in Ancient Mesopotamia?" In *Women's Earliest Records: From Ancient Egypt and Western Asia,* edited by B. S. Lesko. Atlanta: Scholars Press, 1989.

Hartmann, D. *Das Buch Ruth in der Midrasch-Litteratur.* Leipzig: n.p., 1901.

Heinemann, Joseph. *'Aggadot v'Toldoteihen [Aggadah and Its Development].* Jerusalem: Keter Publishing House, 1974.

Herford, Travers V. *Talmud and Apocrypha.* New York: Ktav, 1971.

Heschel, Susannah. "Anti-Judaism in Christian Feminist Theology." *Tikkun* 5 (1990): 25–28, 95–97.

Hesiod. *The Works and Days, Theogony, and the Shield of Herakles.* Translated by R. Lattimore. Ann Arbor: University of Michigan Press, 1959.

Homer. *The Odyssey.* Book 21, Harvard Classics edition (1909).

Hyman, Aharon. *Toldoth Tannaim Ve'Amoraim.* London: Express Press, 1910.

———. *Torah, HaKethubah, Ve-ha-Messurah.* 3 vols. Tel Aviv: Dvir, 1910.

The Interpreter's Bible. 12 vols. Nashville: Abingdon Press, 1952–56.

The Interpreter's Dictionary of the Bible. 4 vols. Nashville: Abingdon Press, 1962.

Jastrow, M. *A Dictionary of the Targumim, the Talmud Babli and Yerushalmi, and the Midrashic Literature.* New York: Pardes Publishing House, 1950.

The Jewish Encyclopedia. New York and London: Funk & Wagnalls, 1904.

Josephus. *Josephus.* 9 vols. Loeb Classical Library. London: William Heinemann. Vol. 4, *Jewish Antiquities, Books 1–4,* translated by H. St. J. Thackeray, 1928. Vol. 5, *Jewish Antiquities, Books 5–8,* translated by H. St. J. Thackeray and Ralph Marcus, 1927.

———. *Josephus: Complete Works.* Translated by William Whiston, 1867. Reprint. Grand Rapids: Kregel Publications, 1960.

Kaiser, Barbara Bakke. "Poet as 'Female Impersonator': The Image of Daughter Zion as Speaker in Biblical Poems of Suffering." *Journal of Religion* 67 (1987): 164–82.

Kee, Howard Clark. "The Testaments of the Twelve Patriarchs." In *The Old Testament Pseudepigrapha.* Vol. 1, edited by James H. Charlesworth. Garden City, N.Y.: Doubleday & Co., 1983.

Koehler, L., and W. Baumgartner. *Lexicon in Veteris Testamenti Libros* and *Supplementum ad Lexicon.* Leiden, Neth.: E. J. Brill, 1958.

Koltuv, Barbara Black. *The Book of Lilith.* York Beach, Me.: Nicolas-Hays, 1987.

Kraemer, Ross S. *Her Share of the Blessings: Women's Religion among Pagans, Jews, and Christians in the Greco-Roman World.* Oxford: Oxford University Press, 1992.

———. *Maenads, Martyrs, Matrons, Monastics.* Philadelphia: Fortress Press, 1988.

———. "Women in the Religions of the Greco-Roman World." *Religious Studies Review* 9 (1983): 127–39.

Kugel, James L. *In Potiphar's House.* San Francisco: HarperCollins, 1990.

———. "Two Introductions to Midrash." In *Midrash and Literature,* edited by G. H. Hartman and S. Budick. New Haven: Yale University Press, 1986.

Kuzmack, Linda. "Aggadic Approaches to Biblical Women." In *The Jewish Woman: New Perspectives,* edited by Elizabeth Koltun. New York: Schocken Books, 1976.

Lachs, Samuel Tobias. "The Pandora-Eve Motif in Rabbinic Literature." *Harvard Theological Review* 67 (1974): 341–45.

Lauterbach, J. Z. *Mekilta de-Rabbi Ishmael.* Vol. 1. Schiff Library of Jewish Classics. Philadelphia: The Jewish Publication Society of America, 1949.

Le Deaut, R. "Miryam, soeur de Moise, et Marie, mère du Messie." *Biblica* 45 (1964): 198–219.

Leibowitz, Nehama. *Studies in the Book of Genesis.* Translated by Aryeh Newman. Jerusalem: World Zionist Organization, 1972.

Lerner, Berel D. "And He Shall Rule over Thee." *Judaism* 37 (1988): 446–49.

Levine, Amy-Jill, ed. *"Women Like This": New Perspectives on Jewish Women in the Graeco-Roman World.* Atlanta: Scholars Press, 1991.

Levine, Lee I. *The Rabbinic Class of Roman Palestine in Late Antiquity.* Jerusalem: Yad Izhak Ben-Zevi; New York: The Jewish Theological Seminary of America, 1985.

––––––. "The Second Temple Synagogue: The Formative Years." In *The Synagogue in Late Antiquity,* edited by Lee I. Levine. New York: JTS/ASOR, 1987.

Levison, Jack. "Is Eve to Blame? A Contextual Analysis of Sirach 25:24." *Catholic Biblical Quarterly* 47 (1985): 617–23.

Levison, John R. "The Exoneration of Eve in the Apocalypse of Moses 15–20." *JSJ* 20 (1989): 135–50.

Lieberman, Saul. *Tosefta Ki-fshutah.* New York: The Jewish Theological Seminary of America, 1955–88.

Loewe, Raphael. *The Position of Women in Judaism.* London: SPCK, 1966.

Maimonides, M. *The Guide to the Perplexed.* Translated by Shlomo Pines. Chicago: University of Chicago Press, 1963.

––––––. *Mishneh Torah.* New York: Shulsinger Bros., 1947.

Marcus, David. *Jephthah and His Vow.* Lubbock, Tex.: Texas Tech Press, 1986.

Margulies, M., ed. *Midrash Wa-Yiqra' Rabbah.* 5 vols. Jerusalem: Wahrmann Books, 1953–60; repr. 1972.

Mazar, Benjamin, ed. *Views of the Biblical World.* Vol. 1. Chicago: Jordan Publications, 1959.

Mechilta de R. Ishmael. Edited by H. S. Horovitz and I. A. Rabin. Jerusalem: Bamberger & Wahrmann, 1930; repr. 1960.

Mekhilta D'Rabbi Yishmael. Edited by M. Friedmann (Ish-Shalom). Vienna: n.p., n.d.; repr. Israel: n.p., n.d.

Mekilta de-Rabbi Ishmael. Edited by J. Z. Lauterbach. Schiff Library of Jewish Classics. Philadelphia: The Jewish Publication Society of America, 1949.

Melzer, Feivel. "Ruth." In *The Five Scrolls,* edited by A. Mirsky et al. Jerusalem: Mosad Harav Kook, 1973 [Hebrew].

Meyers, Carol. *Discovering Eve: Ancient Israelite Women in Context.* Oxford: Oxford University Press, 1988.

Midrash 'Abot. Edited by M. Z. Chefetz. Minsk: n.p., 1896.

Midrash Bereshit Rabba. Edited by J. Theodor and C. Albeck. 3 vols. 2nd ed. Jerusalem: Wahrmann Books, 1965.

Midrash Bereshit Rabbati. Edited by Chanoch Albeck. Jerusalem: Mekize Nirdamim, 1940.

Midrash Eliahu Rabba (Tanna Debei Eliyahu). Edited by M. Friedman (Ish-Shabom). 1904. Reprint, Jerusalem: Wahrmann Books, 1960.

Midrash Mishle. Edited by S. Buber. Vilna: n.p., 1893; repr. Israel: n.p., 1973.

Midrash Pesiqta Rabbati. Edited by M. Friedmann (Ish-Shalom). Vienna: n.p., 1880; repr. Israel: n.p., 1888.

Midrash Rabbah. Translated by H. Freedman and M. Simon. 7 vols. 3rd ed. London and New York: Soncino Press, 1983.

Midrash Seder Olam. Edited by M. K. Mirsky. Brooklyn, N.Y.: n.p., 1988.

Midrash Tanhuma'. Edited by S. Buber. Vilna: n.p., 1885; repr. Israel: n.p., 1972.

Miqra'ot Gedolot. New York: Ktav, n.d.

Mishnah. Edited by H. Danby. Oxford: Oxford University Press, 1933; repr. 1983.

Montefiore, C. G., and H. Loewe. *A Rabbinic Anthology.* N.p.: Meridian Books, 1970.

Moon, Beverly. "Archetypes." In *The Encyclopedia of Religion.* Vol. 1. New York: Macmillan Publishing Co., 1987.

Neusner, Jacob. *Midrash in Context: Exegesis in Formative Judaism.* Philadelphia: Fortress Press, 1983.

———. *The Mishnah: A New Translation.* New Haven: Yale University Press, 1988.

———. *The Talmud of the Land of Israel.* Chicago: University of Chicago Press, 1989.

———. *The Tosefta: Translated from the Hebrew, Order Nashim.* New York: Ktav, 1979.

Niditch, Susan. "Portrayals of Women in the Hebrew Bible." In *Jewish Women in Historical Perspective,* edited by Judith R. Baskin. Detroit: Wayne State University Press, 1991.

———. "The Wronged Woman Righted: An Analysis of Genesis 38." *Harvard Theological Review* 72 (1979): 143–49.

Noah, Mordecai M., ed. *The Book of Jashar.* Reprint. New York: Sepher-Hermon Press, 1972.

Ortner, Sherry B. "Is Female to Male as Nature Is to Culture?" In *Woman, Culture, and Society,* edited by Michelle Zimbalist Rosaldo and Louise Lamphere. Stanford, Calif.: Stanford University Press, 1974.

Pagels, Elaine. *Adam, Eve, and the Serpent.* New York: Random House, 1988.

Palestinian Talmud. Krotoshin edition. New York: Yam Ha-Talmud/ Shulsinger Bros., 1948.

Peritz, Ismar J. "Woman in the Ancient Hebrew Cult." *JBL* 17 (1898): 111–48.

Pesikta de-Rab Kahana. Translated by W. G. Braude and I. J. Kapstein. Philadelphia: The Jewish Publication Society of America, 1975.

Pesikta Rabbati. Translated by William G. Braude. New Haven: Yale University Press, 1968.

Pesiqta de Rav Kahana: According to an Oxford Manuscript with Variants from All Known Manuscripts and Genizoth Fragments and Parallel Passages with Commentary and Introduction. Vol. 1. Edited by Bernard [Dov] Mandelbaum. New York: The Jewish Theological Seminary of America, 1962.

Pesiqta de Rav Kahana, Beshalaḥ. Edited by Solomon Buber. Lwow: n.p., 1868; repr. 1963.

Phillips, John A. *Eve: The History of an Idea.* San Francisco: Harper & Row, 1984.

Philo. *Philo I–X.* Translated by F. H. Colson and G. H. Whitaker. Loeb Classical Library. London: William Heinemann, 1929–53.

Pirqei Rabbi Eliezer. Warsaw (based on Bomberg) 1660; repr. Israel: n.p., 1978.

Plaskow, Judith. "Blaming the Jews for the Birth of Patriarchy," *Lilith* 7 (1980): 11–13.

Prusak, Bernard P. "Women: Seductive Siren and Source of Sin?" In *Religion and Sexism: Images of Woman in the Jewish and Christian Traditions,* edited by Rosemary R. Ruether. New York: Simon & Schuster, 1974.

Rosaldo, Michelle Zimbalist, and Louise Lamphere. *Woman, Culture, and Society: A Theoretical Overview.* Stanford, Calif.: Stanford University Press, 1974.

Rosenberg, A. J. "Ruth." In *Five Megillot.* Revised edition. London: Soncino Press, 1984.

Safrai, Shmuel. *The Jewish People in the Days of the Second Temple.* Tel Aviv: Am Oved, 1970.

———. "Was There a Woman's Section in the Synagogue of Antiquity?" *Tarbiz* 32 (1963): 329–38 [Hebrew].

Saldarini, Anthony J. *The Fathers according to Rabbi Nathan.* Studies in Judaism in Late Antiquity 11. Leiden, Neth.: E. J. Brill, 1975.

Sarna, Nahum A. *Understanding Genesis.* New York: Jewish Theological Seminary/McGraw-Hill, 1966.

Sasson, Jack M. *Ruth: A New Translation with a Philological Commentary.* Baltimore: Johns Hopkins University Press, 1979.

Schuller, Eileen. "Women of the Exodus in Biblical Retellings of the Second Temple." In *Gender and Difference in Ancient Israel,* edited by Peggy L. Day. Minneapolis: Fortress Press, 1989.

Sefer Hadar Zekainim. B'nai Brak: The Institute for Dissemination of the Commentaries of the Ba'alei Tosafot, n.d.

Sefer Ha-Yashar. Livorno: n.p., n.d.

Segal, Moshe Z. *The Complete Book of Ben Sira.* Jerusalem: Mosad Bialik, 1956 [Hebrew].

———. *Ruth: Introduction to the Bible.* Vol. 3. Jerusalem: Kiryat Sefer, 1955 [Hebrew].

Shinan, Avigdor, and Yair Zakovitch. "Midrash on Scripture and Midrash within Scripture." In *Scripta Hierosolymitana,* edited by Sara Japhet. Studies in Bible 31. Jerusalem: Magnes Press, 1986.

Shishah Sidre Mishnah. Edited by Chanoch Albeck. 6 vols. Tel Aviv: Bialik Institute, 1952–58.

Sifra De'Vey Rav, Sifrei D'Vey Rav. Edited by M. Friedmann (Ish-Shalom). Breslau; repr. Israel: n.p., 1923.

Skehan, Patrick W., and Alexander A. Di Lella. *The Wisdom of Ben Sira.* The Anchor Bible. New York: Doubleday & Co., 1987.

Skinner, John, ed. *A Critical and Exegetical Commentary on Genesis.* The International Critical Commentary. Edinburgh: T. & T. Clark, 1969.

Slomovic, Eliezer, and Rosalie [Shoshana] Gershenszon. "A Second Century Jewish Gnostic Debate: Rabbi Josi Ben Halafta and the Matrona." *JSJ* 16 (1985): 1–41.

Sly, Dorothy. *Philo's Perception of Women.* Brown Judaic Studies 209. Edited by J. Neusner et al. Atlanta: Scholars Press, 1990.

Smith, Henry Preserved. *A Critical and Exegetical Commentary on the Books of Samuel.* The International Critical Commentary. Edinburgh: T. & T. Clark, 1899; repr. 1912.

Smith, Louise Pettibone. "The Book of Ruth, Introduction; Exegesis." *The Interpreter's Bible.* Vol. 2. Nashville: Abingdon Press, 1953.

Soloveitchik, Joseph B. "The Lonely Man of Faith." *Tradition* 7 (1965): 5–67.

Speiser, E. A. *Genesis.* The Anchor Bible. Garden City, N.Y.: Doubleday & Co., 1964.

Sperber, A. *The Bible in Aramaic.* 5 vols. Leiden, Neth.: E. J. Brill, 1959–73.

Sullivan, J. P. *Women in Classical Literature.* Los Angeles: UCLA, 1988.

Sussman, Linda S. "Workers and Drones: Labor, Idleness and Gender Definition in Hesiod's Beehive." In *Women in the Ancient World: The Arethusa Papers,* edited by John Peradotto and J. P. Sullivan. Albany: SUNY Press, 1984.

Swidler, Leonard. *Women in Judaism: The Status of Women in Formative Judaism.* Metuchen, N.J.: Scarecrow Press, 1976.

Talmud of the Land of Israel. Vol. 1, *Berachot.* Translated by Tzvee Zahavy. Edited by Jacob Neusner. Chicago: University of Chicago Press, 1989.

Tebat Marqua: A Collection of Samaritan Midrashim. Edited by Z. Ben-Hayyim. Jerusalem: Academy of Sciences, 1988.

The Tosefta. Edited by M. S. Zuckermandel. Jerusalem: Wahrmann Books, 1962–63.

Tosefta according to Codex Vienna, with Variants from Codices Erfurt, Genizah Mss. and Editio Princeps (Venice 1521). Vol. 3, Pt. 2: *Nasim: Sota, Gittin, Qiddusin.* Edited by Saul Lieberman. New York: The Jewish Theological Seminary of America, 1973.

Trenchard, Warren C. *Ben Sira's View of Women: A Literary Analysis.* Brown Judaic Studies 38. Chico, Calif.: Scholars Press, 1982.

Trible, Phyllis. "Depatriarchalizing in Biblical Interpretation." In *The Jewish Woman,* edited by Elizabeth Koltun. New York: Schocken Books, 1976.

————. "Eve." In *Harper's Bible Dictionary.* San Francisco: Harper & Row, 1985.

————. *God and the Rhetoric of Sexuality.* Philadelphia: Fortress Press, 1978.

————. *Texts of Terror: Literary-Feminist Readings of Biblical Narratives.* Overtures to Biblical Theology. Philadelphia: Fortress Press, 1984.

Urbach, Ephraim F. *The Sages: Their Concepts and Beliefs.* Jerusalem: Magnes Press, 1975.

Valler, Shulamit. *Women and Womanhood in the Stories of the Babylonian Talmud.* Israel: Hakibbutz Hameuchad, 1993 [Hebrew].

Van der Toorn, Karel. "Female Prostitution in Payment of Vows in Ancient Israel." *JBL* 108 (1989): 193–205.

Von Rad, Gerhard. *Genesis, A Commentary.* Revised edition. The Old Testament Library. Philadelphia: Westminster Press, 1973.

Vos, Clarence J. *Woman in Old Testament Worship.* Delft, Neth.: Judels & Brinkman, 1968.

Wakeman, Mary K. "Sacred Marriage." *JSOT* 22 (1982): 21–31.

Wegner, Judith R. *Chattel or Person? The Status of Women in the Mishnah.* New York and Oxford: Oxford University Press, 1988.

————. "The Image and Status of Women in Classical Rabbinic Judaism." In *Jewish Women in Historical Perspective,* edited by Judith R. Baskin. Detroit: Wayne State University Press, 1991.

————. "The Image of Woman in Philo." *SBL Seminar Papers.* Chico, Calif.: Scholars Press, 1982.

Weiss, Avi. *Women at Prayer: A Halakhic Analysis of Women's Prayer Groups.* Hoboken, N.J.: Ktav, 1990.

Wertheimer, S., ed. *Batei Midrashot.* Jerusalem: Ketav Yad Yosef; repr. 1982.

Westenholz, Joan G. "Tamar, Qedeša, Qadistu, and Sacred Prostitution in Mesopotamia." *Harvard Theological Review* 82 (1989): 245–65.

Wintermute, Orville S. "Jubilees." In *The Old Testament Pseudepigrapha.* Vol. 2, edited by James H. Charlesworth. Garden City, N.Y.: Doubleday & Co., 1983.

"Women." *The Jewish Encyclopedia,* Vol. 12. New York and London: Funk & Wagnalls, 1906.

Yalqut Shimoni. Jerusalem: Lewin/Epstein, 1941–42.

Young, Robert. *Young's Analytical Concordance to the Bible.* Grand Rapids: Wm. B. Eerdmans, 1970; repr. 1978.

Zakovitch, Yair. "Ruth: Introduction and Commentary." In *Mikra LeYisra'el: A Bible Commentary for Israel,* edited by M. Greenberg and S. Ahituv. Tel Aviv and Jerusalem: Am Oved Publishers/Magnes Press, 1990 [Hebrew].

Zlotowitz, Meir, and Nosson Scherman, eds. *The Book of Ruth.* Art Scroll Tanach Series. New York: Mesorah Publications, 1976.

Zohar. Translated by H. Sperling and M. Simon. London and New York: Soncino Press, 1984.

Index of Names and Subjects

Index of
Rabbinic References